'*The Incredible Teenage Brain* is exceptionally accessible notwithstanding the extraordinary wealth of information it contains on adolescent behaviour. It is perhaps the best book for mental health professionals to recommend to families. But they should also make sure to keep a copy on their shelf.'

– *Professor Peter Fonagy, OBE, Head of the Division of Psychology and Language Sciences Director, Chief Executive, Anna Freud National Centre for Children & Families and National Clinical Advisor on Children's Mental Health*

'This brilliantly written book celebrates the teenager and simply and clearly explains adolescence. By really understanding the teenage brain it is possible to enable our children to navigate this key developmental time without our anxiety getting in the way. This book will empower us all to enable our teens to develop into the best version of themselves while holding strong during some of the inevitable challenges.'

– *Professor Tanya Byron, consultant clinical psychologist, journalist, author and broadcaster, London*

'I'm blown away by this book, I just couldn't put it down. It made me reflect not just on my teenage children, but on my own teenage years. It's so full of useful recommendations that I'll be using it like TripAdvisor in researching my teens for months and years to come.'

– *Valerie Lindsay, mother of teenage children*

'This is an insightful, inspiring and fun book that opens the lid on the often misunderstood and sometimes maligned world of the teenager. It reveals how teenagers are affected by brain development, their expanding social world and self-concept as emerging adults. Invaluable for parents and those who work with teens.'

– *Professor Tony Charman, Chair in Clinical Child Psychology, King's College London*

'Such a useful and reassuring book for parents, carers and anyone working with young people. The authors dismiss the stereotype of the "troublemaker teen". They explain why teens are at the height of their learning potential in all areas of life and show us how, by choosing our words carefully and making shifts in our own behaviour, we can help them shine.'

– *Margaret Rooke, author of* You Can Change the World: Everyday Teen Heroes Making a Difference Everywhere *and* Dyslexia is my Superpower (Most of the Time)

'Your child's teen years can feel like a dark, hazardous path. Here's the guide every parent wishes for, sending up flares of light to ease your way and practical tools to overcome the too-recognisable, real-life pitfalls. The wise authors' compassionate insights will have you bring out the best, rather than suppress, the powerful, joyful potential of your teenager's developing mind.'

– *Sheila Fitzgerald, mother of three now adult girls*

'Any teacher who works with teenagers will find this book fascinating and invaluable. The neuroscience is explained so clearly and offers a new way to look at the rapidly developing brain and how it influences teen behaviour and learning. Bettina, Jane and Tara emphasise the primary need for emotional security as a secure base for learning in school. They give many examples of how stress and anxiety interfere with learning along with ways teachers can create a "positive cycle of learning". What I love the most about this book is that it is written with emotional insight and a great deal of compassion, offering a hopeful and positive way to look at adolescent behaviour.'

– *Sarah Fortna, teacher and learning specialist*

The Incredible Teenage Brain

Everything You Need to Know to
Unlock Your Teen's Potential

Bettina Hohnen,
Jane Gilmour & Tara Murphy

Illustrated by Douglas Broadley
Foreword by Sarah-Jayne Blakemore

Jessica Kingsley Publishers
London and Philadelphia

First published in 2020
by Jessica Kingsley Publishers
73 Collier Street
London N1 9BE, UK
and
400 Market Street, Suite 400
Philadelphia, PA 19106, USA

www.jkp.com

Library of Congress Cataloging in Publication Data
A CIP catalog record for this book is available from the Library of Congress

British Library Cataloguing in Publication Data
A CIP catalogue record for this book is available from the British Library

ISBN 978 1 78592 557 3
eISBN 978 1 78450 952 1

Printed and bound in Great Britain

This book is dedicated to the incredible young people in our professional and personal lives, particularly Ella, Billy, Oscar, Georgie and Bella.

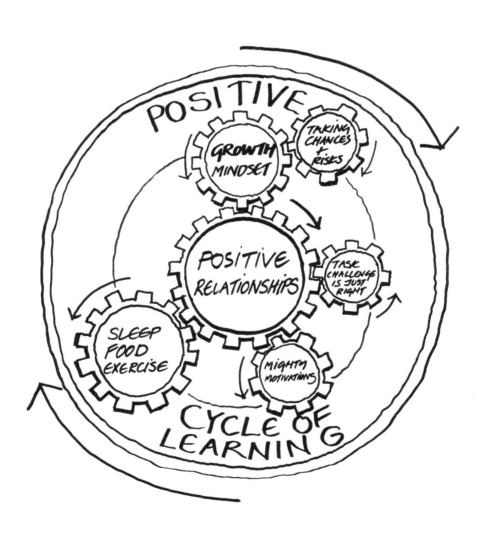

Contents

Part 4: Care and Self-Care for the Teen Brain

Part 5: The Last Word

Foreword

Adolescence comes from the Latin word *adolescere*, which means 'to grow up'. Adolescence starts with the physical and hormonal changes of puberty and ends with adult independence, and it is a time of change: changes to hormones and the body, changes in the social environment and changes to the brain and the mind.

Changes in behaviour that are particularly common during adolescence are increased risk-taking, novelty seeking and being influenced by peers. These typical adolescent behaviours are natural and adaptive processes that help us develop into fully independent adults and are seen in other species of animals, in many different cultures and throughout history. More than 2000 years ago, Socrates wrote, 'They have bad manners, contempt for authority; they show disrespect for elders and love chatter in place of exercise.' One hundred years or so later, Aristotle described 'youth' as 'lacking in sexual self-restraint, fickle in their desires, passionate and impulsive... Youth is the age when people are most devoted to their friends', highlighting the notion that adolescence is a period of fluctuating and intense emotions, in addition to a changing social landscape at this time of life.

For a long time, it was thought that the human brain stops developing in childhood. However, over the past two decades, brain scanning studies have shown that the human brain continues to develop both in terms of structure and function throughout childhood and adolescence, and even into early adulthood (see Tamnes *et al.* 2017 and Fuhrmann, Knoll and Blakemore 2015). Sensory and motor cortices involved in perception and movement mature earlier than other regions, such as the prefrontal, parietal and temporal cortices, which are involved in higher-level cognitive processes and continue to develop into the 20s or 30s.

At the same time that the brain, the body and the social environment are undergoing substantial change, so is the mind. Cognitive skills such as planning, inhibiting inappropriate behaviour and certain forms of memory also continue to improve during adolescence. These cognitive advances provide adolescents with the cognitive machinery to reflect on themselves, what others think about them, and their futures. This is a necessary part of becoming an independent adult, but it also places new pressures on the developing person. Some adolescents may also be vulnerable to experiencing emotions that are hard to manage, or develop mental health problems like anxiety, depression and eating disorders. But the development of the brain in adolescence makes it particularly susceptible to change and that renders this period of life an opportunity for learning and creativity, as well as intervention and rehabilitation.

I have studied the adolescent brain and behaviour for 17 years and am often asked what these mean in terms of parenting or teaching young people. As a cognitive neuroscientist, I feel unqualified to give this kind of advice, and I have been searching for a book that interprets the latest science in terms of what it means for parenting and teaching. This book does exactly that. The authors describe the science in a compelling and clear way, and then place the science in the context of real-life examples of adolescent behaviour and development. How do you handle your teenager wanting to spend more time with friends, taking risks, staying up late? Should you worry about the amount of time they spend on social media? Why won't they go to bed at a reasonable time and why do they find it hard to get up in time for school? When does anxiety become something to seek professional help about? What about other mental health problems like depression and self-harm? This book provides a deep understanding of everyday adolescent issues that touch the lives of everyone who lives or works with teenagers and provides suggestions for how to deal with these.

The authors are child and adolescent psychologists and, between them, have a vast amount of experience working with young people and families. In this ground-breaking book, they provide their combined expertise to help parents and teachers get it right. Adolescence can be a turbulent and challenging time for the adolescent themselves, as well as for the people taking care of them. This is a manual for parents, teachers and anyone supporting adolescents, but it is much more than that, with each issue being deeply seated in scientific rigour. The authors are careful not to oversell the data and are cautious where the science just isn't there yet. But where there is evidence, this book explains what the science shows, how the brain and mind change in adolescence and how this knowledge can be used in positive ways to help young people flourish.

Sarah-Jayne Blakemore, PhD, FRSB, FBA
Professor of Cognitive Neuroscience
University of Cambridge, UK

Introduction

The Incredible Teenage Brain will change how you interact with the teenagers in your life. It will open your eyes to a whole new way of understanding young people and the incredible teenage brain.

We felt compelled to write it, because we are so inspired by the young people in our professional and personal lives. It reflects a seismic shift in the scientific community's perception and understanding of young people, whereby adolescence is coming to be viewed as a time of great opportunity, as well as great sensitivity, and of enormous potential for change. In the past 10 years or so there has been an explosion of research investigating the teenage brain and its unique and positive attributes. There are many pieces of research, books, press articles and radio and TV programmes describing these extraordinary findings – so this book is most certainly standing on the shoulders of giants.

What we do here, for the first time, is take this cutting-edge body of knowledge a step further and consider what it means in a day-to-day context. What can you, as the adult supporting a teenager, do to create the environment that will allow that young person to capitalise on their gifts? At the same time, how can you protect and support them where it is needed, and shore up their vulnerabilities?

One of the most important messages from the latest research is that teenagers are at the height of their learning potential. Here we see learning as a broad concept, beyond but including the school curriculum. Getting the most from formal education, establishing new skills like playing an instrument, developing the ability to navigate social situations, learning to persist with challenges, acquiring emotional self-regulation and developing well-being habits, these are all equally valid learning experiences. Teens have a phenomenal capacity to learn from the environment.

In fact, the teenage phase is increasingly described as 'the new 0 to 3 years' because adolescents explore and learn at the same extraordinary rate that babies and toddlers do. But it's a time-limited offer. After the brain is fully mature (by about the age of 25), we can still learn of course, but the flexibility and capacity to learn – whether through study, or the experience of a life-learning lesson, or shifting an attitude, or an emotional experience – with such mind-blowing speed is lost.

This means that you need to support your teen to get in through that closing door and invite them to engage with life in a way that is enriching and rewarding, during these important years. Making the most of this sensitive period in adolescence is a life-long investment that will continue to pay dividends throughout adulthood.

The evidence from a scientific point of view is increasingly compelling, but there are still gaps and misunderstandings intrinsic to the way that societies and communities view teens. We need to reappraise the teenage years as a time of possibility rather than take the traditionally negative view of teens which is the prevailing narrative.

Search the net for the term adolescence. Within the top 20 hits there are reports of e-cigarette, social media and internet porn misuse; topped off with poor GP appointment attendance. Think about 'Kevin the Teenager', who is unreasonable, ungrateful, foolish and mocked as a figure of fun. Look on the shelves of your local bookstore, there you will find words such as 'blame' and 'attack' in relation to the teenage brain, as though these years are something to endure rather than celebrate. The list could go on, but the 'teen-bashing' ends here.

The scientific facts haven't quite made it into mainstream understanding, where stereotypes about moody, grumpy teens continue to be applied, limiting the expectations of adults and young people themselves. In this book we consider the developmental period of adolescence as optimistic and opportune because that is what the data tell us.

It is this 'rebranding' of teenagers and their incredible brains that lies at the heart of our book. Our message – with the science to back it up – is that it is both inaccurate and unhelpful to consider teens' brains 'broken' or 'deficient'. Some skills are still under construction at this stage, but given their learning potential, teens have abilities that can be channelled into life-long paths of positive development and well-being. In this book we build a bridge between the latest research from psychology, and what is best for young people. As psychologists and parents ourselves, we give hands-on advice about what parents, teachers (and other adults) might think, say and do in the company of teens in order to create an environment in which young people flourish.

At the same time, there are of course potential vulnerabilities to negotiate during adolescence. From the sensitive process of identity formation, to navigating complicated peer dynamics, to experiencing emotions with new intensity, there are aspects of adolescence that need careful handling. Consequently as adults we need to be clued in so that we can step up and step in at the right time.

The very same openness to learning experiences means less productive patterns can develop around this time too. The inherent flexibility that teens have means that if we do so at the right time, we can 'catch' young people who are making negative life choices and support them onto a better path.

Another possible concern among parents is the emergence of mental health problems at this age. We know that if mental health problems are going to occur, they are most likely to appear during the teen years. Recent data from the UK show that teens are three times more likely to have mental health problems than younger children. Difficulties in family communication, social support and issues with self-identity (among other factors) are more likely to be reported in teens who have mental health problems. In this book we also outline communication skills you can use to strengthen your relationships with young people and encourage open and safe discussion with all the protection that that affords. We guide you through ideas that increase well-being and may in some cases prevent more serious mental health concerns developing.

The Incredible Teenage Brain will leave you with a richer under-standing about why your teen behaves in a certain way. It is packed with practical, effective advice which means that you can offer the optimum environment for your teen, so they steer past obstacles and embrace their life-learning and academic potential. The book has a strong scientific background but it is written in plain English so that it is accessible, because we know that most people don't have time to figure out a new vocabulary from the world of neuroscience.

We have divided the book into five parts that guide you through the essential aspects of teen brain development and outline the key learning opportunities for both you and your teen.

Part 1 introduces **the adolescent brain** and we describe the workings of this incredible teen learning machine. In short, young people are primed to learn from the environment efficiently so that they have a better chance of survival as they near independence. We push hard the idea of the teenage years as a learning opportunity, for good reason. It is evidence-based and it means that you can have a hand in shaping the environment around a teenager, so they learn productive and positive lessons for life, and for their school work. We use a highly simplified brain description and divide it into three functions: the *instinctual brain* which puts us in survival mode, the *emotional brain* where our feelings and motivations lie, and the *thinking brain* where we make reasoned judgements. There is only so much brain power to go around – it's a finite resource – so if all the brain activity is in the emotional brain, there's not as much brain power for rational decision making or academic tasks. It's simple physics. Once you have this principle firmly in your mind, you will understand that one of the key roles for an adult supporting a teen is to ensure the young person feels safe and positively motivated – so that all that brain power will be channelled into the thinking brain and the higher order thinking activities.

We consider the way that **the brain thinks, learns and feels** and how *teens* learn moment to moment, day in day out, in the following chapters. We review what happens in the nuts and bolts of the brain; for example, how neurones connect when we lay down a new neural circuit. We discuss different learning styles such as making associations or learning by watching significant others – which of course means *you*. What you do in their presence is dynamite learning material for teens. We consider learning in the broadest possible sense (from formal learning to learning the array of life skills) and illustrate the benefits of a **positive learning cycle**. This includes encouraging a mindset that expects improvement with focused effort and embarking on tasks that are challenging enough to stretch us but not so challenging that we are overwhelmed. Finally – and most importantly for teens – we emphasise the social aspects of the brain. Though we are all social beings, adolescents in particular are highly motivated to connect with others. Given the evidence that the teenage brain is fundamentally social, we close this part of the book by considering the implications of this for a teenager's education.

Here, we also discuss how teenage brain biology acts together with their environment. The **human brain 'seeks out' certain experiences at different times in development**, in a set order so that it can fulfil its potential. You will recognise this principle in babies' language development, for example, or learning to crawl and walk. The window of opportunity to learn the nuances of language, for instance, closes after the infant is about two years old, so babies have to soak up language before the brain moves on from that setting. Evolution uses ingenious ways to keep a baby and caregiver in close proximity, so babies' brains can tune in to their caregivers' speech.

The brain uses this phased technique for learning from our environment in different ways right up until adulthood and the end of adolescence. Our brain essentially aims to get us into the right place at the right time to learn about the topics that are most important and relevant for the particular stage in life we are at. The brain pulls us towards situations using rewarding feelings, for example, to shape learning. It means that we orientate towards different facets of the world at times in our life.

For adolescents, it's almost as if some things (like new experiences or friends) become technicoloured and other things (say childhood pastimes) are fading into black and white. Teens may choose to go to a party even though they have an important test at school coming up, not because they are uncaring about doing well in school but because their brains are drawing them to social experience and their peers. To take another example that may be painfully familiar to parents, a teen whose first choice had always been to snuggle up and watch a film with Mum and Dad on a Saturday night may now prefer to be on FaceTime with their friends in their bedroom. They still love their parents just as much, but their focus has shifted. The teenage brain draws the teen

THE INCREDIBLE TEENAGE BRAIN

towards these new situations so that they will experience, explore and learn about them.

In **Part 2**, we discuss teens with **additional needs** such as those with **mental health problems** or who are **neurodiverse**, with uneven learning profiles.

If you are one of those parents or teachers who has to pull together two skill sets – supporting a young person and one who may have complex needs – you are well and truly in the advanced class. Whether a teen is directly affected or not, readers will find this section essential because the issues we describe are likely to affect a majority of families and schools. We live together in communities and it is important to teach young people to embrace differences in others. We discuss the most frequently occurring mental health difficulties that present in the teen years, helping parents to differentiate between typical emotional highs and lows and more serious concerns that require contact with a mental health service. You will learn what to look for and when to take action. Sudden changes in demeanour or behaviour may be a warning sign that a teen is struggling and protection and resilience come from everyday processes and strong relationships. We can't (and nor should we want to) make emotions go away but we can help teens to understand what is happening and how to manage at difficult times. Teenage brains are primed for all kinds of learning including emotional regulation which is such an important part of well-being. Further, we review some of the most common life-long developmental conditions such as Attention Deficit Hyperactivity Disorder (ADHD), Dyslexia and Autism Spectrum Disorder. We consider how having these conditions might impact on a teen specifically. For example, adolescence is a time of self-concept formation, so how might managing a developmental condition influence a young person? Can they own it, and become empowered by it, or will it make them feel set apart from their peers? You can make a difference to their perception.

We consider what psychologists call the developmental **'tasks' of adolescence** in **Part 3**. By this we simply mean that the brain has priorities during the teen period such as figuring out their social group:

I want to belong but I need to stand out at the same time

personal values:

I think censorship is wrong but social media influencers can be corrosive so the government needs to take action

or self-image:

I thought I was brilliant at French but then I failed my mocks so maybe I'm rubbish.

We consider each of these topics and highlight their importance in contributing to a young person becoming a well-developed adult. We note that as with any work in progress, there are vacillations and moments of extremity before the calibration settles – and therein lies the challenge for us all as adults supporting adolescents. The teenage brain is a force to be reckoned with at times. We consider ways in which you as an adult can hitch a ride on the **mighty motivations** of the teenage brain so the young person is propelled into a successful trajectory of intellectual stimulation, positive relationships and well-being.

The centrality of **social inclusion** and **peer approval** is an intrinsic motivating factor throughout adolescence. The opinions of their peers are a crucial reference point for teens, and that sociability can be a fruitful forum. Peer views can, of course, have more negative effects too and we therefore discuss the influence of the peer group on young people. We take considerable time to re-conceive the notion of risk taking as inherently bad. In fact risk taking is, in and of itself, an essential part of personal development (quite apart from the possible positive outcome following a risk). We discuss finding the balance between **taking risks** and building valuable **resilience**, without dropping into serious adversity. If your teen puts themselves out there by auditioning for a school play, it is a risk because they may be rejected or cast – it's a gamble. Engaging in an experience with an unknown outcome is important. We need to be able to tolerate the unknown to some extent or we wouldn't evolve as people. At the same time, a teen who is auditioning for roles, getting rejected time and time again *and* who takes each rejection as a message that they are lacking personally might develop low self-esteem. We describe the protective benefits of experiencing 'just the right amount of stress'. Like a vaccine, optimum stress experiences inoculate us against the effects of a life event like a major loss because we figure out coping styles, and learn the process of recovery; without this experience, we may fall like dominoes in the face of a major challenge. We explore **pushing the boundaries** to reach new heights of learning in social and school contexts without it becoming overwhelmingly stressful.

Part 4 explores **caring for the developing teenage brain** (and this includes supporting a teenager to develop self-care) during adolescence. We consider the fundamentals of healthy sleep patterns, positive stress experiences and the uses and abuses of technology. These are areas in which the brain interacts with culture in a particularly profound way for teenagers and are common sources of conflict between teenagers and the adults who care for them. We discuss ways you can support your teen to balance their social and academic demands and priorities with learning to look after themselves, from exercising to eating well. Getting this balance right is likely to reap many short- and long-term rewards, while failing to do so can have repercussions, so we believe it is an important area to focus on.

The final section (**Part 5**) revises the main themes of the book and considers your role as an adult central to a young person's life. Here we come to the all-important issue of how you can connect and maintain relationships with young people; this includes practical advice about supporting emotional regulation, identifying when to take action, and just as importantly when to do nothing but simply find time to listen. We have distilled the science and the brain data to provide a checklist for you to use that will give you structure in the moment, when emotions are running high. With persistence, while building new brain circuits alongside your teen, these steps will benefit now and for many years to come. They are the key to unlocking the teenage brain and liberating its potential.

If you would like to get in touch with the authors, please contact bettina@drbettinahohnen.com. Follow us on Twitter at the following addresses:

Bettina Hohnen – @BettinaHohnen
Jane Gilmour – @thechildpsych

In the course of this book, you are invited to learn the fine art of **allowing opportunities for learning** in life and in formal education, while at the same time protecting, supporting and providing important **boundaries**. The teenage brain can grow or contract depending on the quality of the adult **relationships** in a young person's life. Decoding your teen's behaviour will allow you to tap into their brain's power. Like learning any new language, it is hard at first. Consider this book a translation guide. Understanding that **social connection, social sensitivity and social status** underpin so much of a teen's life is tantamount to discovering the Rosetta Stone.

How to use this book

We deliver high quality scientific information in a user-friendly format. We have summarised the issues reviewed in each paragraph with a concise phrase, so that you can get the gist efficiently. You will find the following features in each chapter, clearly signposted with the icons shown below, so that you can easily find the information that is most useful to you.

Long story, short
This icon describes five or six key themes from the chapter. It comes at the start of the chapter so you are primed to the central concepts as you read further.

The science bit: Brain and behaviour
The brain icon describes the research data showing what happens in specific parts of the teenage brain and considers the impact on behaviour. We describe recent neuroscientific insights, and although we think it's fascinating, it might not be for everyone. You could skip this part of the chapter, if you were short of time or inclination, and you would nonetheless get well-researched information and advice.

Translating your teen
The translation section aims to take the science and consider what that might be in terms of the young person's behaviour. This aims to explain why your teen may be behaving as they do.

What does that mean day to day?

This section puts the findings into familiar domestic settings: family times, morning schedules, homework routines and so on.

What does that mean for learning?

Here we consider situations that are likely to occur in school or college and other life-learning experiences.

So, what now?

Given all that we have learnt so far about the teenage brain and behaviour, we go further and consider what we should do about it.

Case study

There are one or more case studies in each chapter that describe real-life case examples, illustrating points from the chapter.

Action point

Towards the end of each chapter there are concrete examples of activities, responses or mindsets you could adopt which are likely to improve your teen's well-being and your relationship with them. Our experience working with families and educational staff suggests that in order to make any real difference, action points need to become habitual, day in, day out. Small-scale changes that are simple and can be integrated into daily life are the ones most likely to become new habits.

The moral of the story is...

In a nutshell, here is what this chapter teaches you about your teen and what it means.

Downloads

At the end of each chapter is a download section, with an exercise to complete. Doing these will help to embed the messages from the chapter and consider how they relate to you, your teen and your situation. Typical scenarios are outlined in a table to help you 'catch' old thoughts and reactions and change them to new ones based on your new knowledge about the incredible teenage brain.

All pages marked with the download icon can be downloaded from https://library.jkp.com/redeem using the code TOUWEBE.

The Incredible Teenage Brain mission statement
Have you ever noticed the diligence with which new parents research the best sleep routine or the most stimulating colours for their precious newborn so they have the best possible start? You may well have done it yourself. Whether you are a parent or a teacher, adolescence is another chance to consider the nurturing qualities in a young person's life environment and re-calibrate so that they can make another great developmental leap, similar in magnitude to infancy, with all the opportunities they deserve. It also means that you are the environment. Your relationship with your teen can augment many aspects of their learning experience. You can offer opportunities in life learning and academic tasks that will launch them into a fulfilling and healthy adulthood. This book gives you the tools to do just that.

PART 1

The Incredible Teen Brain

Chapter 1

The Incredible Teen Brain – Time to Upgrade

Long story, short

- Teenagers are incredible. Here we 're-brand' the adolescent years as an exciting and optimistic time, with enormous potential.
- Teenage brains are going through a significant and dynamic neural upgrade making the brain acutely sensitive to the environment.
- The changes in the teenage brain are a double-edged sword – great things can happen but it is also vulnerable to potentially damaging lasting changes, including mental health difficulties.
- Different parts of the brain mature in ordered 'steps' so it is ready to make the most of particular learning experiences at different stages of life.
- The teenage brain is orientated towards five priorities: peers, self-identity, independence, emotionally driven learning and novel experiences.
- Getting the environment right, at the right time for teens, is the key.

Introduction

Teenagers are incredible in every way

Teens are incredible but yet we hear daily examples of people bad-mouthing them; young people are described in ways that would not be tolerated for any other group in society. Someone who is unreasonable is described as 'teenagery'; when a teen misbehaves, you might hear 's/he was such a teenager this morning', as if negative behaviour is to be expected from teens and something they need to get over. As we write this book a new advert characterises teenagers as *grumpy* and *sullen* creatures who slam doors and are mean to their siblings – the advertised adventure holiday will 'cure them' of their teenage ways. This conceptualisation needs to change. In *The Incredible Teenage Brain* we show you the much more positive view of the teenage brain that's emerging from science, and we show you how you can completely change the way you think about, and interact with, the young people in your lives as a result.

Quick question: What do you mean by teenager?

While the term 'teenager' strictly speaking refers to ages 13–19, it is used in common parlance to refer to a broader developmental period which begins with the onset of puberty and ends around the time a person reaches independence.

As we learn more from science it is clear that there are particular changes to the body and brain that occur during the period of life. We use the terms teenagers and adolescence interchangeably to refer to this broad period of development (Ron Dahl 2004).

Considering the complex brain systems that undergo fine tuning and the complicated life skills that need to be mastered, it makes sense that evolution devoted such an extended period of time to the period of adolescence. Our knowledge of the teenage brain has grown exponentially since the turn of this century when research revealed adolescence as a time of enormous neural change and growth. Previously the brain was believed to do most of its developing before the toddler years, but we now know the brain goes on developing until well into our third decade of life and this has revolutionised the way we understand typical teenage behaviour.

The brain develops in cycles according to a timetable

Brains get *upgraded* in a specific order throughout development, predetermined according to what we need to do to learn and survive in discrete stages in life. Regions and circuits of the brain develop at different times, within an ordered hierarchy, according to a developmental timetable. In other words, the brain develops in cycles and is 'expecting' to receive certain experiences at particular stages of development. Genes play an important role in brain development by signalling to different brain areas to be supremely sensitive to the environment. The teenage brain is primed for learning. Adolescence is a time when the brain is highly adaptable and ready for change.

Biology and the environment interact to drive brain development; teens are motivated to have specific learning experiences

An inherent part of brain adaptation, therefore, is the interaction of biology (when a part of the brain is sufficiently mature and ready for learning) with the environment (the learning experience) (see Figure 1.1). This is a reciprocal relationship because the environment facilitates brain development and, in turn, the stage of brain development maximises the learning experiences available in the environment. The brain drives us to seek out specific environmental experiences at different times in development and it is highly sensitive to these 'target' experiences. These are commonly referred to as 'sensitive periods' of development. Knowing which parts of the brain are going through their final upgrade during the teen years gives us insight into adolescent behaviour so we can unlock their incredible potential. The recent body of research shows that teens are driven towards five areas of learning experience. They are motivated to: integrate with peers (see Chapter 8: Cracking the Social Code); take risks and have new experiences (see Chapter 9: Risk Taking and Resilience Making); learn using emotion, so-called 'heartfelt' goals (see Chapter 10: Powerful Feelings and Mighty Motivations); work out self-identity (see Chapter 11: Self-reflection); and gain autonomy and independence (see Chapter 12: Ready to Launch (with Your Support)). The brain wants adolescents to learn about these issues because – as far as evolution is concerned – they are the most important given their stage in life. These are the brain's priorities, and teens are likely to be most motivated to learn in the context of these as that is what is, and what *feels*, important to them.

The brain needs the right experiences at the right time to develop fully

If a brain is not exposed to a given experience at the right time then it will not develop fully. For example, using an extreme but clear example, if a child has a cataract from birth (which occludes their sight), vision will be permanently impaired. They will develop sight if the cataract is treated by mid-childhood, so some capacity to learn to see still exists in the brain, but sophisticated visual skills such as depth perception will never develop fully. We can't say exactly what the consequences would be if teenage brains are not exposed to their target experiences. However, we can say with certainty that learning safely with boundaries and adult support in these areas during the teen years is a crucial part of a teenage brain's development and is important for long-term well-being.

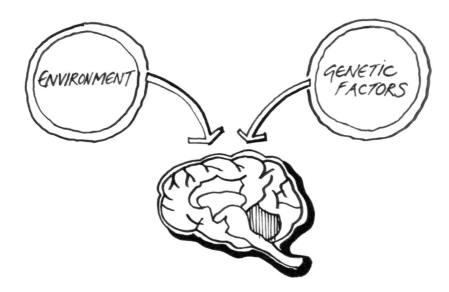

Figure 1.1: Biology and the environment both have an important role to play in driving brain development

Adolescence can be a turning point for mental health

As Lucy Foulkes and Sarah-Jayne Blakemore say, 'By averaging across participants [in research], we are not addressing the fact that adolescents, and their brains, develop in meaningfully different ways' (2018, p.315). Individual differences are caused by the interaction between genetic factors (characteristics we inherit from our parents) and environmental factors (life events or experiences). These differences and interactions can manifest in a multitude of different ways, but in terms of mental health they come to the fore in adolescence. Adolescence is physically the healthiest time in a person's life, but it is also the time when a person is most likely to develop a mental health problem. As we discuss in Chapter 6: Teen Brains Overwhelmed, about 75 per cent of mental health problems, such as depression, anxiety, eating disorders and schizophrenia, develop during the adolescent years and it is likely that this is related to the extraordinary changes occurring in the teenage brain. We will discuss ways in which you can shape the environment so the chances of mental health problems emerging are decreased, at least to some degree.

The science bit: Brain and behaviour

Neural upgrade for adolescence

The teenage brain is incredible certainly, and also unique. Recent research findings show that there are characteristics that are specific to the teenage brain and do not occur in the brains of younger children and adults: how it is structured, how it processes information and responds to the environment. The upgrade creates more efficient and specialised systems that will set the individual up for life.

Neuroplasticity

At the turn of the 21st century very little was known about adolescent brain development. Since then, our understanding has grown due to the advent of exciting new technologies that allow us to watch brains while they are thinking or doing something. Technologies such as Magnetic Resonance Imaging (MRI) have changed the face of neuroscience. One of the amazing findings is that the brain changes when we learn something. It physically changes. In fact, it is highly adaptable, shifting and changing throughout life in order to make sure it is the best brain it can be for the environment in which we live. The term used to describe this ability to change is *neuroplasticity*, which simply means 'the brain can change in response to experience'. Being adaptive is the single most important function of the human brain – we 'strive to survive'.

The final stage of development fine-tunes the teenage brain according to what is happening in the environment

Another aspect of the teenage brain upgrade involves specialisation. Imagine a start-up company which sets up many different services, hedging its bets to cover all the bases. As it matures, it will only keep the departments that are needed in the current marketplace. Ultimately, to function efficiently, the company specialises, losing under-utilised departments so that it can be as streamlined as possible and offer a service efficiently. In a similar way, the brain produces many more connections than are needed in childhood and then, in the final teen phase of maturation, 'pruning' occurs, in which connections that are redundant are lost. Experience dictates which connections are useful. Brain connections remain if an activity is repeated, and those which are not used are surplus to requirements and will wither away. You may have been fluent in French in high school, but if you haven't spoken it since, the chances are you are not fluent any more but may be able to recall a few well-learnt phrases. You brain has pruned back your 'French connection' so that it does not waste valuable resources on an obsolete activity. This makes for a highly efficient brain that is adaptive to the environment. Pruning fine-tunes the brain according to the environment it is in, so it is set up for adult life to be as responsive and adapted as possible. How an adolescent spends their time is therefore very important: you want your teen's brain to specialise in response to an enriched, diverse and nurturing environment. Now is the time to get the environment right.

Translating your teen

Expect teen behaviour to be different

An adolescent is different in many ways from a pre-teen. Your teen's behaviour, motivations and focus change as their brain seeks out the developmental tasks and experiences that it needs to prepare for independent living as an adult. With the onset of puberty teens are driven towards different experiences in life. Parents and teachers may marvel at the speed of change in the behaviour of teens, which may happen overnight. Bewildering as it may be for an adult, it can be equally so for the young person. It can feel like a loss to adults, but there are so many gains to be had from spending time with adolescents and it really is extraordinary to watch their potential unfold. While they may look like adults, adolescents, and their brains, are still under construction, so the first step in translating their behaviour is to use your *teen lens* and view events from their perspective. Take a moment and, if you can, reflect before acting; your response will be more thoughtful, which means that day on day your teen will get a more enriched and nurturing environment (see Chapter 17: May The Force Be With You, Luke). Adolescents are learning; they are trying new experiences and, as with all new experiences, there will be many false starts and mistakes. This trial and error behaviour will not define their character for life. They are just learning.

 ## What does that mean day to day?

Teen's brains invite them into new areas of learning, and different behaviour

Because the adolescent brain has particular learning priorities, we can predict with pretty fair accuracy what teens are likely to be interested in day to day. The American paediatrician Ron Dahl calls these priorities *natural attractors* (Dahl *et al.* 2018). Consider the determination toddlers muster when they learn to walk, getting up time and again despite falling on average 100 times a day. Nothing can stand in their way – they are driven by their brain telling them to 'walk'. Walking is a natural attractor for toddlers. Teens are driven to explore the world in a different way but with no less enthusiasm. Classically, teens will turn their attention towards friends rather than towards their family. They spend more time with peers, place importance on being accepted by them and greater value on what their friends have to say. This is because the new generation is getting ready to form a new community in time, so it's crucial to find a place in that group. Typically adolescents become more self-conscious and interested in what they look like and how they fit in. Pre-teens might consider mirrors a bit pointless, whereas teens will spend many hours in front of a mirror considering and adjusting how they look. This is because their brain is sending signals that it's important to think about how you look to the outside world. Teens begin to question authority because it is useful, in evolutionary terms, to ask questions of the status quo – it may lead to a better outcome and they are testing out their capacity for independence. Young people are drawn to new experiences that produce strong emotions and high arousal. They will likely fall in love with someone or something with deep intensity. Their brain is wired to learn on the basis of these powerful emotional experiences. Life with your teen changes. Buckle up, it might be a bumpy ride, but it is a privilege to be on this journey with your teen. Watch and get ready to be amazed.

Getting the environment right really matters at this time in life

While plasticity in the brain is there for life (phew!), adults' brain circuits are predisposed to resist modification, as the natural state of the adult brain is stability. In contrast, the structures of the teenage brain are highly malleable, ready to be modified by experience. Learning happens easily and experience shapes the teenage brain, and that is why young people learn from watching others, and more quickly and easily than adults. This also means that the environment has a more powerful impact on the teenage brain than on either the adult or pre-teenage brain. Adolescence is a time of great opportunity because any experience a teenager has will influence brain-wiring deeply. Teaching life skills and healthy habits at this time is likely to have life-long benefits. But when things are changing, as the saying goes 'moving parts get broken', presenting a double-edged sword. Great things can happen to the brain, but a difficult path can also be trodden that can have a lasting impact. If we miss opportunities or expose our young people to impoverished or even aversive experiences, it will be much harder to go back and make changes later. That is not to say it will be impossible, because we know plasticity remains for life, but it will be harder as the circuits are less amenable to change in adulthood.

Adolescence is perhaps the time when we have the greatest

opportunity to tip the balance in a direction that limits the possibility of a negative spiral in a person's life. As Ron Dahl points out, just as the impact of malnutrition is devastating during periods of accelerated growth, so the impact of a poor social, emotional and psychological environment could have similar long-term consequences during the teen years. This is a sobering thought, given that this is also a time when teenagers may be pushing away parents or teachers and challenging authority in their drive for independence. Adolescents need a stable, predictable and nurturing environment at the very time that their quest for autonomy and the resulting confrontation is at its peak. As supporting adults, we need to consider what this means for day-to-day life; we need to give them space and hold them tight all at the same time. No one said this was easy.

What does that mean for learning?

The learning potential is massive – the teen years are a crossroads

Adolescence is a springboard for learning progress. Good brains can become great brains. Ensuring teens are engaged in learning is key, making it important for parents and teachers to use tactics that activate their huge motivation to learn about the world. This is an opportunity for teaching diverse academic topics, learning an instrument, debating abstract conceptualisations of a theory or mastering foreign languages. Teaching might be through informal exploration techniques – which harness their interest in autonomy, for example – or formal instruction.

We need to consider ways to harness motivation and drives to aid learning

In most Western countries, adolescents sit pressured gateway exams between the age of 16 and 19 years. Curriculums are often highly circumscribed and there is little room for the adolescent to choose or express individuality in their learning, which is counter to their natural priorities during adolescence. Perhaps we need to consider ways to harness the teenage brain's drives and motivations, rather than fight against them. As Mary Helen Immordino-Yang, Linda

Darling-Hammond and Christina Krone put it: 'Structured opportunities to teach and learn from others; to explore, discover, and invent; and to test out the predictive power of their reasoning and calculations, help children construct a sense of scholarly and personal agency' (2018, p.7). A 2018 study by Christopher Bryan and colleagues illustrates the power of harnessing teen motivation in teaching life skills: using a process that immersed them into complex 'backstory' information, decision making and understanding the consequences of behaviours was more efficient than traditional didactic teaching. Importantly, these same programmes emphasise that errors are part of the learning process, part of the growth mindset (see Chapter 3: The Teen Brain Learns and Believes). If possible, be flexible with topics and carve out specific opportunities for students to follow their passions. We discuss teaching strategies that tap into teen motivations in more detail throughout the book. The challenge in education is how to capitalise on the energy, drives and vitality of the extraordinary teenage brain.

So, what now?

In this book we pull together aspects of development that are characteristic of adolescence, but we need to hold in mind that each teenager matures at a different rate and the path that each of them moves along will differ. We must also consider individual differences in personality and approach.

Supporting a teen takes a different set of skills from helping younger children, so you may need to regroup and rethink your approach in adolescence. Take a look around and see what motivates the teenagers you know. Their brain is sending them strong signals to push along their learning at this most sensitive of time in their life, so their behaviour is likely to be a response to those signals.

Parents, teachers or any significant adult supporting a teenager can shape their environment and that means *you* can influence the way their brain develops. It is a daunting prospect but also a precious opportunity. The following chapters will bring together evidence-based ideas about how to implement the information in a day-to-day context and make the most of this valuable chance.

Case study: Molly

Molly was the most adorable child. David and Devaki's firstborn, she was a loved and loveable girl, engaging, witty, doing well at school. She adored and protected her younger brother, loved nothing more than a 'jammies' day with her mum and dad, snuggled on the sofa together, talking and laughing. In her last year at primary school, when asked to write about 'Where you want to live as an adult' she wrote 'I always want to live with my mum and dad. They are the best parents in the world.'

Then, seemingly overnight, just before she turned 12 she seemed to change. Staying home was suddenly 'boring' and every Saturday she wanted to sleep over with her friend. She seemed to be most interested in speaking to her friends, on her phone, with her bedroom door firmly shut. She cut her beautiful long blonde hair, trying a new style that she thought was cool, but her parents thought she didn't look like 'their Molly'. She began wearing mostly black, using make-up and listening to bands that they had never heard of. It felt like they were losing her.

Molly had always been close to her dad, but she stopped laughing at his jokes and spoke back to him; she chose to go to her friend's party to which boys were invited, rather than go out sailing with him. David felt heartbroken. He had given her everything – his heart and soul. Had they spoilt her? Should they have given her that new iPhone? How could she be so cold and rejecting, someone who didn't know how to consider other people's feelings? He was upset, concerned for her future and he felt rejected. Suddenly he felt like he didn't know Molly or how to be a parent.

A good resolution

As Molly's parents started to understand more about the teenage brain, they began to realise this was a typical and necessary part of her development. It helped for David and Devaki to discuss these feelings of rejection together and they also thought about them alone. They spoke with their friends who had children of a similar age who bravely shared similar sentiments. Although it still hurt at times, Molly's parents were able to see her behaviour as part of a process of development rather than a rejection of them or a permanent state of her character. They needed to put some firm boundaries in place regarding make-up and clothing and speaking rudely to them, but they understood that her desire to be with friends was developmentally appropriate. They thought with her about things she might like to do as a family and made adjustments to take into account her new motivations and interests. They invited her friends round and made their home a fun place for all the gang. Things settled down, and while she was different, she was by no means lost. In fact, this new phase of family life was beginning to be fun.

What might get in the way?

Conversations with young people about clothes and make-up don't always go so well. Making sure that you listen and hear the young person's point of view before setting the boundary is essential. Try to give something back, perhaps offering a time when they can wear the make-up they like (e.g. in the house), suggesting a level of make-up that would be acceptable, or finding another way in which they might express themselves.

Feelings of rejection as a parent can also be real. When a child who has held onto your skirt or trouser leg for 10 years suddenly prefers other people's company, it is not easy. Talking this through with a partner, friend or even therapist can help you to put things in perspective. And remember, you are the most important person in your teen's life, even if it doesn't always feel that way. We know that from many years of research.

Case study: Anuska

Anuska had always loved horse-riding. This worried her mother as Anuska was born pre-term at 31 weeks' gestation, weighing little more than a kilogram, and she was quite a delicate child. She appeared physically to be younger than her three older sisters, was sicker more often than her siblings and seemed to worry more. However, now she was 15 years of age, she had become stronger and more able physically and academically. Her dream was to compete in the Olympic Games as an equestrian. However, Anuska's progress had not been predictable or consistent, and while she worked hard at it, her talents were somewhat limited. Anuska's horse-riding teacher had a conversation with her mother about this. It concerned both adults that Anuska often gave up on other aspects of her life, such as friends and foreign languages. Anuska tried at school but she found maths and foreign languages particularly difficult, and they were concerned that she could easily give up on them.

Anuska's mother worried that the horse-riding world, which is highly tough and competitive, may be a difficult path for her to take. She was also frustrated at the disproportionate effort Anuska wanted to put into horse-riding compared to her school work and worried that putting all her eggs in the 'horse-riding' basket was a risky choice.

A good resolution

Anuska's parents worked very hard to promote her confidence with horse-riding. They used every means that they had to support her in attending competitions, enjoying the care of the animals and engaging with the friends that she made in the stables.

Interestingly, when she turned 18, Anuska changed her mind about continuing a career with horses and decided to apply for a university course. Inside, her parents breathed a sigh of relief. It wasn't that they hadn't believed in her, rather that they wanted to protect her. However, with time, Anuska had seen what was a good path for her and what might work better. She was able to apply the skills of determination and persistence she had developed through her horse-riding to her academic pursuits and did well. Her parents were patient for this maturation to occur. In the end, they worked together to facilitate a gap year in which Anuska travelled and worked in various stables through Latin America. This satisfied Anuska's love for horses and, with time, she found a way to enjoy this passion of hers while pursuing a more realistic career. It was her parents' role to support her through this phase of her life.

What might get in the way?

Parents want the best for their child. Nobody doubts that. In their quest to secure the best future for their child (or perhaps a path they wished they had taken themselves...), parents often panic when a teenager falls in love with something they deem unsuitable. Finding the balance between watching and waiting and intervening so a young person doesn't lose out on opportunities is tough. It requires careful thought and holding on tight as things unfold. As we will see later (see Chapter 12: Ready to Launch (with Your Support)), unfortunately, top-down authoritarian parenting has its side effects at this age. It may produce short-term results, but there may well be longer-term problems. Stay strong, trust in the process of development and read on.

Action point: Guide, support and maintain curiosity to promote teen learning – it's a new skill set

Teenagers need a different set of rules and expectations. Even though you have the wisdom of your own experience and can imagine the long-term path, you may need to adopt a new skill set and be less directive than you would be with younger children. Supporting teens is much more about guiding than being in the driving seat. At the same time, taking the back-seat is too far behind. You are aiming to be a bit like a fabulous driving instructor or co-pilot, who sits alongside their young learner, encouraging them, keeping them calm. Know to expect the occasional stall and sometimes warn them about the road ahead, but only take over the controls in a real emergency.

Action point: Teenagers need to be looked after – and to develop independence

The most difficult aspect of support is often about balancing two competing demands. It's not 'either/or', it's more 'both/and'. For example, teens need to develop independence, but don't assume that they think just like adults or treat them as a friend, they still need looking after and in some ways need you more than ever.

Action point: Understand that teen motivations are powerful and surf on the crest of that wave

Tune into a teen's motivations and desire to learn and see where that leads you. For example, if they have suddenly fallen in love with playing guitar in a band, support that in any way you can. Respect and understand the power of their need for new experiences and work with them to use their motivations in a positive way. At the same time, provide boundaries to keep them safe.

Action point: Work hard to get the environment right for teens

Now is the time to get the environment right for the young people in your life. Their brains are primed ready to learn new experiences, particularly in a social context. Learning good life-long habits during adolescence is low hanging fruit; *if* the environment is right then a positive path will form.

Action point: Educate teens about what is happening in their brains

Teens benefit enormously from understanding something of their experience. They need you to understand their behaviour so that you can support them to understand what is going on themselves. Being a teenager is hard at times, but educating them respectfully about what is happening to their brains can be extremely empowering for everyone and can give you and your teen a shared understanding and language for some of the challenges of adolescence.

The moral of the story is...

Behaviour, motivations, priorities and drives change in the teenage years. Their academic and life-learning potential is great, but teens are vulnerable because of the changes happening in their brain. You can scaffold and facilitate a successful journey through adolescence.

Downloads: The Incredible Teen Brain — Time to Upgrade

Teenager's brains are going through a significant upgrade with enormous potential for high-impact learning. Their brains are highly sensitive to experience, so it's important to get the environment right for them. Teen behaviour, motivations, priorities and internal drives change in adolescence, so once puberty kicks in, the same young person will act differently. The changes in the incredible teenage brain are an important part of a process and are a step towards becoming well-rounded and fully formed adults.

Exercise

The next time the teen in your care behaves in a way that challenges you, puzzles you or makes you concerned, stop and take a moment to be curious. Might this event be explained by the changes happening in the teenage brain? First take the teen perspective. Understanding an event as a result of the changes in motivations and priorities that occur in adolescence can take the heat out of challenging behaviour or give meaning to behaviour that flummoxes you and help you think about the most efficient way to address it. Don't mix up understanding with excusing behaviour. It's always a good strategy to try and understand behaviour, but we don't recommend that you allow disrespectful or self-destructive behaviour.

Note down three changes you have noticed in your teen's behaviour, priorities or motivations since reaching this important stage of life. Which ones unsettle you?

Change 1

. . . .

. . . .

Change 2

. . . .

. . . .

Change 3

. . . .

. . . .

When this happens...	Instead of thinking this...	Try this...
If your teen sings night and day and dreams of being a singer...	She will never make any money if she becomes a singer, what a waste of her time...	I'm so glad she has found something she enjoys so much. It is building her confidence and it doesn't mean she is going to drop out of school.
		 Use a teen lens and appreciate teen passions
If your teen rushes to look at her phone as soon as she arrives home from school...	I wish she would just come home and start to revise instead of talking to her friends, she's got so much to do.	She seems so much more interested in friends than doing well at school, but that is expected as her brain is wired towards friendships right now and doesn't mean she will never be focused on her work. A catch-up with friends is important before she gets down to work.
		Use a teen lens and notice teen natural attractors (e.g. friends)
If your teen is grouchy all through a family lunch...	Oh yes, here comes the grumpy teen. I am not going to tolerate this behaviour, it's plain rude. I will just ignore him until he pulls himself together.	I wonder what he felt so strongly about when he was grumpy? It's important I try to help him understand himself, so I must try to find a way to gently talk it through when he's calmer.
		Use a teen lens – be empathetic to less-than-perfect behaviour. The changes the teen is going through are tough.

Chapter 2

The Teen Brain Thinks and Feels

Long story, short

- There are three different 'brains' (groups of structures), each with a different job:
    - the instinctual 'brain' dominates in a crisis
    - the emotional 'brain' feels and motivates
    - the thinking 'brain' thinks and reasons.
- The brain considers things in the following order of importance: safety, emotions, then thinking.
- The emotional brain remembers and can quickly trigger a response.
- Understand brain functioning and you will understand teen behaviour.
- Teenage brains learn best when the emotional brain is calm and content.
- Getting young people in the right 'zone' for learning facilitates the thinking brain; you can help engender this situation by communicating with them effectively.

Introduction

*Why did you do that? What were you **thinking**?*

said the adult to the teen, the world over. How many of us have felt so angry that we behaved reactively in a way we regretted later? All of us. Well, that's because all of us have brains that don't always **think**. In effect, our brain considers thinking a luxurious pastime, feeling takes precedence.

The science bit: Brain and behaviour

The Triune brain helps us understand behaviour

Behaviour is a window into the functioning of the brain and by understanding the brain we have a better understanding of behaviour. The Triune brain is a framework that describes the brain in terms of three distinct regions (each termed a sub-brain) each with its role in brain functioning. The model was formulated by an American neuroscientist, Paul MacLean, in the 1960s. The three 'brains' – instinctual, emotional and thinking – follow an evolutionary path, which means they have evolved successively as humans have developed.

Warning: The Triune brain is a highly simplified model of brain organisation and activity but is a useful rubric to understand behaviour, particularly for non-neuroscientists.

THE INSTINCTUAL BRAIN – DOMINATES IN A CRISIS

Brain functions essential for survival – such as breathing, heart-rate and body temperature regulation – take place in the instinctual brain. This set of brain structures, in the lower regions of the brain, towards the rear, is the brain stem. The brain stem monitors us, and keeps us safe by taking over when we are in danger. When we are under threat (in the modern day world this can include when we feel very anxious or stressed), functioning in this part of the brain will take precedence over any other brain activity and we go into a state of 'fight, flight or freeze'. When this part of the brain is most active (in a state of anxiety), behavioural responses are quick, instant and protective. At these times there is no reflection or careful thought. Brain signals are sent straight to the body to act quickly in order to ensure our survival. Instinctive responses – such as hitting out at someone in response to a threat (fight), running away (flight) or standing still (freeze) – are driven by this part of the brain? These are simple, impulsive behaviours, usually carried out in defensive, uncertain and fearful times. This is as true for you as it is for the young person in your care.

THE EMOTIONAL BRAIN – FEELS AND MOTIVATES

At the top of the brain stem and buried underneath the top layer (the cortex) is an area known to scientists as the limbic system, which we will call the emotional brain. The emotional brain houses structures responsible for safety, emotions and motivation. It is an important region for forming the relationships with others – so fundamental to human experience. Parts of the emotional brain (the amygdala) light up when we have a strong feeling such as anger, anxiety, sadness, guilt and happiness. Other parts (the hippocampus) hold event memories, so emotional memories can be used in the future to help keep us safe and enable faster learning. Another emotional brain structure (the ventral striatum) lights up when we are motivated to do something and drives behaviour. It is unconscious but together our emotional brain structures help us get what we want from the environment.

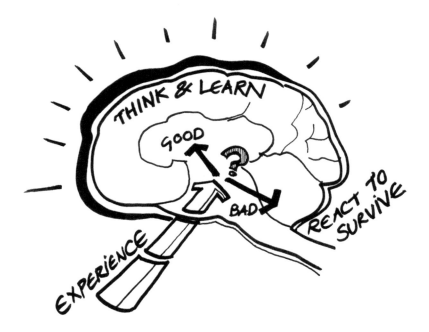

Figure 2.1: How the brain functions in response to experience

Judy Willis (2009), a neurologist from the United States, calls the emotional brain the 'switching station' because it determines where brain activity goes. A person's response to any experience is filtered through the emotional brain. For example, if a person is extremely frightened, the emotional brain essentially assesses the signals, and as it considers 'fear' a crisis it sends a message to the instinctual brain to switch on the survival mechanisms. Note that brain activity is pulled away from the thinking brain. Emotions are like big sirens. They are hard to ignore because they tell the brain to pay attention. But if the emotional and instinctual brain judge a situation to be calm and safe, the brain is free to work in the higher parts of the brain and do careful thinking.

THE THINKING BRAIN REASONS

Thinking and reasoning is done in the highest part of the Triune brain, the thinking brain (the cortex). It is made up of folded brain matter which forms an outer layer over the top of the brain covering from front to back. It allows us to speak, reason, calculate and decide. It is where our intelligent thinking takes place – the clever bit, although it is facilitated by complex circuitry below. It is more developed in humans than in any other living organism.

The thinking brain is highly immature when we are born and goes on developing and shaping itself until full maturity around the age of 25. A particularly important region in the thinking brain, just above the eyes, is known as the prefrontal cortex (PFC) and is the seat of judgement. This is where we make decisions, direct our attention and it helps us think before we act. We discuss this region a lot throughout the book as it is important.

Translating your teen

The emotional brain is the link between the thinking and the instinctual brain

The emotional brain is fundamental to brain function and guides us towards things that are important to us (motivators) and away from things that may be harmful (threats). There are many critical circuits linking the emotional and thinking brains, with particularly strong connections to the PFC. Animals don't have a PFC like we do and so are driven by their emotional brain. Your pet dog simply follows her desires for food, fun, love and attention. We have a thinking brain so that we can moderate our responses – wait until everyone is seated before we eat, read another person's mood before giving them a hug, do our chores before we have fun and think through and consider what is driving teens' behaviour before we shout at them. Teenagers are learning to use their thinking and emotional brains together, but it's a highly complicated process for the brain. The emotional brain signals are sometimes so loud in adolescence (and for good reason – see Chapter 10: Powerful Feelings and Mighty Motivations) that they drown out the reasoned behaviour messages from the thinking brain.

The thinking brain can only function when the environment is right

Paul Gilbert (2010) describes three important aspects of the environ-ment which are fundamental to engaging the thinking brain. The first is **safety**. When a young person feels safe they are more able to engage their thinking brain. The second is **motivation**. A teen's performance in tasks can improve exponentially when they are motivated to do well. The third is **feelings**, an important source of self-protection. Feelings are there to give us quick signals about the environment so that we can act and react to be safe. Just like motivation, feelings can be a friend or foe to learning. If a child is feeling anxious (about being judged in a learning situation) or angry (at the way they have been treated), their emotional brain draws energy away from their thinking and learning brain. If they feel supported by those around them, content and able to take on a task, their thinking and learning brain can fire on all cylinders.

The emotional brain has a strong memory

A small structure in the emotional brain called the hippocampus (we've got two: one in each brain hemisphere) stores memories of past events. This ensures we remember and learn from past experience, which is often very helpful (if you got burnt last time you touched the stove, you will remember not to do that again) but can also be unhelpful for learning. If a maths lesson was stressful last week, even before a young person begins work, their emotional brain is remembering maths = stress. If homework is always a time of stress, shouting and tears, your teen may have a meltdown as soon as they hear the words 'it's time to do your homework'. The meltdown can be explained like this: brain activity rushes to the emotional brain (the switching station), which sends the brain power to the instinctual brain because it is considered a crisis ('This situation is bad news. Run! (flight) or make it stop (fight)'). Brain power is not directed to the thinking brain, the area in which the homework is done. Think again if you believe their meltdown 'came out of nowhere'. Meltdowns never come out of nowhere, but a stressful memory may well trigger an instant emotional response.

What does that mean day to day?

The Triune brain helps us understand behaviour

As adults it is important to bear in mind that your teen's negative or impulsive behaviour may be driven by strong brain signals. The young person is still learning how to manage their impulses and drives. Providing a safe environment is important to young people so they can access their thinking brain to regulate their behaviour and responses or to learn. Motivation is extremely helpful to aid learning, and threatening situations block learning.

Internal motivation (they want to do it themselves) is by far the most effective way to get a brain going but it isn't always available, so we often have to get their motivational system in line by offering rewards. If they are motivated towards the reward their emotional brain gets in line more easily, making for a more efficient brain and more effective performance.

Emotional memories are stored to help predict the future

The brain readily stores emotional memories, so if homework, for example, is often stressful, the teenage brain will automatically be less receptive before the teen even starts their homework. For repeated stressful situations, take time to work out what is going on and use the Triune brain model to find the best solution.

Vulnerable young people have had difficult experiences and their instinctual and emotional brains may dominate

Some young people are particularly vulnerable. The brains of young people who have lived through terribly unsafe and scary times may be wired to trigger to fight or flight easily. This response has protected them in the past, but it is not conducive to learning if the brain is primed to react for survival. Others may have lived through a difficult event (e.g. being bullied at school) or fear they have lost a significant adult's love (e.g. after a divorce). These young people may behave in extreme and unpredictable ways because their emotional and instinctual brains are used to being in charge. Adults need to help the young person to understand their experience and develop an environment in which they feel secure and stable so that the emotional brain considers it safe enough to activate the thinking brain and learning can take place.

What does that mean for learning?

Use your brain knowledge to create the right environment for your teen to engage their thinking brain

Learning can be hard. If we are learning, by definition we don't know the answers, and that is a vulnerable position to be in. Young people can be fearful of failure in learning tasks, and in a culture of high stakes for school grades, teens' emotional and instinctual brains can easily dominate. What adults need to know is how to facilitate effective functioning in the thinking brain to help with learning. For all of us, all the time, the thinking brain and the emotional and instinctual brains are competing to dominate our actions. Our brains cannot instruct the body to run away while also processing algebra. One or the other has to take precedence. Safety is of primary importance – there is no point in doing algebra if our life is threatened; remember the hierarchy of instinctual, emotional and, finally, thinking brain. Avoid delivering your incredibly important, wise and powerful lecture about how to get into university when your teen is upset, ashamed or angry. Their brain power won't be their thinking brain, so their ability to listen and learn will be significantly reduced.

Getting the task level right is important to promote optimal learning

Most teachers are familiar with the **Zone of Proximal Development**, a concept developed by a Russian psychologist, Lev Vygotsky, at the turn of the 19th century, which says we need to get an individual in the right 'zone' to stretch their learning (Vygotsky 1978); this occurs when the task feels hard, but just about achievable with concerted effort and possibly support from others.

Tom Senninger (2015) used Vygotsky's ideas and described three different zones:

- the 'comfort' zone – learners feel safe but they are unchallenged and so aren't learning
- the 'learning' zone – learners are stretched and grow
- the 'panic' zone – learners are stressed and learning is blocked.

Senninger's description of different learning behaviours fits with what we know about how the brain works. If a task is undemanding (comfort zone), the young person will disengage, lack motivation and the emotional brain will dominate, their brains will not grow and they will not move on to more challenging tasks. If a task is too hard (panic zone), they may become fearful and the emotional brain will dominate. With the thinking brain disengaged it's unlikely that their brain will grow. However, if the teen is stretched sufficiently (learning zone), they will engage their thinking brain, experience brain growth and also grow in confidence. As we will see in Chapter 10: Powerful Feelings and Mighty Motivations, teens have learning priorities, and using these is the key to success in helping an adolescent to learn.

So, what now?

The Triune brain helps us to understand teen behaviour. Understand how the brain functions and you have an important part of the key to unlocking the potential of a teenage brain.

The next two case studies show different perspectives of a young person's experience at school, and how those around them work to support them.

Case study: Mercia

Mercia, a secondary school head teacher, was reflecting on what was happening with students in her school. When they misbehaved in class the form teacher would send the young person to Mercia, both as a kind of punishment but also a chance to reflect on what they had done. Mercia was bemused because there often seemed to be a mismatch between the behaviour the form teacher reported and the behaviour she saw in her office. By the time the young person was with Mercia they were often reflective, repentant but often unable to say *why* they had behaved as they had. Yet often the same person would be in the same position a week later. What was happening?

Mercia decided to sit in on some classes to observe. What she saw was quite amazing. Young people often started well in class, but then there would be a trigger that would put them off course. For example, they might stumble over a learning activity or a friend might tug at their jumper and annoy them. The young person then seemed to change and a much less thoughtful part of the young person took over. If Mercia tried to talk to the young person immediately after the incident, they seemed unable to reflect or consider their actions. This was very unlike the situation she'd encountered in her office once they had had a period of calm. After reading about the Triune brain Mercia realised what was happening – these young people were often unable to control their behaviour and make good choices in that moment because their lower brain had taken over.

A good resolution

Mercia called a staff meeting. She taught the staff about how the brain functions and ran an interactive workshop where all the teachers were given a chance to think about when they seemed to 'lose it' and lower brain regions took over. Mercia told staff that young people needed a period of calm when their behaviour was going awry. Staff began to notice the 'fight or flight' response in their students after a bad grade, a fight with a friend or an angry remark from a teacher and stopped trying to get answers in that moment. Young people were helped to understand that while they couldn't necessarily change the way they felt, they could change their behaviour if they understood it better. Over time, behaviour improved and relationships in the school strengthened.

What might get in the way?

Teachers want all children to achieve. There is no doubt about that. Teaching is probably one of the toughest jobs out there. It requires real devotion to the cause. However, as teachers fight to deliver an over-packed curriculum, they see behaviour as an interference pulling them off course. We must remember that a brain ripe for development is at stake here, and while academic learning is important, the ability to understand emotions and behaviour is a skill that will serve a young person long-term, ultimately supporting learning of all kinds. If a young person is struggling with their emotions and behaviour, it is worthwhile spending time enabling them to understand why and giving them the skills to manage.

Case study: Skye

Fourteen-year-old Skye became very overwhelmed at the beginning of each term thinking about the exams at the end of the term and all of the work she needed to do to get there. The worries would plague her and she found it difficult to deal with them. Her father would reassure her that it would work out fine, but this was not enough. Skye would become upset – in fact, so upset that it affected her digestive tracts, resulted in headaches and meant that she was tearful and frustrated. Her academic achievement was important to her and she really wanted to perform well. She put a lot of pressure on herself. It became increasingly difficult for everyone at home. Her two brothers did not share the same concerns but were finding her emotional presence hard to deal with. Her anxiety was beginning to affect all aspects of her life. She struggled to choose where to sit in the classroom and she found it hard to see her friends socially, even though she wanted to spend time with them.

A good resolution

Skye's parents decided something needed to be done to help her. They called a meeting with her teachers. The first thing was to acknowledge that it was difficult and then they needed to be very clear about what was the exact content of her anxiety. Skye shared her negative, anxious thoughts easily (e.g. if I don't do well at school I won't go to university and everyone will be disappointed in me). She was distressed and it was hard, but she felt relieved afterwards. Skye and her teachers planned out a work timetable and gave her some control over when the various submissions were required, based on the previous school year. Clear boundaries were put in place for 'work' time to ensure she had 'down-time' every day when she could relax. If the work wasn't quite finished, that was OK. She was paired up with an older student mentor who she met with twice per week; her mentor gave her advice on the pitfalls of high school, describing which teachers were approachable and which subjects and clubs might be most enjoyable. At home, Skye's father took time each morning and evening to speak with Skye, to challenge her negative thoughts and work out what was going well and what she struggled with. They talked a great deal about her feelings, which was new territory for both of them but with practice became easier. Their relationship was closer and Skye told her father that she often felt that she could not manage the school work and doubted herself. The worries remained present, but were much more manageable. The physical symptoms reduced significantly.

What might get in the way?

Once you recognise that a young person is struggling emotionally, conversation is key along with a plan for how to manage going forward. Over time it can be hard to keep this up as the stresses of life take over. It is important for parents and staff to keep meeting regularly to check in with young people and not to remove the support too quickly. Early intervention is much more helpful than waiting until there is a crisis, and we know that support for anxiety is far more likely to produce a positive outcome.

Action point: Notice a teen's behaviour to read their brain

You can figure out which sub-brain is in the driving seat by looking at a young person's behaviour. Faced with homework, if a young person starts acting up, messing about being rude or doodling on the page, it is likely that their emotional brain is in charge and their thinking brain is struggling to keep up. Take note of this and change what you are doing so that they can engage their thinking brain.

Action point: If emotions are in charge, your teen can't think

Barked instructions ('Stop messing about!') or irritation ('What is wrong with you, why can't you just start your homework?') are not effective ways to facilitate the thinking brain of a teenager. We need to work out why the emotional brain is dominating and calm them. Chapter 17: May The Force Be With You, Luke offers some tips for what to do in the moment, which will help switch the thinking brain back on. We all respond with our instinctual brain from time to time. We are all works in progress, but offering teens the chance to understand their behaviour will mean they are more likely to be able to behave logically and reflectively, and this will serve them well.

Action point: Motivate, don't threaten

The most engaged teenge brain is one that is motivated. Motivation is a natural drive towards pursuing a goal and achievement. While threat-based learning can sometimes draw short-term rewards, it is likely to do long-term damage to mental health. As we will learn, teens have mighty motivations and, while it may not always be possible, tapping into internal motivation is always going to be the most effective way to engage the learning brain.

Action point: Consider whether the task level is right

When presenting a learning task, it is crucial to get the level right so the teenager is in their 'zone of proximal development'. If a young person is not engaged or making progress, consider whether the task level is right for them and support them when they get frustrated, or invite them to take a step up in complexity if they are not engaged.

The moral of the story is...

Understanding how information enters and is processed in the brain can be very helpful. At a fundamental level, we need to pay attention to the emotional brain signals so that the brain power can be channelled into the thinking brain for learning. The order is important here. Learning is a luxury in a world where survival is essential, so the emotional brain functions get first pick at the brain energy store. It takes time to be able to cope with the frustrations of learning. Your job as adults caring for teenagers is to provide an environment that invites the thinking brain to switch on. This book is about showing you how to do this.

Downloads: The Teen Brain Thinks and Feels

Understand how the brain works and you will understand your teen's behaviour – and yours

All brains, teenagers' included, prioritise safety before thinking. Of all the possible influences on the brain, the drive to stay safe will call the shots on brain activity. If the teen feels unsafe physically or emotionally, their brain is focused on dealing with threat and pushes activity to the emotional brain. A safe, calm and motivated brain works best for learning and making good choices, because the brain can allow resource into the areas that think and reason (the thinking brain).

Getting the teenage brain in the right 'zone' for learning is key to making the most of teen learning potential.

Exercise

Sometimes fear or anxiety can 'look like' anger. Keep this in mind and note down three situations in which your teen appeared anxious or angry, when they seemed 'all over the place', possibly out of control. This is when your teen's brain is dominated by the emotional brain. Ask yourself: What were they doing? Who else was there? What happened just before? What else was significant that day/week/month for your teen? What did you say? How did you react?

Anxious or angry – Situation 1

. . . .

. . . .

Anxious or angry – Situation 2

. . . .

. . . .

Anxious or angry – Situation 3

. . . .

. . . .

Now make a note of three situations in which your teen is best able to regulate their emotions and engage their thinking brain. Answer the same questions.

Best able to regulate emotions and engage thinking brain – Situation 1

. . . .

. . . .

Best able to regulate emotions and engage thinking brain – Situation 2

. . . .

. . . .

Best able to regulate emotions and engage thinking brain – Situation 3

. . . .

. . . .

Do the same exercise for yourself.

Anxious or angry – Situation 1

. . . .

. . . .

Anxious or angry – Situation 2

. . . .

. . . .

Anxious or angry – Situation 3

. . . .

. . . .

**Best able to regulate emotions and engage thinking brain –
Situation 1**

. . . .

. . . .

**Best able to regulate emotions and engage thinking brain –
Situation 2**

. . . .

. . . .

**Best able to regulate emotions and engage thinking brain –
Situation 3**

. . . .

. . . .

When this happens...	Instead of this...	Try this...
Your teen is avoiding studying for their exams due to start next week.	If you don't do well in that exam next week you can say goodbye to that party at the weekend. I need to see some commitment to your studies, now.	Your exams next week are important and I know you can do well. Focus is going to be key this week. What can we do to make sure you work well this week, so you can enjoy that party next weekend?
		Motivate, don't threaten
Your teen gets his books out to study, then suddenly shouts, 'I'm dropping Chemistry. I'm done with this', and chucks his book on the floor.	That explosion came out of nowhere. What is his problem?	He must have been triggered by what happened last time we sat down to do chemistry homework together which, I must say, didn't go well. Let's see how we can change it, together.
		Recognise triggered behaviour – feelings never come out of nowhere
Your teen failed a test despite having studied for it for many hours at home and school.	She seemed to revise for hours and still didn't do well in the test. She must be weak at that subject.	I wonder whether she spent all that revision time in her 'comfort' zone. If so, it would not have challenged her and stretched her learning sufficiently to do well. I want to go through her study techniques in detail.
		Time on task is not the best predictor of success, it's what young people do in that time that counts

Chapter 3

The Teen Brain
Learns and Believes

Long story, short

- Our brains are immature at birth and grow by linking neurones together to build circuits.
- Repetition is the key to building stronger circuits for learning – this changes the brain.
- Beliefs we hold about ourselves change the way our brains work.
- Teens need to be in a positive cycle of learning to build their brains.
- Having a growth mindset makes young people take on new challenges and their brains grow strong when they make a mistake.
- Adults create a positive environment for learning by using growth mindset language about themselves and their teens.

Introduction

Brains grow when we do things repeatedly

We are always learning. It is a natural part of the human condition because we have **neuroplasticity** (see Chapter 1: The Incredible Teen Brain – Time to Upgrade). Learning is not always comfortable. Indeed, if we are going to get really good at anything, there will inevitably be some discomfort while we learn and an effort required to bridge the gap between the existing level and the learning goal.

Michelle Obama describes this very well:

When you think hard about something or you struggle to solve a problem – whether it's math or science, or a problem in life – your brain is actually growing. (Michelle Obama 2014)

Knowing the nuts and bolts of how the brain develops and what changes underlie learning can be extremely helpful because we can visualise what is happening in the brain when, for example, a young person learns a new task or makes a decision that bewilders us.

We hold beliefs that affect our brain and behaviour

Human beings hold a set of beliefs that have a powerful influence on how we interact with the world. The way we think influences what we do and feel; this is known as a mindset. The field of *mindsets* was made popular by Carol Dweck (2012), an American psychologist, who first championed the idea that an individual's belief about whether intelligence is fixed (a fixed mindset) or can be grown (a growth mindset) might be an important determinant of success.

More than a decade of research has proved the power of mindset in shaping a person's feelings, thoughts and behaviour towards many aspects of life. As Jo Boaler, a professor of mathematics education, puts it: 'When people change their mindsets and start to believe that they can learn to high levels, they change their learning pathways and achieve at higher levels' (2016, p.ix). As you read through this book you will see the power our beliefs have over how we respond to stress, setbacks in learning, difficult social experiences and how we interpret other people's abilities, including the young people we work with.

The science bit: Brain and behaviour

When we learn, we build new brain circuits

The brain contains approximately 86 billion neurones, cells which form the building blocks for learning. We are born with approximately the same number of neurones that we die with, but the difference between an immature brain and a mature brain is the number of connections between neurones. A newborn baby's brain has few connections. You are probably aware of the rapid speed of brain development from birth to three years, particularly if you have watched a baby and toddler master a series of complex tasks rapidly. This proficient growth is due to the brain making circuits which connect areas of the brain together, linking parts together to develop different skills.

While genes play a role in determining which part of the brain is ready for development, as we saw earlier, day-to-day experience is the driving force behind learning, a process called 'brain wiring'. When we do something for the first time, an electrical signal is sent down one neurone and links to another with a chemical compound, the electrical signal then continues to the next neurone, and so on, linking billions of neurones together in circuits. As the saying goes, 'Cells that fire together wire together' (Carla J. Shatz 1992, p.64).

The first time your teenager uses a new App on their phone or learns the controls on a new computer game, they are building a brain circuit. Every time they repeat it, the circuit becomes stronger and the behaviour becomes faster and requires less effort. During the learning process, the brain wraps a fatty layer around the brain circuit so the signal moves more quickly and efficiently (a process called myelination). Just watch the speed of an adolescent texting on their phone to observe evidence of a very well-myelinated circuit. The bottom line is that any repeated activity or thought pattern makes lasting changes to brain pathways.

A person's mindset has a big impact on how they feel, think and behave

Intelligence (IQ) is not the most important factor when it comes to academic performance, many factors contribute including mindset – a well-replicated finding. Students with a 'fixed' mindset about intelligence believe ability is carved in stone and determined at birth. These youngsters wilt and shrink in the face of a challenge, feel threatened by failure and stick with what they know. Young people with a 'growth' mindset believe skills and achievement are grown through effort, persistence and repetition. These youngsters believe they can learn anything, persevere when it's hard, purposefully seek challenges and can be motivated by an obstacle. When researchers discovered they could manipulate a child's mindset and influence achievement and behaviour, it was a revelation.

Translating your teen

At least 10,000 hours are needed to be an expert

Understanding how the brain learns at a cellular level fits with the '10,000 hour rule'. Canadian journalist Malcolm Gladwell popularised this idea in his book *Outliers* (2008), but the research was actually done by Swedish psychologists Anders Ericsson, Ralf Krampe and Clemens Tesch-Romer (1993), who wanted to know what made talented people so good at what they did and studied skilled people in all kinds of fields. Whatever their skill, the experts all had one thing in common – they had all put in a minimum of 10,000 hours' practice in their chosen field. It needed to be what he called 'deliberate practice', in which the person identifies areas of weakness, seeks critical feedback and improves technique. Ericsson was not a neuroscientist, but his notion of deliberate practice is supported by findings from neuropsychological research. Skill comes from repetition – the more a circuit is fired, the more efficient it becomes. No one becomes an expert without hours of work.

Our aim is to get teens into a positive cycle of learning

A positive cycle of learning (see Figure 3.1) occurs when you do something, feel a sense of achievement and as you experience a state of 'flow', momentum builds along with brain circuits. You feel great, and then you do that activity again and again, getting more expert. Repetition builds brain circuits. Those circuits become more efficient as they get myelinated, building competence. When we are good at something we are keen to do it again and so the skill develops further.

Teach young people what is happening in their brain when they learn. Enable them to understand that when they do something for the first time, they will not be very good at it because they don't yet have the brain circuit to support that skill (useful to know when one experiences failure). If they want to be good at something, repetition is the key. It's a simple idea but it is fundamental to neuroscience and learning. If you say 'she's just talented at x, that's why she did well', it inadvertently teaches a young person they either *have it* or they *don't have it*. If you don't have it, then what's the point of trying? The thought gets in the way of learning. The right environment gets teens into a positive cycle of learning. We come back to the environment again and again as it's so important. Even though brains are built to learn, this cycle is easily disrupted by an unfavourable environment.

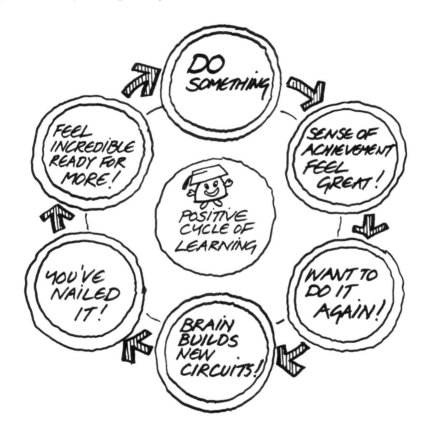

Figure 3.1: Positive cycle of learning

People with a growth mindset embrace challenges and try harder

Many things, including a fixed mindset, can knock a person out of the positive cycle of learning. A young person may be merrily working on a task and growing brain circuits but then they come to a challenge or experience failure. What happens next is key. Individuals with a growth mindset understand this as part of learning. They are challenged but believe repetition will get them there if they persist. Those with a fixed mindset read challenge as a sign that the task is not for them. Changing a young person's mindset gives gratifying results; it teaches teens about brain growth and reaching their potential.

With a growth mindset, mistakes cause the brain to spark and grow

Jason Mosner and colleagues (2011), a group of psychologists, studied what happens in the brain when we make a mistake. They found there is more activity in our neurones because most brain growth happens when our brains are struggling. It also turns out that people with a growth mindset show greater brain activity, and therefore growth, when they make a mistake than people with a fixed mindset. They literally learn more by their mistakes. A growth mindset predicts greater learning and might be just what is happening when people do their 10,000 hours of deliberate practice.

What does that mean day to day?

All learning requires practice – it takes time to learn to boil an egg

When we think about learning, we must ensure we keep in mind a broad definition of what we mean. We are not just referring to academic learning, but also to learning how to do the washing up, prioritise, make our beds, devise our schedule, work with our emotions, support someone in need. Teachers might consider teaching study skills or revision scheduling or how to manage exam anxiety. For parents, teens won't magically know how to do household chores, or manage their emotions and behaviour, unless they have had practice, with a supportive, instructive adult alongside them. If you find yourself saying, 'I can't believe I have a 17-year-old who can't boil an egg', ask yourself honestly, have you taught your child to boil an egg? Actually, it is quite a difficult skill at first, especially with the all-important toast soldier option, so give them a chance to build that circuit.

Watch your (mindset) language

Teens don't just learn about mindsets by being told about them. They discern this information from our behaviour and language. We tend to label young people as being *good* or *not good* at things. As it turns out, both are unhelpful. When a young person does something well and you give them a virtual pat on the back saying 'Gosh, you are such a talented musician' or 'You are so clever, you don't even have to try', you are reinforcing a fixed mindset. Similarly, when a young person does badly in a test and you say, no doubt to reassure them, 'Ah, don't worry about it, you are just not good at maths. Nor was I when I was younger. It's just how we're built', you are doing the same. Both messages convey there is little that they can do to change the course of their destiny, but they run against what science tells us about how the brain develops and grows.

Genes do have a small role to play. We can inherit a natural inclination for language, say, but if you don't have the opportunity to learn it, or don't value the effort needed to become really good, you will never be an expert. Growth mindset language focuses on effort: 'You did so well in your maths test, you must have worked really hard,' or 'That wasn't your best grade, so let's focus on how best to help you prepare for it next time.' These are small but very meaningful changes to your teen's environment that will help your child's brain grow to its optimal potential.

What does that mean for learning?

Watch out for fixed mindset triggers

The concept of the growth mindset has been embedded in education in recent years and the majority of teachers have had some exposure to its ideas. Many educationalists are implementing growth mindset concepts in their classrooms and using 'growth mindset' feedback, but the latest research offers important updates to the approach.

Recent research in this area warns about the dangers of mindset triggers. Certain events may cause us to revert to a fixed mindset. For example, if a student continues to get a poor grade in a subject, as their teacher you might begin to believe they just aren't good at that subject. It is important to monitor these beliefs, because students need teachers who believe in them. A teacher's words and the beliefs they hold about their students are powerful predictors of student success. In fact, psychologists Jason Okonofua, David Paunesku and Gregory Walton (2016) described a one-session intervention inviting an empathic mindset in teachers which had a significant impact on pupil engagement and vastly improved student–teacher relationships. As many teachers will know, it only takes one small change or one person to turn a child's learning around.

Be aware of triggers for a fixed mindset about yourself, which are particularly likely in high-pressured situations. You don't meet a deadline and you think, 'I'm never any good at time management, I'll give this to colleague X next time.' Don't get tricked into that kind of thinking. If you keep trying, your neuronal circuits will fire and you will get better at it, slowly but surely. Only 9,999 hours to go.

Students need teachers who actively encourage them to make mistakes

Making a mistake feels horrible and may be particularly painful for a teen and their developing self-concept (see Chapter 11: Self-reflection), but it is important to embed a culture in a learning environment that values errors. A mistake? Fantastic! Now your brain is *really* growing.

So, what now?

Teenage brains have neuronal circuits ready and waiting to grow with efficiency. We can use our knowledge of science to support young people to grow their brains if we tell them how it works and reinforce a growth mindset. Be careful how you phrase feedback and don't slip into a habit of thinking either you or your students *can't* do it. When it comes to the brain, there is no such thing as can't. It's just that you haven't learnt to do it yet.

Case study: Reo

Reo was a young man, aged 19, who came to see a psychologist following a bout of trichotillomania, an anxiety-related condition which causes people to pull out their hair. Reo was from a small, loving family and had been an all-round high achiever throughout his school career. He was told from an early age how academically capable he was and teachers regularly said, 'You are so clever, you will no doubt go to a top university.'

Reflecting on his time at school, Reo said he had always been a well-behaved student who had met parental and teacher expectations. He had been top of the class academically and said he didn't need to work that hard for it. He loved hockey and had played throughout his school life, usually in the A team at school. He had some friendship problems during adolescence, partly due to competitive jealousy between him and his friends who were all trying for the sought-after top team spots in hockey. He had struggled with the conflict of being close friends with peers while also competing with them. It got nasty at times. He was made head boy in the final year of school.

Reo was completely shocked and upset when he did not do as well as expected in his final school exams, nor get a place at the university of his choice. His parents and teachers were similarly surprised, although they tried hard to not show it. Reo did go to a good university and found friends and settled well. Although he loved the adults in his life very much, the separation from his parents and teachers had been good for him and he was developing autonomy and independence in a healthy way. Peer relationships had gone much better at university and he was working out who he was and what he wanted to do with his life. However, when applying to study law, he became overwhelmed with anxiety. This is when the trichotillomania had begun and he couldn't control it.

As Reo talked with the therapist and worked through his thoughts, he realised he was terrified of the possible rejection he might get by applying for legal placements. It was a highly competitive process. He reflected on how traumatic what he saw as his 'failure' in the final hurdle at school had been and how he felt publicly ashamed. He did not want to risk that again.

A good resolution

Reo is a good example of a young person whose parents had been keen to bolster his confidence throughout childhood by telling him how inherently capable he was. While this was done with good intentions, combined with his desire to please, it meant he never got a bad grade throughout his school career. He had developed a fixed mindset ('I am clever'), and when he did not do as well as expected, he believed this meant his parents and teachers had got it wrong. He believed it confirmed that he wasn't as bright as they had said. Looking back, he saw some behaviours that might have limited his growth at school. He only ever wanted to try things he knew he wouldn't fail at, so perhaps didn't push himself. If he didn't do so well in a topic he would quickly move on, telling himself it just wasn't 'his' subject. After all, he was clever and didn't have to work at things. He remembered struggling in class but being scared to ask a question because he feared he might lose his place as the 'clever' boy.

In therapy, Reo learnt about a growth mindset and thought about how it impacted on his approach to new and difficult tasks. He also learnt that failure did not equal 'not clever'. He was scared but, with a psychologist alongside him, found the courage to apply for law and risk not getting the highly competitive places on the course. He was rejected, as many candidates are first time, but with his new growth mindset he was able to pick himself up, work hard and try again. Next time, he did have success, and with it a growth mindset and whole new approach to life.

What might get in the way?

It was brave of Reo to seek help from a psychologist and supportive of his parents to encourage it. To begin with, it was hard for him to think in any critical way about his childhood, which he had thought was perfect. But he soon realised that this was not about criticising his parents and teachers.

Recent research in this area has helped us to understand

how adult language and well-intentioned encouragement can hold young people back. This was not about blame, it was about reflection and understanding.

Action point: All learning comes from repetition, so support and encourage teens to keep going

Use your new neuroscientific knowledge to support the young people in your care to build circuits that they need for life, not just for achieving academically but also for life skills. If they can't yet do something you consider a basic skill, don't look exasperated, teach them and then give them opportunities to do it again and again.

Action point: A cycle needs to occur and recur

Learning is a cycle and will require several attempts to be efficient – that's OK. The key elements must be present though. Find what builds a sense of success and achievement in your teenager and think about what you can do to enable them to feel this more. Read on to find out what might mitigate against entering this positive learning cycle and how we can get young people back on track.

Action point: Teach young people how the brain grows and foster a growth mindset

Familiarise yourself with the signs of a fixed and growth mindset and make sure your teen knows about them too. Pay attention to the detail of your language to ensure you are not inadvertently reinforcing a fixed mindset. Watch out for traps and triggers to support your teen. Grow your brain; believe in yourself and in them.

Action point: Help them find a new way to practise their learning

If the young person is struggling with a task, support them to also think about *how* to work next time. 'You must try harder' can be demoralising and isn't specific enough to be useful. Support a review of their strategy, where they study, when they do their practice and so on. Changing the practice **approach** may make it purposeful and move the learning to the next level.

Action point: Talk to young people about your own mistakes
Talk to them about your challenges and triumphs. Normalise mistakes, talk about your experiences of frustration and wanting to give up. Then revel in the joy of when you broke through and how great that felt. Young people need role models – you can show them growth is as much about failure and getting back up to learn again as it is about working hard. Of course, struggling and making mistakes are difficult experiences, but say it loud, proud and often – these experiences add value and are rich learning opportunities.

The moral of the story is...

Brains build circuits through repetition, which leads to competence. The environment for, beliefs about and responses to learning challenges can make or break the path into the positive cycle of learning.

Downloads: The Teen Brain Learns and Believes

Brains learn by doing, and we develop skills by repetition and practice. Teenage brains are particularly primed to learn but, to make the most of this potential, they need to get into a positive cycle of learning. What we believe about learning and our belief about ourselves as learners predicts how we react in a learning experience and thus how much we will learn.

Pay attention to your language to support a growth mindset and teach young people that mistakes are an inherent part of the learning process. Your mindset about your own learning and about your teen's learning capacity will influence their mindset about learning.

Exercise

Note three situations when things didn't go so well for your teen. Think about academic tasks and life skills. Are you triggered into a fixed mindset such as 'They are no good at this and never will be? They might as well stop trying'?

It didn't go so well – Situation 1

. . . .

. . . .

It didn't go so well – Situation 2

. . . .

. . . .

It didn't go so well – Situation 3

. . . .

. . . .

When are your teens in the best positive learning cycle? (Think broadly about any activity – it might be programming the games console.) Is your mindset still fixed? What is different in comparison to the learning experience that didn't go well?

It went well – Situation 1

. . . .

. . . .

It went well – Situation 2

. . . .

. . . .

It went well – Situation 3

. . . .

. . . .

When your teen tries something for the first time, do they seem upset when they are not instantly successful? It might indicate a fixed mindset about their own learning. What is your response?

. . . .

. . . .

Now do this exercise with yourself in mind.

It didn't go so well – Situation 1

. . . .

. . . .

It didn't go so well – Situation 2

. . . .

. . . .

It didn't go so well – Situation 3

. . . .

. . . .

It went well – Situation 1

. . . .

. . . .

It went well – Situation 2

. . . .

. . . .

It went well – Situation 3

. . . .

. . . .

When this happens...	Instead of this...	Try this...
Your teen tried to wash his clothes for the first time. He put his new blue shirt in with his whites and now everything is tinted blue.	He is never going to cope alone. He is 18 and can't even wash his clothes without ruining them.	New skills don't just appear from nowhere. He is learning something new where we expect mistakes to be made. He'll get there – brain circuits take time to build.
		Remember, **mistakes** are an important part of learning
Your teen aces an English assessment.	Wow, you did so well in your English test. You are just really good at that subject, the same as me.	Wow, you did so well in your English test. You must have worked really hard at that.
		Consider your language carefully to support a growth mindset about **performance**
Your teen has stopped following her study time-table, saying it is totally useless.	You'll never pass your exams with that attitude of 'I can't'.	Your workload is so big right now, it must feel overwhelming and make you think you can't do it. Remember, the brain learns by repetition, so the more you practise, the better you will become.
		Be careful to reinforce a growth mindset about the approach to **task preparation**

Chapter 4

The Teen Brain Connects, Watches and Absorbs

Long story, short

- We learn by associating two events, experiencing consequences and/or watching others (modelling).
- We are actively teaching our teens when we are with them – whether we think they are watching or not.
- Young people's brains are primed to reflect their own learning processes, through metacognition (thinking about thinking).
- By modelling our learning behaviour, we can invite adolescents into the positive cycle of learning.

Introduction

We are always learning from each other

For many years psychologists have studied how we learn from each other, leading them to identify some patterns. Understanding these patterns can play an important part in enabling us to unlock the potential of the teenage brain. Learning – in the broadest possible sense of acquiring new behaviours, habits, attitudes or skills – can be positive, enriching, harmful or negative. It can launch you into a mind-blowing orbit or hinder your progress. But whatever the learning context, adults are often intrinsically involved in the mechanisms underlying a teen's learning.

The science bit: Brain and behaviour

Two events can become linked, even if we don't want them to be

The brain has multiple systems for 'learning'. While many of the skills and procedures that come under the guise of 'educational' learning take thousands of hours of practice to build circuits, other kinds of learning can happen very quickly and passively. Learning through association is referred to as classical conditioning. Ivan Pavlov (2011), a Russian physiologist, made the famous observation that dogs would naturally salivate at the sight of food fed to them by a lab worker in a white coat, but that after a while the dogs also began to salivate at the sight of the white coat alone. Salivating at the sight of a white coat did not happen spontaneously, the dogs learnt to do it – it is a **conditioned response**. In a young person's world the equivalent learning experience might be that fear is the conditioned response to school because they have been bullied and so have learnt to respond with fear at the very thought of it. By the same token a student will dislike a subject if they have been punished by the teacher. This conditioning can be very strong, and a dislike of the subject might continue throughout the academic career of the student or even their life.

Table 4.1: *Conditioned responses mean we learn through association*

Unpleasant object	Neutral object	Change in behaviour (conditioned response)
Being bullied (at school)	School	Fear and avoidance of school
Being scolded (in maths lessons)	Maths	Low confidence in maths
Conflict with parents (when doing homework)	Homework	Dislike of homework

When one thing follows another, it can increase or decrease the chances of it happening again

Another important pattern of learning develops from the consequences of our actions, known as **operant conditioning**. American behaviourist B.F. Skinner (1998) described learning experiences that made the person feel good (reinforcement) or bad (negative consequences, or what Skinner called punishment). Experiences immediately after a behaviour can increase or decrease the likelihood that the behaviour will happen in the future. For example, getting a laugh from friends in a class when being cheeky to a teacher increases the chances of the teenager trying to make friends laugh again – the laughing has positively reinforced the cheeky behaviour. By the same token, having a curfew brought earlier for arriving home late after a party decreases the chances of them being late again. The reduced curfew is a negative consequence of the behaviour (arriving home late).

But we know that a teenager's brain responds differently to negative consequences than children's or adults' brains. Studies show that teenagers are much more likely to respond well to a positive reward or motivator (e.g. if you can get home on time you can earn the right to stay out later next month) rather than negative consequence (e.g. if you don't get home on time you will be grounded for the month). Moreover, negative consequences can disrupt positive adult–teen relationships. While there are going to be times when negative consequences are needed, using positive motivation is a better strategy at this time in a young person's life. As we learn more about neuroscience, it is becoming clearer that positive relationships form the bedrock of learning and any strategy that strengthens this should always be the first choice.

Table 4.2: *Operant conditioning means experiences immediately after a behaviour can increase or decrease the likelihood it will happen again in the future*

Behaviour	Experience that follows	Effect
Teacher smiles when an ordinarily shy student asks a question	Feel more encouraged (positive experience)	More likely to ask a question next time
Parent gives in when teen demands more gaming time	More gaming time (positive experience)	Teen more likely to demand more gaming time in future
Parent moves curfew back by half an hour when teen arrives home later than agreed	Less time out with friends (negative experience)	Teen more likely to stick to curfew next time

Modelling behaviour is very powerful

American psychologist Albert Bandura (1976) developed a theory called **social learning** in which an individual observes another person (the so-called model) and learns without encouragement (reinforcement) because the individual notices the consequences of the behaviour on the model. Bandura had children watch video clips of adults interacting with an inflatable Bobo doll. In some of the experiments, the adults ignored the doll, in others they punched it. Children who saw adults punch (or ignore) the doll were likely to follow suit when they spent time with the doll, even if it was some time later. Role models and the power of observational learning that goes on through the steps of attention, retention, reproduction and motivation are significant. It's true that peers influence teen behaviour (see Chapter 8: Cracking the Social Code), but role models like you, who are older and of a more senior status in the community, will have a significant impact on young people. What you *do* – much more than anything you *say* – is highly influential on adolescents.

Table 4.3: *Social learning theory means that teens learn simply through observing others*

Behaviour observed	Modelled response	Change in behaviour
Parent giving up when a task is challenging	Stop when it gets hard	Teen is more likely to give up on homework, for example, when challenging
Teacher shouts and bangs the desk when feeling irritated	When you feel 'wound up' – shout and act out (poor emotional regulation)	Teen more likely to lose their temper when other pupils frustrate them in group lessons

Thinking about thinking and developing strong strategies helps students get unstuck

Recently, educators have been helping young people understand the *processes* of learning as well as the content. Knowing and reflecting on *how* we learn, it turns out, can be very important. When a young person comes across a problem that seems insurmountable – writing an essay, giving a talk, asking someone out on a date – metacognition can help.

Metacognition is literally thinking about thinking. Teach young people to imagine they were standing above themselves, observing what they are doing, to help them to think about why they were stuck and what they need to do to get unstuck. We use metacognition a lot of the time, but by training young people to be metacognitive about difficult tasks, we can help them proactively overcome obstacles in their lives.

The growth mindset concept, introduced in the previous chapter, is an example of a metacognitive strategy. Another encourages young people to understand their 'executive functioning' skills which enable us to perform a task (see Chapter 7: Thriving with Neurodiversity) by overseeing our functioning, a bit like the conductor in an orchestra, telling us what to do when. Success in school is strongly dependent on these skills working well, so teaching teens what they are, what happens when they falter and helping them develop future strategies is highly effective for successful learning and independence. These self-regulation skills will serve them well for life.

Table 4.4: *We can teach teens to be 'metacognitive' so they learn what went wrong and what they can do next time*

Behaviour	Executive function challenge	Strategy	Growth mindset
Teen forgets homework set	Keeping information in mind (known as working memory)	Follow instruction as soon as teacher gives it to them	If I use information when I hear it, then it's off my list and it's done
Teen runs out of time in an exam	Planning when to do tasks and time management	Form a detailed plan at beginning of exam and use a timer	When I organise myself at the start I finish it well

Translating your teen

We learn to connect experiences unconsciously, and it is a highly efficient learning process

In day-to-day life, when two experiences co-occur they become paired unconsciously and then have influence even beyond the pairing. This is really important because we learn to like or dislike something based on the actions and events that come afterwards. Within the positive cycle of learning, this connection is strong. When a student has a positive experience of learning, their brain delivers a reward. The next time they are in that situation, they experience reward again – sometimes before they've even started. By the same token, negative experiences can prime a young person to feel fear and therefore practise avoidance. If piano practice is a time of shouting and upset, the young person will soon learn to dislike the music session and likely avoid it.

You can change young people's behaviour by changing yours

Young people will naturally avoid things they dislike, particularly during the teenage years when emotions are acutely felt (see Chapter 10: Powerful Feelings and Mighty Motivations). As an adult in their life, try to add positive experiences following behaviours you want to increase (allow them to have a treat after they have finished homework) and remove experiences that are keeping undesirable behaviour going (finish their homework for them when they have procrastinated so they can go to bed on time). These things matter in shaping their behaviour.

What lessons are you teaching your teen with your day-to-day activities?

Be aware that your teenager will copy what they see you do. This may not be conscious or ever discussed. Saying 'don't do this' as you do something is not effective. Actions trump words. Think about what you are 'teaching' your teen without even realising it. This applies to how you manage yourself when you are angry or anxious, how you approach a challenging problem and how much compassion you show for other people. What messages are you sending your teen with your day-to-day activities?

Young people are ready to learn how to learn

Teenage brains are ripe and ready to learn to be metacognitive. Now is the time to help them reflect on the processes of learning. What went well? What didn't go so well? Comment when they use a good strategy ('I liked the way you planned your time this evening, it worked well') or suggest strategies if they need some prompts ('Maybe try testing yourself on the material without looking'). This will hand them the keys to their own success.

What does that mean day to day?

Being thoughtful about the learning environment at home pays off

It's hard for anyone to be on best behaviour all the time at home or work, but do remember teens are watching you all the time and your behaviour shapes theirs. This is not about being perfect but about establishing good habits to provide an environment that is responsive, consistent and thoughtful. A mother who loves her work and spends hours reading and taking notes in any spare minute or down-time will soon notice her children will do the same – handing them an efficient, lifetime study habit.

Give a consequence for poor behaviour, but not an impulsive punishment

It is very important for young people to have clear boundaries – there should be clear expectations about rules, being polite, kind and so on. However, remember that teens have heightened emotional experiences (see Chapter 10: Powerful Feelings and Mighty Motivations), and if emotions run high in the moment, particularly just after a boundary has been crossed or a rule broken, they may struggle to tell you how they are feeling. It can be tempting to give the young person a punishment on the spot following a transgression (parents often grab straight for their phones as a punishment). You are likely to be feeling very emotional too, which is not the best state for considered action (see Chapter 2: The Teen Brain Thinks and Feels). However, it is better to wait, watch and listen first. Your responses as a parent, family member, teacher or professional working with the young person are very important and can have a significant impact on how they learn to integrate their emotions and motivations towards learning goals. Appropriate consequences for behaviour may well be in order, but protect your relationship by giving a thoughtful response. See Chapter 17: May The Force Be With You, Luke, for some more top tips.

What does that mean for learning?

Teens still learn from adults even when they are more interested in peers

A classroom teacher has to manage many young people at one time. The social element at school is particularly powerful, and teens are influenced more by peers than adults in certain contexts. However, don't be fooled by their apparent lack of interest in you as an adult in their life, they are still watching and learning from teachers and mentors.

Adults can inadvertently reinforce behaviour they want to reduce

Adults create the environment in which young people learn and grow. You can inadvertently associate two events together (maths lessons and boredom), encourage problem behaviour (giving more screen time after a teen gets angry or behaves rudely) and model inadvisable behaviour ('lose it' by shouting when the class gets out of hand). If you understand these mechanisms and are conscious of your behaviour, particularly at this sensitive time of teenage brain development, it's another step towards liberating your teen's full potential.

So, what now?

Teens are watching you and learning from you even though it often doesn't feel like it. If you understand the learning processes, you can make the environment the best it can be for your teen to spend time in the positive cycle of learning, growing and building their incredible brains.

Case study: Jack

Jack was 13 and loved his Playstation. He was given it for his birthday and he and his parents had agreed that he could have a play every night, but only after he had done his homework. This was working well, except his parents started to notice that he rushed through his homework rather quickly and his marks were dropping. They talked this through with him and he admitted that he was often so excited about going on his Playstation that he just wanted to get his homework out of the way. They were inadvertently reinforcing him rushing his homework as he then got more time on his Playstation. Though hard to admit, Jack did see that this was not going to be a good strategy going forward. They reflected that time management was hard when Jack was on the Playstation, as he was so distracted by the game. He could be on it for hours and hours. They also thought about all the things Jack was no longer doing because of his Playstation, such as drawing, playing cards with his Dad after dinner and reading a book. Together they came up with a plan that allowed Jack to still have time online with his friends (1 hour a night) but it was dissociated with homework (it was always from 4.30 to 5.30pm and not later) and he would find something fun to do with his Dad (who he didn't see much) after they'd all had dinner, such as reading, watching some TV or playing cards together.

A good resolution

Jack's parents were able to step back from the situation, think about what was being reinforced, perhaps reflect on mistakes they had made in setting up the system they had for homework/Playstation use at home, come to an agreement and model a problem-solving solution. Not all families agree to Playstation in the week, but this family found a way that Jack could have some time doing what he loved (which was also social as he met his friends online), he could get his homework done and he could spend positive family time with his Dad. It didn't always go smoothly and sometimes he wanted to push the boundaries and get more Playstation time, but with calm consistency it soon became a habit.

What might get in the way?

It would have been easy in this situation to get cross with Jack, tell him he didn't care about his homework and ban the Playstation. But this would have modelled poor emotional control to Jack, damaged the relationship and blamed Jack for something he probably wasn't even aware of. Instead, this family was able to dissociate two unhelpful events (rushing homework and Playstation time), model problem solving and model the willingness to reflect on previous choices and review them. These incidents and events in a family life have the potential to erode positive relationships in the family and build resentment, which is unhelpful at a time when teens need parents so acutely and parents need to build their teens' trust in them so they will be approached at times of danger.

Action point: Beware the connections you introduce
Think carefully about situations that may have negative associations for your teen. Be thoughtful in how you respond and what associations are being encouraged by positive reinforcement. Can you change a negative association into a positive one?

Action point: Lead by example and they will take care of the rest
Modelling is the most powerful form of adult-to-child teaching. Take time to reflect on what behaviour you are modelling to the teens you are with. Model the behaviour and reactions you would like to see in your teen – you might have to fake it till you make it.

Action point: Teach your teen to be metacognitive
Help your teenager to view their thinking through an active, involved and potential-enriched lens. Encourage them to think about the processes they use and develop strategies for next time if things didn't go well.

The moral of the story is...

Much of a teen's learning will happen through three different processes: watching others, linking an event with a subsequent experience or by association. Use your understanding of these processes to change your behaviour so you can shape your teen's.

Downloads: The Teen Brain Connects, Watches and Absorbs

There are many different ways to learn. It takes thousands of hours of practice to learn skills and develop competence, but some other learning processes happen quickly, passively and unconsciously. Adults play an important role in all types of young people's learning.

Events can become linked in our minds, even if we don't want them to be (e.g. being bullied at school can lead to a fear of school). When one thing follows another, it increases or decreases the chances of it happening again (e.g. if parents give in when their teen demands more gaming time it means the teen is more likely to ask again in the future). Modelling behaviour is very powerful (e.g. a teacher who shouts and bangs the desk when feeling irritated is demonstrating an apparently appropriate way to express irritation). Teens' brains are ready for self-reflection and 'metacognition' (thinking about thinking) and now is the time to help them learn to self-regulate. Help them learn good habits and become aware of their learning patterns.

Exercise

Note three situations where your teen has associated one event with another (e.g. waking up and immediately checking phone now always seem to go together, when they were not related before).

Situation 1

. . . .

. . . .

Situation 2

. . . .

. . . .

Situation 3

. . . .

. . . .

Note three situations where your teen's behaviour has been reinforced by what followed the behaviour (with a positive or negative outcome).

Situation 1

. . . .

. . . .

Situation 2

. . . .

. . . .

Situation 3

. . . .

. . . .

Note three situations where you have modelled behaviour you don't like in your teen (be honest, it's OK, we all do it).

Situation 1

. . . .

. . . .

Situation 2

. . . .

. . . .

Situation 3

. . . .

. . . .

When this happens...	Instead of this...	Try this...
Your teen has said she has to 'check something' the last few times she's due to do her Japanese homework, and disappears.	Why does my daughter disappear when doing Japanese homework? I have been calling her for ages and she is simply ignoring me. She knows it's got to be done, so why avoid it?	She finds languages hard. In the past, I have been impatient when she seemed to be slow on the uptake, resulting in tears. No wonder she avoids Japanese homework.
		Be mindful of associations that come from **past experience**
Your teen is so disruptive in your Physics class he is sent out of most lessons.	He is such a bad influence. I have to send him out of the classroom or the others can't learn. He doesn't want to try, he won't listen even when he is in the lab.	Maybe sending him out of class when he messes around is inadvertently reinforcing his bad behaviour – he escapes the situation he struggles with. Perhaps I should check his level of understanding and get him support.
		Make sure you are not **inadvertently reinforcing** behaviour that is unhelpful to learning
The internet goes offline again. Your teen sets it up for you – again.	I can't remember how to do it, but the kids can. It's just easier, they are better at these things.	I struggle with technology but I must model persistence to my teen, not give up and find a way to remember the set-up (and have a growth mindset).
		Model behaviour that you **would like to see** in your teen

Chapter 5

The Teen Brain Loves Other People

Long story, short

- Social connections are a fundamental need for our survival.
- The brain's default setting is social.
- Social pain really hurts and social reward is particularly valuable to teens.
- Teens' social brain network undergoes fundamental changes after puberty.
- Social aspects of a learning task will increase engagement, particularly for socially aware teens.

Introduction

Social connection is fundamental to humans

As we learn more about the brain, we are learning more about us as a species. For many years scientists have known that we evolved to live socially, in packs, but now neuroscience can add to that by showing that the human brain has evolved so that *social* needs are primary. In his 2015 book *Social*, Matthew Lieberman, a neuroscientist, discusses the major brain adaptations that have taken place over evolution to show how fundamental the social world is to our survival and existence. Consider how helpless an infant is and how completely dependent they are on caregivers for survival – they simply wouldn't survive without other people. The brain continues to develop rapidly for around 25 years, during which time the young person needs others to help them grow and protect them from danger. It turns out social connection is not just a luxury, it is essential throughout life.

The science bit: Brain and behaviour

Our brain's default setting is social – social understanding is key for survival

Some of the strongest evidence that we are fundamentally social comes from findings about what happens to our brains when we do nothing. Many of the most interesting findings in science come from accidental observations. Researchers noticed that when participants taking part in MRI experiments were not actively thinking about anything in particular, in the down-time between testing procedures, there was still a lot of activity in the brain. More than simply random activity, there are highly consistent areas of the brain which light up during times of free thinking. This area of activation is known as the **default mode network**, initially identified by American neurologist Marcus Raichle and his colleagues (2001), but researched by many neuroscientists since. It has been compared to the screensaver mode on a computer.

The default mode network consists of regions of the brain that are involved in thinking about ourselves and other people, including our past and planned experiences. It is as if our default setting is inherently social. This default state is seen in newborns and is like a reflex that 'switches on' as soon as a demanding task is complete. Our brain spends a high proportion of its life orientated to a social world – whenever it gets a spare moment – and so, as Lieberman says, children have put in their 10,000 hours of social practice before the age of 10. Why would the brain prioritise social processing over any other kind of processing? Lieberman argues it must be because of the fundamental need for expert social and self-understanding in order for us to survive and thrive.

Social and physical pain are equally important to the brain
Another amazing brain adaptation that shows the importance of social experience is that the brain reacts to social threat and physical pain

using the same set of neural mechanisms. This finding comes from results from the Cyberball experiment carried out in an MRI scanner. The individual plays a virtual ball throwing game with two other people, then suddenly they are left out and the ball is no longer thrown to them, emulating social exclusion. The parts of the brain that light up when a person is socially excluded during this game are the same parts that light up when someone is in physical pain. The implication is that, as far as the brain is concerned, cutting our leg is the same as not getting an invite to the party. If we think about the purpose of pain – it is an alarm bell that tells us to take action to protect ourselves – we see the value of social inclusion to the brain. The overlap of neural mechanisms suggests the brain considers social pain *as important* to our survival as physical pain.

This predilection towards the social is true for us all, but it is at its height in adolescence. As we will learn, teens are programmed to turn their attention towards socially relevant information, and part of that means that social exclusion is more painful for them. Given the fundamental importance the brain gives to social information and its part in our survival, it makes good sense for young people, as they embark on independence, to be acutely socially aware.

Social and physical reward are treated the same by the brain and we like to be kind to others

Need more convincing? Another reason we know that social information is crucial for the brain is that social needs and physical reward share the same neural network. You might guess that getting money is more rewarding than praise, but it turns out that is not the case. The brain registers both in the same way, even if the comment is from a stranger. Social reward in the form of positive regard from others is of high value to human beings. More surprisingly, perhaps, studies have shown greater activation in the reward centres of the brain when we give money away than when we choose to keep money. Altruism is highly rewarding for the brain. Perhaps we are not fundamentally selfish after all.

Biology drives attention to the social world when networks are developing

The networks in the brain devoted to processing and rewarding social information undergo significant structural changes with the onset of puberty. There is a biological and environmental partnership which persists throughout development in which brain networks that are undergoing the most development and are most malleable correspond with the aspects of the environment that the teen is driven towards. Biology drives environmental experience to offer optimal potential for growth.

The social brain may have untapped memorisation power

There are fascinating emerging data illustrating the benefits of playing to our social strengths, if we engage the social brain when learning. For example, one study showed that people who were asked to 'form an impression of the person' who was reading a newspaper article to them remembered more information later than those who were asked to 'memorise' that same information in preparation for a test. Follow-up MRI studies found the former group engaged their social brain network more, with the intriguing possibility that the social brain offers enhanced memorisation power.

Translating your teen

Social exclusion is painful for teens and needs your empathy

When a teenager is not invited to a party (with their friends' Snapchat Bitmojis milling around together without them adding insult to injury), they are in social pain. Their brain experiences this like a physical injury. Knowing this, it seems important that we empathise with and listen to their social difficulties. Offer an emotional bandage and support them as we would naturally if they injured themselves.

Social rewards work for teens

Praising a teen, ideally with remarks that are specific to the situation (not just a generic 'well done' or pat on the back), is just as pleasurable for them as receiving presents; in fact it gives a less materialistic message, enriches your relationship and will be just as effective. While they may not always show it, they care what you think of them. Remember the value of relationships, relationships, relationships.

Gossiping may have a serious purpose

As teenage brains learn about the social world, teens are driven to their friends for good reason. Yuval Harari, in his 2015 book *Sapiens: A Brief History of Humankind*, argues that gossiping and sharing social knowledge is the foundation of our species' survival. 'Gossiping' teens are actually practising the rules of their social group – commenting when two friends hook up or if a friend is caught out being insincere suggests they have understood their peer group norms, and that's good preparation for future community membership.

What does that mean day to day?

High quality social relationships predict well-being

At Harvard University, George Valliant (2012) and his group carried out a study to track individuals over their lifetime – a study following people over their lifetime is a researcher's dream because it tells us so much rich information. The researchers asked: What keeps us healthy and happy as we go through life? They found that the key determinant of happiness is good social relationships. Socially connected people are happier, healthier and live longer. Loneliness is toxic: it is linked with reduced physical health and happiness, brain function decline (including memory loss) and shortened lives. Importantly, it is not the number of friends *per se* that determines positive outcome; rather, it is the quality of those close relationships that matters. This suggests that living in isolation is the single most important impediment to long-term well-being. It also shows the power of positive relationships. Your relationship with your teen is something to strengthen and treasure for if there was a magic formula for mental well-being, it exists in the relationships we have with others.

Teens tend to feel lonelier than others and need to be amongst their group

According to a recent survey in the UK, adolescents are the most likely age group to describe themselves as lonely, though their lifestyle means that they spend most of their time in a group, so their loneliness is to do with their need for social connection, which is at its peak at this time of life. There is a uniquely strong pull at this age to be part of a social group, and when teenagers are not with the group, they feel more lonely. As we will go on to discover, social isolation is more damaging during the adolescent years than at any other time in life.

Maybe our irritation with teens is because we feel socially rejected by them?

We all have social brains and find social rejection painful. As our teens turn their attention towards their peers and choose their friends' company over ours, we can feel rejected. Look after yourself but don't feel offended or get caught in thinking they are ungrateful for all you have done. They are just fulfilling their developmental job – peer integration means they are getting ready to form a new adult community. Neuroscientist Sarah-Jayne Blakemore (2012) wondered whether we mock teenagers in a way that we wouldn't with any other group in society because deep down we are hurt that they want to separate from us.

What does that mean for learning?

Use positive social bias in the classroom to optimise learning across the curriculum

Given our understanding of the social brain, Lieberman (2012) questions our traditional teaching methods, describing them 'as a zero-sum battle between actual learning and social distraction' (p.5). Currently we tell teens to leave their social brains outside the classroom and switch off their social thinking – an aspect so important to them. Lieberman believes we should leverage that bias, introduce social elements to teaching methods and use the 'social encoding advantage'. This has a number of practical implications that he draws out.

TAP INTO THE SOCIAL BRAIN POWER IN WRITING TASKS

Students should write to a specific person when they write a narrative, because writing to a person, rather than in a vacuum, becomes a task of writing from one brain to another, tapping into social brain power. In their evidence-based review (July 2019), the Education Endowment Foundation concluded: 'If students love to write, because their peers as well as their teachers are eager to see what they have to say, then they will write with energy and pleasure' (p.26).

TAP INTO THE SOCIAL BRAIN POWER IN MEMORISATION TASKS
Rather than stripping learning tasks to a list of facts, draw on the social motives behind actions and decisions. Developing a narrative enables consolidation and retention in memory, tapping into the social brain power.

Figure 5.1: The brain is most powerful in a social context

TAP INTO THE SOCIAL BRAIN POWER TO CONSOLIDATE UNDERSTANDING
With more abstract topics such as science and maths, Lieberman suggests using the 'learn-for-teaching' approach. Get young people to learn material in order to teach it to someone else and the social element of the task will capitalise on the brain's social power. Traditionally, the more able teach the less able, but this task is actually more beneficial for the person teaching, so where appropriate, explore the ideas that young people who are *less* able teach the *more* able teenagers on new topics.

So, what now?

We are all fundamentally social animals and need to be part of a group. Our brains feel real pain when we are left out and feel good when someone praises us. This is particularly acute in teens, and their need to be with friends is a normal part of their development.

Case study: Lethabo

Lethabo was a bright, popular 15-year-old, with excellent verbal skills, but he tended to tune out when a subject focused on visual material, especially symbols. He 'hated' maths, and his teacher, Dlamini, had watched his grades fall steadily over the last year. She was an enthusiastic, energetic teacher and prided herself on her ability to find a way to connect with her pupils. She didn't enjoy the idea of an able pupil slipping away from her. She met with Lethabo and asked him why he thought his grades were slipping. Lethabo said it just didn't make any sense to him, and he was beginning to feel embarrassed because 'all his mates knew it all and he never got it'. She watched him tune out about five minutes into every lesson. With important exams on the horizon, Dlamini was beginning to feel hopeless.

Lethabo's parents contacted Dlamini as they were concerned and indicated they wanted her advice and a new plan for the final term. She had an idea, remembering all she knew about the social brain. She was perfectly honest with Lethabo about how worried she was and said she was planning something she had never tried before. She asked him if he would help her teach the Year 8 students fractions. At first Lethabo was reticent, fearing that he wouldn't be able to do it, but he knew he could be funny and entertaining and so agreed cautiously. Dlamini said she wanted him to teach fractions to his Granny at home first and use as many jokes and metaphors as he liked to get his ideas across. That went well, and as he was keen to appear smart in front of the younger kids he prepared well for his teaching responsibility and it was a huge success. He surprised himself, his teacher and his friends and absolutely nailed it. He left the lesson feeling good about himself, and of course much more confident about the topic. Dlamini planned to ask Lethabo's help on future occasions, but in the meantime, he found that teaching a difficult topic to others, including his Granny, seemed to tap into a maths super-power and boosted his confidence. He had found the secret to his grade improving in maths and a new way for his brain to grow.

A good resolution

Dlamini drew on the ideas of Lieberman, that the social task of teaching activates the social network, so increasing the richness of encoding information. Further, she knew that given Lethabo's motivation to increase his status, he was likely to put some time and effort into preparing for his own session with the Year 8 students. Finally, confiding in him somewhat was likely to make him feel valued. Having a good experience was important because it started him on a positive trajectory with the teaching to learn technique. Nothing breeds success like success.

What might get in the way?

Young people can be unkind to each other and it would be important in this situation to make sure the young person was ready and confident in teaching non-peers so it was successful when they started to link in with peers. Having Granny be the guinea pig was important so Lethabo had a chance at a run through with a non-critical person. A difficult experience like this could knock a young person's confidence more. If teaching a whole class is not possible, simply pairing students up in class could also lead to success and tap into the power of the social brain.

Action point: Prioritise the social world

The brain prioritises the social world and so should we. Recognise the power of relationships: both adult-to-teen and peer-to-peer. Don't dismiss an ongoing problem in your relationship with a teen as unimportant or put it down to their being 'teenagery'. This is missing a trick. Find ways to solve social problems, as the quality of teen relationships matter and relationships underpin success in adolescence and throughout life.

Action point: Take social pain seriously, it really hurts

Take note when a teen says their friend has upset them; empathise when they are in tears at not having been invited to a party. Social exclusion really hurts.

Action point: Use the power of social reward as it is so easy to access

Social rewards like a smile, an encouraging comment or a hand on a shoulder are available to you every minute of every day, so use them. Social reward has power. Get creative because that will raise the visibility of the praise and make it more potent: use emojis or drawings. Leave a note on the bathroom mirror, send an e-mail or a GIF on the school's virtual noticeboard.

Action point: Make academic tasks socially relevant

Emphasising the social relevance in academic tasks is likely to have a positive impact, increase motivation and liberate brain power and potential. This does not require a whole new curriculum, but small adjustments can move a child into a different realm with their learning such as using narrative, prioritising the social aim of a task or peer-to-peer learning.

Action point: Recognise social awareness as a high value skill

Social capacities are increasingly understood as high status skills – it's a velvet revolution. Show your admiration for social awareness explicitly or implicitly by the way you react to your teen's observations or comments about social issues.

The moral of the story is...

Our brains consider social information fundamental to our survival. Teenagers are acutely attuned to social signals, so include a social element into learning tasks to increase their engagement.

Downloads: The Teen Brain Loves Other People

Social connections are fundamental for our survival. Social understanding is key to making these connections. These crucial social brain networks are developing during adolescence, so much of a teenager's attention is focused on the social world. Teens experience social pain if they are isolated, particularly by their peer group, whereas strong relationships help teenagers to thrive. Social pain and reward are felt more acutely during adolescence than at any other time.

Tapping into this 'social power' is essential for learning. A crucial task in facilitating the incredible brain is to understand teens' need for social connection and fear of social pain.

Exercise

Note down a social situation your teen was in that caused them to feel upset, left out and overwhelmed.

. . . .

. . . .

. . . .

Consider ways you could help your teen if they were in that same situation again and use these ways in the future.

. . . .

. . . .

. . . .

. . . .

When this happens...	Instead of this...	Try this...
All the class are talking about a party on Snapchat. Your teen hasn't been invited.	She's making such a fuss over not being invited to that party. For goodness sake, there will be hundreds more parties.	She is really in social pain over not being invited to that party. I know she will recover, but right now I need to support her. It is real distress even if it is short term.
		Recognise that **social pain is real pain** and teens feel this more acutely
The first thing your teen does when she gets home from school is to reach for her phone and call her best friend.	How is it even possible for them to have anything more to say to each other on the phone all evening? They have been together all day.	It's important for her to feel connected with her friends – maybe to make sense of what's happened in the group today. She is learning all about the social world.
		Remember that **it takes a long time** to be socially competent, and teen gossiping is how they build those circuits
There are two teens who talk incessantly in class. They catch each other's eye even if they are separated.	I am so irritated by these two. Yes, it's great to have friends but save it for break-time. I need them to be silent and listen to me or how can they learn?	I wonder if I can use their social connection and brain power to help them understand this topic by getting them to 'teach' each other one of the concepts?
		Tap into the social bias in classroom tasks

PART 2

A Different Teenager

Chapter 6

Teen Brains Overwhelmed

Long story, short

- A small (but notable) percentage of teenagers have significant mental health difficulties.
- Strong emotions are typical in adolescence, but persistent emotional distress which impacts on day-to-day activities might indicate a mental health problem.
- The way teens express their emotional needs is different from children, so may need decoding.
- Teenager's mental health difficulties can interfere with learning and growing.
- You can help support teens' good mental health by helping them recognise and manage emotions and providing clear boundaries.
- If you are worried about an adolescent's mental health, consult your GP or primary physician.

Introduction

Life is full of ups and downs for any teenager. It is not unusual for teenagers to have several hours or days of sadness, anxiety or other strong emotions. However, some young people have sustained periods of emotional turmoil and become so mentally unwell they cannot function in their daily lives and their learning, growth and development suffer.

Such difficulties can get in the way of teens achieving their potential, entering the positive cycle of learning (see Chapter 3: The Teen Brain Learns and Believes) and making the most of the enormous opportunity that the incredible teenage brain offers. As with any human characteristic, mental health is on a continuum and it can be hard to define exactly where the cut-off is between typical and atypical, so this chapter aims to help you develop an awareness of what constitutes a mental health problem. Knowing what to do and when to get professional help is essential for any adult caring for a teenager.

Mental health waxes and wanes as a normal part of life

Mental health waxes and wanes, just like physical health. We all have times of getting a cold or flu or a stomach bug. By the same token, we all have times of feeling a bit low or anxious or have unhelpful thoughts such as being worried about our body shape, lacking social confidence or struggling with our relationship to food. Emotions are important signals that warn and prepare us mentally and physically to take certain actions (see Chapter 10: Powerful Feelings and Mighty Motivations). Experiencing emotions, even strong emotions, does not mean that your teen has a mental health problem. It is only when emotions impact on a person's life to such a degree that they cannot manage daily tasks and are unable to recover from or overcome difficulties for an extended period of time that this falls outside the normal pattern.

Expectations of behaviour change with age

Emotions, and the expression of them, vary according to age. For example, it would be appropriate for a two-year-old to cry if their parent left them with a stranger. This would not be appropriate for a 16-year-old. A toddler on the floor may be shouting if they didn't get their own way. If a teenager did this we would be concerned and might consider them in need of some support.

Societal attitudes to mental health are improving

Awareness of mental health difficulties is on the rise and finally the media is bringing the debate into the mainstream. Increased awareness is sometimes confused with increased rates of mental ill-health, but this is not necessarily true. Population surveys carried out in the UK over the past 20 years show that there has been a slight rise in the number of teens with mental health conditions in the past 20 years, but not a significant increase (Department of Health and NHS England 2017).

The slight increase is mostly accounted for by a rise of reported anxiety and depression in secondary school-aged teens. However, our knowledge about mental health has increased, and adults caring for teens are currently far better informed than ever before. Indeed, some argue that the increase in rates might actually reflect a decrease in stigma: in other words, rates of mental health problems have remained stable but teens are more likely to come forward and ask for help, so reported rates appear higher.

Too many young people suffer from a mental health problem

Before we pat ourselves on the back too much, it is important to remember that while society's understanding of mental health difficulties has improved, there are still significant numbers of teens with mental health problems. The most recent NHS population survey shows that there is work to do (Department of Health and NHS England 2017). One in eight young people aged 5 to 19 years have a mental health disorder (emotional, behavioural or developmental – we'll get into this later). It is concerning that young people aged between 17 and 19 years of age show the highest rate of emotional disorders overall (17%), with girls in that age group being twice as likely as boys to have this type of difficulty. A similar pattern is found in other high income countries.

Many factors combine to cause mental health problems in young people

Mental health problems don't have a single cause – many factors play a part. Genetics play a part. This means that if people in your family have a history of mental health difficulties, your teen is more likely to develop them too. This is not a done deal by any means, because the environment has a significant influence on brain development too.

A young person's life events (loss, trauma), the way they are parented, even in infancy, peer difficulties like bullying or the school environment can all contribute to the likelihood of a mental health problem. A teenager's temperament is also a factor. Vulnerabilities such as a propensity for perfectionism or anxiety traits may increase the chances of mental health difficulties.

There are many studies from the National Institute of Mental Health in the USA looking at young people's brain and behaviour development over time. The ambitious Adolescent Brain and Cognitive Development (ABCD) study is of particular interest (Nora Volkow *et al.* 2018). Scientists are tracking 10,000 children aged 9 to 10 years old over the next decade of their lives with state-of-the-art brain imaging techniques. The study will look at their behaviour, hormones, genetics, brain development and day-to-day life experiences, including use of screen time, alcohol and drugs, which will give us a much better understanding about mental health and brain development in a few years' time.

Protective factors are powerful and, in the teen years, relationships are critical

While we are still uncertain about what might cause mental health problems, we are much more certain about what we can do to protect young people from developing these difficulties. Some teenagers are highly resilient and do not show mental health problems despite challenging high-risk circumstances. What protects them? If we can find that out, we can 'bottle it' and offer it to the wider population.

American psychologist Professor Anne Masten, has studied widely in the field and believes that resilience is made of ordinary, everyday processes (Masten 2014). These include: positive thinking patterns (hope, motivation), good self-regulation and stress management, supportive social networks, extra-curricular activities, satisfaction with school and strong family relationships. These all add up to form protection against incoming adversity, like Harry Potter's Patronus.

The evidence is gathering strength – in the teen years, relationships may be one of the most important factors protecting young people from mental health difficulties and enabling them to develop strong resilience for the rest of their lives. For example, we know that positive relationships protect girls at risk of anxiety or depression, whereas poor relationships, lacking in nurture, significantly increase the chances of a mental health difficulty.

The science bit: Brain and behaviour

While adolescence is physically the healthiest time in a person's life, it is also the time when a person is most likely to develop a mental health problem. Many serious mental health disorders, such as schizophrenia, first present in adolescence, which has caused scientists to question why teenagers are particularly vulnerable to developing these potentially life-long difficulties.

There are documented childhood experiences that are associated with later mental health problems including abuse and neglect in childhood and bullying in school. There is growing evidence that cannabis can increase the risk of psychosis when consumed during the teenage years, but the mechanisms of influence are not well understood. Genes clearly play a role, increasing the risk of a mental health problem for some individuals, but it is a complicated area. Environments and genes interact together so that genes can be 'switched on' in certain environments and individuals can seek out certain experiences, meaning that experiences have a genetic loading. We do know that some young people are remarkably resilient and maintain strong mental health despite significant negative life events. Researchers are keen to identify what factors offer resilience to young people.

We know that there are differences in the brains of many people who have mental health problems, but the implications of this are not well understood. Some findings are disorder-specific. We also know that an MRI scan is not yet able to detect a mental health problem. Diagnosis of mental health disorders is done through consultation with a professional such as a child and adolescent psychiatrist or clinical psychologist.

Translating your teen

This means that though the chances of mental health conditions occurring are small for your teen, if mental health problems *are* going to emerge for them, it is most likely to happen in adolescence. The plasticity and steep trajectory of teenage brain development is likely to be part of the story explaining the vulnerability at this stage of life. At the same time, there is strong evidence that past experiences and the multitude of demands on a teen's life are part of the explanation too. The point here is that you need to hold in mind that mental health problems are relatively unlikely but are a possibility. Consider the possibility seriously if your teen's behaviour changes markedly.

We have chosen to focus on anxiety, depression and conduct disorder because they are the most commonly occurring disorders for teens. Other mental health problems such as eating disorders, obsessive-compulsive disorder or, very rarely, thought disorders are also more likely to emerge at this time. Again, this is probably due to the sensitivity of the brain while dealing with the formidable tasks of the teen years. Two or more mental health conditions could emerge at the same time, so be aware that there are many different presentations.

Anxious teens avoid situations they find scary

Anxiety disorders present in different ways. Some of the most common conditions in adolescence include: generalised anxiety disorders (worrying about things all of the time), obsessive-compulsive disorder (use of actions to counteract worrying thoughts or feelings) and phobic disorders (intense fear of a particular experience or object). In the teen years, when friends are all-important, social anxiety can increase quite significantly.

Anxiety means there is an experience of feeling worried and often a thought that something terrible is going to happen, along with physical symptoms such as headache, increased heart-rate, dry mouth, sweating or tremors. People with anxiety disorder often manage by avoiding the situation they find frightening, but in the long run this only increases anxiety, resulting in a cycle that is hard to break because your brain learns, pretty quickly (remember, an adolescent's capacity to learn is fast and efficient), that anxiety decreases as soon as you avoid the situation, so triggering the false idea that avoidance is the only way to feel better. In fact gentle exposure to the situation you are anxious about, and facing your fears, may be the best way forward.

There are good evidence-based treatments for anxiety disorders, particularly Cognitive Behavioural Therapy, which helps to challenge anxiety-provoking thoughts, and gradually helps you to re-learn that anxiety will decrease after a while even if you are in a scary situation.

Depressed teens often retreat from everyday life

Depression or low mood can present in many ways including increased irritability, poor sleep and concentration, negative self-image and, in more severe cases, self-harm or suicidal thoughts. Depression can affect relationships with family and friends as the young person may lack motivation to take part in social events. Early symptoms of depression can eat away at relationships as a teen retreats from interactions with friends and family, making the teen more vulnerable. This is perhaps not surprising given all we now know about how fundamental our social connections are and the importance of strong relationships for well-being. Depression can impact on learning and sleep to such a degree that learning slows or stalls. For less severe cases of depression, structured psychotherapies such as Interpersonal Therapy (which focuses on managing and improving relationships) or Cognitive Behavioural Therapy (which links thoughts to feelings) have a good evidence base, but a combination of medication and Interpersonal Therapy is usually indicated when a young person is really struggling with a low mood, at least initially while they work through their difficulties.

Angry teens can push the boundaries

Angry teens can present with challenging behaviour or appear argumentative. While we may not intuitively think of these 'externalising' behaviours as an emotional issue, actually the behaviour may reflect your teen's difficulty articulating their emotional discord. The thinking brain is at the mercy of the emotional brain, remember. It's as if the thinking brain has been hijacked. While aggression towards others, rule-breaking and lying or stealing are never acceptable, it's important to understand the roots of the behaviour in order to change it. Being curious and understanding does not preclude clear, consistent boundaries. As we know from our learning models (see Chapter 4: The Teen Brain Connects, Watches and Absorbs), punishment, without understanding why a behaviour has occurred, is unlikely to be effective. If your previously compliant teen suddenly becomes oppositional, it is most likely a communication issue.

Teens need help differentiating between emotions experienced and emotions expressed

The teenage brain is primed to feel deeply (see Chapter 10: Powerful Feelings and Mighty Motivations). As teens learn to manage these strong emotions they may overreact initially and may lose control for a brief time. Who is in control all of the time anyway?

It is important to help teens differentiate between what they feel and what they do. Allow them to feel angry, name the emotion most certainly, but not to act out and be rude. Allow them to feel sad and cry, but not sit alone for hours in distress. Allow them to feel anxious, encourage them to say it out loud, but don't give them permission to avoid the anxiety-provoking situation. Feel the fear and do it anyway, because that means the fear will dissipate. At the same time, help them to understand that just because something feels good, it doesn't mean it is good. Eating is an example: our brain signals reward when we eat, but there needs to be limits to any hedonism or we may develop negative habits. This all amounts to understanding our emotions and ultimately emotional regulation (see Chapter 17: May The Force Be With You, Luke), which is an important part of well-being.

When to take action

If a young person is regularly very upset or anxious and it is impacting on their ability to take part in school, social activities or home life, then it's time to ask for help. Another red flag would be a step-change in behaviour or demeanour. As a first step, concerned adults could talk to a family member, a teacher, a friend or a faith leader.

In order to get support from mental health services, usually a primary health physician, such as your GP, is the first port of call. Psychologists and psychiatrists are mental health professionals who have the tools to help your teen work through this difficult time. 'Therapists' are often highly trained, but be aware that anyone in the private sector working independently can call themselves a therapist in theory, so be careful about checking out their qualifications with professional bodies – perhaps take the advice of your GP for a good recommendation. A practitioner psychologist or psychiatrist will reliably have high levels of mental health training and expertise. If the young person is talking about or has actually tried to harm themselves or others, or if repeated attempts to help them to manage their emotions are not helping, then we recommend that you seek out mental health services.

Warning signs that your teenager may need professional input include persistent problems lasting more than a couple of weeks, or the following:

- a significant change in the young person, such as irritability, social withdrawal or lack of self-care
- unexplained weight loss, disrupted sleep or loss of appetite
- unexplained physical harm, such as cuts or burns on the skin
- inability to take part in social or school activities.

What does that mean day to day?

Teens may need support to understand their emotional experience

The teen years can be emotional. Strong emotional experiences do not equate to mental health problems, and though often teens do need the adults in their lives to help them manage difficult times, this is a typical part of adolescent development. It is not your job to fix every problem or make the emotions go away. It is your job to support your teen to understand what is happening to them and find ways to cope, with you alongside. By teaching them to process their emotions rather than by denying them or erasing them, they will learn to do this independently, building well-being and resilience. This is a healthy and good long-term plan for your teenager.

Early intervention is the best option

Though attitudes are improving, some stigma still exists around mental health, and for some people it holds some societal 'shame'. It is important to be open and honest about sharing any concerns. Stigma can lead to secrets and might prevent a teen seeking help. There are very good treatments available for many mental health difficulties, and the earlier treatment is sought, the better. The more a mental health difficulty becomes entrenched, the harder it can be to shift the symptoms and recover.

What does that mean for learning?

Emotional brains are not learning

The brain has a hierarchy of activity (see Chapter 2: The Teen Brain Thinks and Feels). Our emotional responses are there to protect us if we feel scared or unsafe, so in those situations the emotional brain dominates, leaving us little space to reason or think, and so we move away from the positive cycle of learning. In that emotional mode teenage brains are not able to learn. For this reason mental health needs must be a priority in teenagers or their opportunity to learn will be compromised.

Teachers play an important role in teen mental health care

A recent survey in the UK found that teachers are the professionals who are most likely to come into contact with people with mental health difficulties. Teachers are frontline mental health workers in many ways. There is a government initiative in the UK to increase formal mental health training in recognition of the need for teachers to know how to spot mental health difficulties and what supports to put in place. While it is not the job of a teacher to treat a mental health problem, knowing what to look for, how to support a young person and how to direct them towards professionals who can help would augment the experience of vulnerable teens in school significantly.

So, what now?

A small proportion of teenagers have significant problems with their mental health. In order to know how to support young people, it is important for adults to be familiar with the signs of mental health conditions, how to support a struggling teen and when to refer them on to a professional.

Case study: Hasan

Sixteen-year-old Hasan had always been a sensitive boy with a gentle sense of humour that entertained the family. He was close to his mum, Fatimah, dad, Fajar, and little brother Hilman. Hilman was very bright and usually top of the class, whereas Hasan began to fall further and further behind at school. His mum got an e-mail to say he had begun to miss classes. He denied it and insisted that the school register was wrong. Fatimah suspected money was going missing from her purse and he began to stay out late, without letting his parents know where he was. The family had never had any contact with mental health services before. They were a hardworking law-abiding family that had a strong religious faith and prided themselves on contributing to the community.

They were keen to try and deal with the problems themselves and were grounding him frequently, but when Hasan was arrested for stealing a computer from school, the school welfare officer suggested a referral to the local Child and Adolescent Mental Health Services (CAMHS). The police caught him riding his bike with the computer balanced on the handle bars. It was almost as if he wanted to get caught.

The psychologist at CAMHS took a history from all the family. It was clear that Hasan's attitude to life had changed dramatically. The behaviour had escalated rapidly and was very much out of character. It soon emerged that the pressure of school was weighing on Hasan. He was likely to fail all of his end of school exams according to a school report. His parents were understandably anxious, angry with him and fearing disaster for him. Fatimah tended to raise her voice around him because she felt that Hasan was not listening to what she was saying.

A good resolution

The psychologist had sessions with Hasan alone, and with his parents and the whole family. In these sessions she raised the idea that Hasan's behaviour was serving a function: if his behaviour was extreme enough he would be excluded from school, which was preferable to failing his exams, which he felt was more shameful. (Remember from Chapter 4: The Teen Brain Connects, Watches and Absorbs, one behaviour can inadvertently encourage another. Here school exclusion reinforces the difficult behaviour by avoiding the shame of academic failure.) This idea moved the problem along considerably because it gave words to his behaviour. The family learnt to facilitate ways of improving communication so that all family members could discuss their views and be heard. Hasan began to gain more independence, such as later curfews, in return for taking responsibility for household tasks. His status in the family was re-established and raised. The next step was figuring out a way back into education or training while making sure the family's expectations for Hasan were realistic.

What might get in the way?

Challenging behaviour such as stealing and ignoring parental boundaries is serious and cannot be left unchallenged, clearly. However, we must remember that young people don't always express their needs directly or understand what is going on for them. It is the job of adults who are supporting teens to 'decode' their behaviour. Hasan's parents could have just got angry and his teachers could have simply excluded him, rather than being curious and asking why he was behaving in that way. Young people are under a lot of academic pressure at a time when their self-concept is vulnerable. This is a difficult situation for everyone, but there are always solutions. Look underneath the behaviour to find the clues.

Action point: Understand what constitutes a mental health problem to know when to seek help

Parents and teachers might want to wait and watch for a while if they suspect a teen is struggling or if their behaviour suddenly becomes out of character. But don't wait too long. If your teen is not functioning well and shows key signs of distress, don't delay in asking for help.

Action point: Use your relationship to build resilience in your teen

Many factors combine to cause mental health difficulties in teenagers, and many factors are protective. Put relationships in your toolkit – they are a mighty powerful piece of equipment.

Strengthen your relationship with your teen, because whatever the circumstances, a strong connection with your teen is the most valuable resource you have to support or guide them.

Action point: Help your teen differentiate between emotions and behaviour

As emotions dominate a young teenager's experience they may not always understand what is happening to them or feel in control. Help them to 'read' and name their own emotions so they can act accordingly and express themselves appropriately. Model it yourself in the classroom and at home, normalising everyday ups and downs and teaching your teen the breadth of emotional experiences we humans have.

Action point: Take time to decode teen behaviour

Teens give us clues that they are struggling (slamming doors, being unusually quiet, suddenly not doing homework, avoiding a party), but they don't always tell us. Be prepared to look carefully and decode. When they are ready, be available to talk to them.

Action point: Tend to emotional needs before learning

An emotional brain draws energy away from the thinking brain and positive cycle of learning. Tend to emotional needs first, even if it is just to connect with a young person and acknowledge their difficulties. If a teen isn't thinking or engaged, take a moment to check in with what is happening for them and give them a time out (not a punishing time out, but a moment to recover) before getting to the learning task at hand.

The moral of the story is...

Teens are vulnerable to mental health difficulties. A well-informed supportive adult alongside them can empower teenagers to develop emotional regulation and good mental health habits.

Downloads: Teen Brains Overwhelmed

Strong emotions are common in adolescence, but persistent emotional distress which impacts on day-to-day activities might mean a mental health problem. Mental health difficulties can interfere with learning and how your teenager copes with challenges in their future.

The way teens express their emotional needs is less easily interpreted compared to younger children, so they may need you to decode it. As an adult supporting a young person, it is important to help teens develop good emotional regulation and mental health habits.

Exercise

Note down the ways in which your teen expresses the following emotions: anger, sadness, anxiety, excitement, guilt and disappointment

Anger

. . . .

. . . .

Sadness

. . . .

. . . .

Anxiety

. . . .

. . . .

Excitement

. . . .

. . . .

Guilt

. . . .

. . . .

Disappointment

. . . .

. . . .

What everyday habits or rituals do you have to support your teen's mental robustness? A daily or weekly check-in? Given that teens may not always be ready to talk things through, do you have a code word so they could signal they are feeling down but aren't yet ready to talk about it?

. . . .

. . . .

. . . .

. . . .

. . . .

. . . .

How do you help your teen differentiate emotions experienced and emotions expressed? Can you help them to see that noticing emotions is a good daily goal, although acting on all of them may not be appropriate or helpful?

. . . .

. . . .

. . . .

. . . .

. . . .

. . . .

. . . .

When this happens...	Instead of this...	Try this...
Your teen tripped over in school in front of her class. She is crying and upset, feeling so embarrassed.	She needs to just get over it. She only tripped up. What's the big deal? Gosh, she makes such a fuss!	It is horrible to feel embarrassed. I will put myself in her shoes and spend some time talking it through with her. Afterwards, and when she feels ready, we can move on.
		Allow teens to express emotions
Your teen doesn't want to go on the school trip. He's not sleeping and tearful.	You don't have to go on the school trip if you are that scared. Stay home with me.	I can see you are really worried. It's important to go and not let worry be in the driving seat. What's the worst that could happen on the trip? Avoidance is never the answer and you might get into a habit where you only feel OK at home. Let's think of ways to make you feel more comfortable about going.
		Don't be scared of teen emotions
Your teen is rude to you in front of your friends.	(Shouting) How dare you speak to me like that? No more screens for you for the month.	It is absolutely not OK to speak to me like that. I feel really cross right now. Before I say something I regret, I'm going to take some time to feel calmer and **use my thinking brain.**
		Teach and model emotional regulation
Your teen seems to be in a really bad place and you have been increasingly concerned about what he might do to himself because he has been so unhappy for the last month or so.	Maybe it's nothing. I'll leave it and see if things get better. He seems OK today.	He seems able to cope some days, but the pattern is more often bad days than good. I'm concerned about him. As his distress is recurring, I am going to seek help from a professional.
		If you are concerned, **speak to your doctor**

Chapter 7

Thriving with Neurodiversity

Long story, short

- The impact of a neurodiverse condition may be mild or significant but it will be life-long.
- Even if your teen is 'neurotypical', an understanding of neurodiversity and conditions that can affect their friends and classmates will stand you – and them – in good stead.
- Neurodiverse conditions run in families – be aware of any positive or negative associations and use stories of resilience in affected family members to inspire your teen.
- Teens may re-evaluate what a long-known condition means to them as part of their self-image development.
- Secondary school requires a step-up in executive function skills and these are often vulnerable in neurodiverse conditions.
- Encourage your teen to own their neurodiverse learning profile so they can get out there and access the learning support that belongs to them.
- Navigating a neurodiverse profile *positively* with your help will likely result in added value for your teen: a growth mindset.

Introduction

Neurodiverse means that the brain develops in a different way

Everyone is different. In this chapter we review neurodiversity, sometimes called 'neurodevelopmental conditions', which means the brain has a pattern of development that might impact on a person's day-to-day functioning. The impact might be very mild (and the symptoms barely noticeable) until school years, for example (like Dyslexia). The symptoms might get less impactful in adulthood (like Attention Deficit Hyperactivity Disorder or ADHD) or have positive aspects (the skills to notice fine detail associated with Autism Spectrum Disorder), but the brain's development is different from a typically developing brain, and this difference remains throughout the individual's life.

If your teen has already been identified as neurodiverse in some way, we will assume that you have a good level of knowledge about their given condition.

According to the UK's Department of Education, the vast majority of individuals who are neurodiverse are in mainstream school, and while they are more likely to have specific learning needs, they do not have general learning difficulties (where all aspects of learning are affected). This reflects a policy of inclusion that has had significant impact in a short period of time. For example, in the USA, only a minority of young people with Autism Spectrum Disorder were in mainstream school in the early 1990s, whereas now 70 per cent learn in regular schools.

In this chapter we consider what it might mean to have both a neurodiverse brain and a teenage brain. This meeting of minds is no less of an opportunity to learn and flourish than for any other teenager, but the combination of a neurodevelopmental condition and a teenage brain does throw up some issues which may prove difficult for both of you to manage at times – and it will keep you on your toes as the supporting adult. We will consider two central adolescent issues, self-concept and the academic demands of secondary school, with some common neurodevelopmental conditions in mind, but it is not an exhaustive list. You may need to begin with the broader themes we raise in this chapter and then extrapolate to your specific circumstances.

'Neurodiverse conditions' is a shorthand term, not a stigmatising label

We use terms currently accepted in education and young people's services, although we understand that some people have strong feelings about expressions such as Specific Learning Difficulties, considering them stigmatising labels. This is a valid debate but it is outside the scope of this book. We use the mainstream terminologies in this book as we believe they provide a shared understanding about the challenges that a young person with Developmental Co-ordination Disorder, ADHD or other difficulties might have.

Neurodiverse presentations can reduce a young person's ability to demonstrate what they know in a one-size-fits-all public exam system. Because of this, they are often entitled to compensation or Access Arrangements (e.g. extra time, use of a laptop, reader or scribe). In the UK, young people don't need a specified condition to gain Access Arrangements as decisions are made based on evidence of 'educational need' (e.g. slow speed of processing, below-average reading skills). In the USA, a diagnosis is essential in order to access support. Some families describe feeling concerned that their child will hear the word 'disorder' and make negative assumptions about themselves. Though it is understandable, you do have some influence over how it is received by your teen. Your tone and response will influence your teen's perception of any words used. Avoiding the topic or telling them to keep it a secret will inadvertently give them the message it is something to be ashamed of. Searching out positive information, finding support groups and watching films or reading books related to the diagnosis are all ways of helping your teen to embrace it, understand it and accept it is a part of them.

Having two or more neurodiverse conditions is common

If you are familiar with neurodiverse conditions, you are probably aware of the idea of co-occurrence, in which a person has two or more conditions. Co-occurrence of neurodevelopmental conditions is the rule rather than the exception, partly because the suspected causes for many of these conditions are common across the neurodevelopmental spectrum; the pattern of difficulties is simply expressed in a variety of different ways. For example, Tourette Syndrome, ADHD and obsessive-compulsive disorder share a genetic link which may be expressed by having the full triad or a combination of those disorders. That understood, it means that young people, and indeed the adults supporting them, may identify with one or another of their co-occurring conditions at different times in their lives depending on its salience in their day-to-day lives.

Neurodiversity runs in families

All the conditions that come under the umbrella of neurodiversity have a strong genetic component – in most cases the specific genes involved are not known, but there are robust data to show that where one person is affected in a family, there is a higher chance that another family member will also be, as compared to the patterns in the general population. The closer the relation, the higher the chances, so first-degree relatives are most likely to have the same sort of difficulties. This means that parents and teens may share the same condition, or variants of it, which may have some pretty far-reaching emotional implications day to day. We will consider these later in the chapter.

The science bit: Brain and behaviour

The neurodiverse brain has specific patterns of brain development

There are many studies which explore the brain regions associated with specific neurodevelopmental conditions. There are general principles common to all: the degree or speed of connection between brain cells or brain regions is different from those of the typically developing population. The nature of that difference and severity varies from condition to condition. We are not yet able to use brain scanners such as MRI to identify neurodiverse conditions that require an educational assessment.

The prefrontal cortex shows extraordinary rates of development in the teenage period

The executive functions, often vulnerable in neurodiverse conditions, but central to many higher order tasks in secondary school, are housed in the part of the brain known as the prefrontal cortex (see Chapter 2:

The Teen Brain Thinks and Feels). MRI scans show us that this area is developing very quickly throughout adolescence, kick-started by the onset of puberty. Specifically, the number of neural connections within the prefrontal cortex and between this region and the emotional centres of the brain is growing exponentially. It is a rocket-fuelled trajectory of growth. This is as true for neurodiverse teens: though the development may take a different path or speed, there will be the same phenomenal upgrade in your teen's abilities to plan, divide attention, think strategically, plan and organise themselves.

Similarly, the prefrontal cortex is also associated with self-reflection and the development of self-image, so it's no coincidence that self-identity becomes a preoccupation in the teenage years (see Chapter 11: Self-reflection). The high levels of connectivity observed in MRI scans may be because so much self-reflection occurs in teens, or it may occur *so that* the teen can make judgements about themselves, or it may be a bit of both, which is the most likely scenario. As is so often the case in describing brain development, figuring out the relative contributions of biology and environment is a bit like figuring out if the chicken or the egg came first.

Translating your teen

The only thing that is constant is change

Adolescence means change – it's a dynamic time of physical, mental and social development: new demands, new friends, new school subjects, different bodies, emotional high and lows, changed expectations, moving trends. Coping strategies that were successful before adolescence won't do the job for many teen tasks. The transition from primary to secondary education is considered one of the most challenging experiences for typically developing young people precisely because it requires a step-up in social, emotional and cognitive domains, and all at once. In secondary school, the requirements of the curriculum become more abstract and there may be significant effects for some teens in the neurodiverse community. Primary education relies to a degree on rote memory skills, but in secondary school, the demands move beyond simple rote learning onto strategy, analysis, deduction and argument formation.

Executive functions are often vulnerable in neurodiverse teens – but are central to secondary school

The academic demands of secondary school, college or university have a particularly heavy load on executive functions. The term 'executive functions' is an umbrella term describing between eight to eleven (depending on who you listen to) skills. These include the capacity to plan, switch flexibly between topics, hold information in mind for a short period (called working memory) and concentrate on two activities at once (known as divided attention). Secondary school tasks demand a significantly increased amount of executive function skills, and this is likely to be particularly challenging if your teen is neurodiverse.

For example, taking notes in class is usually introduced for the first time to students in secondary school and it relies on holding information in mind for long enough to write it down (working memory) while paying attention to what the teacher is talking about next (divided attention). Add to the pot two further executive function skills – emotional regulation and impulsive control – and you will agree that the secondary school soup is quite a spicy one. For many young people with neurodevelopmental conditions – ADHD, Developmental Co-ordination Disorder, Dyslexia, Autism Spectrum Disorder, Tourette Syndrome and so on – these executive function skills are vulnerable and impact on day-to-day functions. It means that transitions from primary to secondary school and then on to college potentially include additional challenges for neurodiverse young people. What we have discovered in recent years is that, with the appropriate support, mindset and positive self-belief, teens with neurodiversity can and will thrive in education. Just as for the neurotypical population, the teenage years offer a great opportunity for growth and learning for the neurodiverse population.

What does that mean day to day?

Family members share genes and memories – how does that impact on you and your teen?

What are the day-to-day implications of family traits and neurodiversity? One important repercussion is that you or your teen are likely to have first-hand experience of a given condition from other family members, whether you know the condition by name or not. If you see behaviour in your teen that you recognise in yourself, it can be highly emotive, so it's important to be aware of any positive or negative association linked with a particular condition.

So, for example, if your teen has a paternal uncle with ADHD who, despite being very able academically, dropped out of school and has had neither a long-term job nor personal relationship, ADHD may become firmly linked in your mind with this life path. Of course, there are numerous studies to show that the majority of young people with ADHD have fulfilling careers and relationships, with a marked improvement in functioning as they go into adulthood. However, in this particular family context, it might mean that if your teen with ADHD has one poor school test result around the age their uncle dropped out of school, your reaction is highly expressive and way out of proportion to the event because perhaps in the back of your mind ADHD leads inevitably to adjustment problems in adulthood.

Parents may be supporting their neurodiverse teen to deal with difficulties that they themselves also have

The second important consequence of neurodiverse family traits is that if you are related to a neurodiverse teen, you may share aspects of that condition in your own profile. Young people on the autism spectrum may need some guidance about how to manage small talk, for example, but they may be asking a parent who finds managing these unstructured social situations extremely hard as they too have social communication difficulties.

Similarly, young people with ADHD respond particularly well to routine, structure and clear, explicit boundaries. If a parent has any ADHD traits, they will find providing such an environment particularly testing, because they themselves may have problems with organisational skills. If you are outside a family, supporting a teen in an educational setting, bear in mind the additional challenges that parents may be facing as they support a teen who has the same needs.

On the other hand, affected family members will have developed useful coping strategies over their lifetimes, and they will have messages of resilience to share, precisely because they have had the same challenges earlier in their life. Share your family's stories of persistence, because doing so will let young people in. When as a supporting adult you reveal your own vulnerability, this can be very galvanising for a teenager, as it implies power equivalence, and that increase in social status will engage your young person in the conversation. They will also respond to your openness about difficult experiences.

Neurodiversity can be a positive and, while accepting it can take time and support, understanding can bring resolution

Parents, teachers and teens can feel worried when they are told about a teen's neurodiversity, but there may well be advantages: 'It's a general principle that whenever a disadvantageous condition is widely dispersed throughout the population, one must ask whether it's a purely unfavourable phenomenon or whether there's some counter-vailing advantage' (Norman Geschwind 1982, p.21).

There are many valid theories suggesting that as we need biodiversity for a flourishing planet, so there are good adaptive reasons for neurodiversity in the population. Information introducing an audience to any given condition will often include high-profile, talented, successful people with a particular disorder. Mozart and Einstein seem to have had the full house of neurodevelopmental conditions between them. The point is that, in certain contexts, the quick-thinking, fast-acting style that comes along with ADHD, for example, might mean a new and productive idea is generated.

At the same time we appreciate that, for a teenager, the experience of embracing neurodiversity is neither inevitable nor immediate. The impact of learning that your teen (or you) has a condition is often considered similar to mourning in some ways as there is a loss, of sorts, of what was expected. As they move into their teenage years, for example, young people who may have been aware for many years that they have Dyslexia, say, may re-experience the first impact of their diagnosis on a more complex and painful level. This is because their cognitive skills and capacity to think about longer term consequences develop so dramatically in the adolescent period. Accepting what a condition means is a process, and it is to be expected that many individuals will have unresolved feelings at first.

Given that a teenager's self-concept is being formed, evaluated and re-evaluated (see Chapter 11: Self-reflection) during adolescence, we need to consider how your teen might understand the implications of a given neurodevelopmental condition and how it might impact on their self-concept during this sensitive time.

Teens may re-consider their condition and what it means to them

The behaviours that suggest a person has unresolved feelings about a condition include being in complete denial about it (e.g. your teen getting cross or hiding when the diagnosis is mentioned), obsessively searching for reasons why it affects them (beyond appropriate curiosity) or using it as a blanket explanation for anything going wrong in life, whether it is relevant or not (e.g. the teen who says their ADHD means they can't focus, so there is no point in even trying to do their homework).

In the context of the self-identity calibrations that happen frequently during adolescence, we might expect some element of unresolved feelings reflecting an increase in understanding about a condition of which your teen may have been aware since early childhood. Features of neurodiversity which may have simply been accepted by the young person in middle childhood are likely to be re-evaluated by teens. This could be considered a progression, as it demonstrates an increased capacity to think, reflect and plan about the future.

Social nuances take on greater importance as peer groups develop, and girls tend to interact using more facial expressions and implied social meaning in their communication style. These aspects of communication are classically difficult for young people on the autism spectrum. Exclusion from peer groups is particularly difficult for a teen. Some teens with Autism Spectrum Disorder might want to be part of their group but may prefer slightly less intense relationships. They may question what that social preference reveals about them. Are they 'weird'? Why do they flinch if another kid tries to hug them when they score at football? These self-reflections are core to every teen's life.

What does that mean for learning?

Adolescence is all about transition; secondary school is a major transition

The challenges and demands of secondary school transfer represent a step-change for any teenager. Young people with brains which work differently need particular support, as this is likely to be a testing time. Watch out for rigid behaviour which may signal anxiety about the change.

Executive function challenges increase exponentially in secondary school and university

Young people with ADHD are likely to find the demands of secondary school a major challenge. They will likely need considerable support over and above their peers to find new ways of coping with the basic organisational tasks such as moving from class to class, using different books and dealing with specific homework tasks and teacher demands.

The tasks of school learning become more abstract in the teen years – either a challenge or an opportunity

Young people with good memory capacity usually do well in elementary school, but in some cases neurodiverse students, particularly able teens on the autism spectrum, or those with a language disorder, find the abstract requirements hard to manage. They may have had a robust self-concept as an academic student in primary school, but find that this is challenged in secondary school with the new expectations of the curriculum. On the other hand, some able neurodiverse students find that more abstract academic demands showcase their higher order abilities in a way that was not apparent in primary education. Spelling still matters in a history essay assignment, but it's not the point – instead the capacity to analyse information is central.

So, what now?

Young people with neurodiverse brains need special consideration. Their potential is enormous but their path can be rocky along the way as they navigate the adolescent years. As the support, you will need to keep your eye on the ball.

Case study: Hiro

Hiro was a 14-year-old boy who was diagnosed with ADHD at eight years of age, before he moved to secondary school. Looking back, his mother could see that the difficulties he had with thinking before he did something, focusing on and completing tasks and staying still had been there since birth. She had called him her 'pocket rocket' as a toddler as he would climb on furniture, stairs and anywhere that was exciting.

Hiro's father, Akira, had similar traits. He worked as a stock broker and loved the rush of his work. He had a secretary who planned his days and appointments, and reminded him of anything that he needed. He found that his butterfly mind could generate great concepts but he needed his team to get him through. He had failed horribly at school and gone on three gap years before he managed to get into college. He dropped out of his degree and then spent a few months in prison for drink-driving. When he was released from prison he met Hiro's mother, Emica, who loved Akira's energy and worked very hard to organise him, setting boundaries and limits. Emica made expectations very clear and encouraged him to use shared technology to keep a calendar and to know his whereabouts. When they met, she strongly influenced his decision to seek a diagnosis. He took medication, and together they tried to work out new patterns of behaviour. She realised that by supporting him rather than criticising him, he managed far better and their life was much easier.

After Hiro's diagnosis at eight, adults had understood his behaviour better and he had managed the transition to high school quite well. However, the work load was increasing and the academic stakes were higher at the age of 14, and Hiro's parents were worried. He struggled to complete his homework, fell out with his friends and found it difficult to think about how to repair the relationships. He had a gentle nature and fast humour, but his father Akira was worried he might be going down a similar route to himself as a teen. One of the most difficult aspects of Hiro's behaviour was his quick temper, particularly towards his younger brother, Eiichi, who was only 11 months younger. Moreover, his parents knew parties, alcohol and drugs were only round the corner and he was an impulsive boy.

A good resolution

Hiro's mother asked to have a series of sessions with the clinical psychologist and to involve Akira. She felt that she needed the support to problem solve with Hiro and wanted her husband involved too. She was also keenly aware of the impact of Hiro's behaviour on Eiichi and wanted to make her input as useful as possible. She learnt about structuring Hiro's day and how to give him feedback quickly to focus on the positive aspects of his behaviour. She talked to him a lot about his feelings and behaviour. With time he started to feel less angry and frustrated with his own behaviour and how other people responded to it, and trust built between parents and son. A large focus of the work with the psychologist had been for Akira to work out his response to his son, to rein in his natural proclivity to react and to check his catastrophising thoughts when he saw a reflection of himself in his son. Hiro talked with his parents about the temptations at parties and they made plans for how he would manage. Part of the conversation was helping Hiro understand the interaction of his teenage brain with his ADHD brain which made him more vulnerable to being led down a bad path. The most valuable tool they had in their toolkit at this stage was their relationship, and it was growing from strength to strength.

What might get in the way?

Hiro's behaviour could easily be interpreted as that of a 'naughty' child. A 14-year-old can often be adult size, and when a younger teen is in the firing line, parental emotions can be hard to control. Hiro's behaviour seemed developmentally inappropriate, particularly as his younger sibling was acting in a more emotionally controlled way. If his parents had responded to the behaviour and not been curious about what was going on, the opportunity for understanding and solutions would have been missed. As it turned out, understanding how his ADHD brain was coping with the tasks of teenage life and building their relationship to support him was the best way forward.

Action point: Name it – it is the first step towards embracing it

Naming a neurodevelopmental condition, and providing accessible and accurate information about it for your teen, is an important part of resolution, as it increases feelings of control and competence in the young person. In the case of Dyslexia, the earlier a young person learns their diagnosis, the higher their self-concept as a learner will be. If you are keeping 'it' a secret or using a euphemism, it is important to ask yourself, why? Secrets (as opposed to private information) often mean shame. Unspoken issues sometimes take on a life of their own – both young children and teens often sense there is something afoot and may imagine all sorts of serious and inaccurate scenarios. They may wonder if having the condition is a secret in the family – does that mean it is something of which they should be ashamed?

Action point: Be proactive with information about the condition

Expect and encourage a number of conversations – perhaps years apart – about what the condition means. The young person may find it easier to digest information in their own time, at their own pace. Direct teenagers to reputable websites and highlight, as is ever true, that the web is a magnificent resource but also includes magnificent amounts of rubbish, including sites that scaremonger using extreme cases or include someone's opinions presented as fact. Books can be helpful too.

Action point: It's all in the delivery – if you believe it's OK, so will your teenager

If you give the message with your words and actions that a diagnostic label, such as 'Dyscalculia', is simply a way of summarising that number tasks are hard for some people, your teen is more likely to feel at ease with it. Indeed our clinical experience is that naming a condition can be an empowering process, as the young person can find an explanation for the struggles they have had. Having a neurodiverse condition is not an excuse for lower expectations, but it is an opportunity for additional praise when the young person reaches their goals.

Action point: Positive relationships predict positive resolutions

An adult's level of understanding about the consequences of a given condition is stable, but your teen's understanding and self-identity are still under construction, so their levels of resolution might fluctuate. Interestingly it is not the severity of a condition which predicts a healthy resolution for *parents*, rather it is the quality of relationship that they have with their child. It is highly likely that this is true for young people too, which means that you can facilitate an empowered experience of neurodiversity using your superpowers as a key adult. It's yet another good reason to invest time in fostering a positive relationship with your teen.

Action point: Own it – teens can shape their own learning environment

Aim to encourage the young person to shape their own environment – it's part of the path to being an independent adult. Hitch their wagon to the idea that they have a right to have their learning needs supported. It is a matter of social inclusion and equality. Your teen can be a trailblazer for the neurodiverse community. For example, teens with Developmental Co-ordination Disorder are likely to take longer to complete written work. If someone dictates information and they are taking notes, encourage them to speak up and say 'slow down', rather than struggling to overcome their difficulty without compensatory support.

Action point: Model a growth mindset and a tenacious learning style

Neurodiverse teens might not always take the most direct route, but given the right context, they will get there. Indeed the neuro-diverse route might be considered more enriched. Individuals with Dyslexia are often described anecdotally as creative. There is not much empirical evidence to support it, but what evidence exists points towards it being somewhat true (partly because it's hard to measure creativity). Having to pedal harder to get the same academic outcome as peers could be considered unfair or it could be understood as a valuable life lesson in resilience, finding alternative routes to success and the power of tenacity.

The quality of your teen's experience will be shaped by you. Model your own experience with a growth mindset in a wide variety of contexts. Being neurodiverse sometimes means finding extra energy. It is important to acknowledge the additional effort it takes to write the list, re-check work, or remember to make eye contact. It is time-consuming and sometimes frustrating. Your dyslexic teen might feel justifiably dispirited having to do yet another grammar edit on that politics essay. You can 're-frame' the experience without discounting their feelings. ('Yes, it is a bit dull, but grammar is a conduit so that the world understands the meaning – the world needs to know about these political ideas, so nail that grammar edit or how else are you going to change the world?') You get the idea.

The moral of the story is...

You and your teen may have to find a new relationship with their neurodiversity during adolescence. There may be additional challenges particularly during transition periods, but with the right support, your teen can reach their goals with added value: the opportunity to develop skills for life in tenacity and resilience.

Downloads: Thriving with Neurodiversity

Young people with neurodiverse brains and learning profiles need special consideration. The impact of a significant learning difference may be mild or significant and will be life-long. Teens may re-evaluate what having the learning challenge means to them as part of their self-image development and ability to thrive. Now is your chance to frame their abilities in a positive way to build resilience and teach them to own their learning profile, get out there and access support that belongs to them.

Exercise
Note three main challenges your teen faces at home and at school because of their neurodiverse brain.

Challenge 1

. . . .

. . . .

Challenge 2

. . . .

. . . .

Challenge 3

. . . .

. . . .

Name three strengths your teen has to help them to cope with their specific challenges.

Strength 1

. . . .

. . . .

Strength 2

. . . .

. . . .

Strength 3

. . . .

. . . .

If you have traits of that neurodiversity, do the same exercise for yourself.

Challenge 1

. . . .

. . . .

Challenge 2

. . . .

. . . .

Challenge 3

. . . .

. . . .

Strength 1

. . . .

. . . .

Strength 2

. . . .

. . . .

Strength 3

. . . .

. . . .

How does your neurodiverse teen cope with executive functions, such as being able to plan, divide attention, think strategically or be persistent until a task is finished? What systems could you put in place to help them do these tasks independently?

. . . .

. . . .

. . . .

. . . .

What do you do or say that helps your teen frame their neurodiversity as a positive?

. . . .

. . . .

. . . .

. . . .

When this happens...	Instead of this...	Try this...
Your teen has Dyslexia.	He's never going to be good at English because his Dyslexia means he can't write well.	He's going to have to work harder than others, and we will need some support and accommodations in place. He has strength in oral skills. How can we use that to develop his writing?
		Keep a **growth mindset** – whatever the learning profile
Your teen with Autism Spectrum Disorder says he doesn't get most of the jokes at school. He got the funny stuff in primary school, but not now.	There's nothing wrong with you. Other kids are mean.	Autism Spectrum Disorder means some types of conversation are harder to understand. It's annoying but it's OK. Don't ever think it's because you are not smart.
		Name the condition to empower your teen
Your teen has ADHD. She doesn't have her notes to do her assessment.	School knows you have got ADHD. Why hasn't the teacher given you the notes? It's hard enough for you to learn without these other things to do.	Your teacher will try to always give you notes from the lesson, but if they forget, make sure you remind them. She is there to help, but it is your responsibility to make sure you have them all.
		Teach your teen to self-advocate to get the support they need
Your teen has Tourette Syndrome. He has forgotten homework twice this week.	He has such a hard time trying to manage his tics. I'm letting him off again, I know, but he's got such a lot on his plate.	Tics take up a lot of his resources when they happen so often, but they are a bit lower this week. He's bright, so I'm doing him no favours if I don't expect him to complete tasks all the time. Part of academic success means finding a reliable system for homework.
		Have (appropriately) high expectations – don't allow a neurodiverse condition to be an excuse day to day

PART 3

Teen Developmental Priorities

Chapter 8

Cracking the Social Code

Long story, short

- Social motivation changes over time.
- For teenagers, peers' presence and acceptance have great impact.
- Social signals (e.g. tone of voice) may be so powerful to a teen that the content of what we say can get lost.
- Harness the power of the teen social brain and peer orientation to achieve positive goals.

Introduction

Understanding the social world is highly complex and takes time to master

Brains are fundamentally social (see Chapter 5: The Teen Brain Loves Other People). This chapter untangles the processes that are involved, given that teens are particularly social beings. Consider the intricate social signals involved with interacting with another individual. Social signals are numerous and complex, and relationships have different values and degrees of influence: some are about power and authority, others about nurture and care. As we negotiate each relationship we might be influenced by our past experience, we need to work out our place in the group, we need to recognise others' emotions...the list goes on.

Cracking the code of the social world takes many years. In fact, it takes 25 years for the brain to sculpt its circuitry to manage the complexity of social information. Interesting that logical reasoning reaches maturity much sooner than social reasoning.

The focus of our social relationships changes as we grow up
Although social relationships are important across the lifespan, there are dramatic changes in the *focus* of relationships (see Figure 8.1). We are driven towards change, and the impact of those relationships (or the lack of them) varies according to age.

During **infancy** the key social relationship is the main caregiver. The baby or toddler is inherently driven towards the parent or other caregiver for *care*. Decades of research has shown extended maternal separation during infancy without a consistent caregiver has life-long implications for building relationships. John Bowlby's attachment theory, developed in the mid-20th century, has transformed our understanding of the importance of relationships with a significant other in the early years of life (Bowlby 2005).

During the **juvenile** phase (around 4 to 10 years), the focus of social development is the *playmate*. Children are driven to play with other children, moving from playing alongside to co-operative play with other children. Primary school children are learning how to play with friends, but they remain strongly connected to their parent.

During the **adolescent** years, teens are driven to *integrate* with their peers, and being part of the wider group is the learning task. This is different from just playing or hanging out with friends or interacting with their classmates. It's fundamentally about fitting in, finding their place in the group and working out where they belong. This is one of the key drivers for your teen – to integrate with their peer group. No wonder then that teen behaviour with peers changes so significantly with the onset of adolescence.

The teen years seem to be a sensitive period for social integration
The distinction between these stages of childhood is important, because it gives us the code for unlocking the needs of young people of all ages and unlocking the incredible teenage brain. Understanding *why* teens are so drawn to their friends and peers, and what they are, at a fundamental level, trying to achieve, enables us to support and facilitate this aspect of their development. Importantly, research shows us that isolation from your peer group is most detrimental during the adolescent years. Both animal and human research show that extreme social isolation at this time in development results in

long-term difficulties in cognitive, social and emotional regulation skills which are linked to structural differences in the brain. We might consider adolescence a sensitive period for social integration. Just like we discovered that there is a sensitive window of opportunity for developing language, or learning to walk, early in life, it may be that social integration is developmentally sensitive and critical to the adolescent period of life. If this is true, we need to get this aspect of the environment right for teenagers.

Figure 8.1: Social focus changes – peer integration is key for teens

The teenage brain is programmed to orientate towards social information – learning as much as possible before independence and adulthood

With the onset of adolescence, both the quantity and quality of social relationships change dramatically. From an evolutionary perspective, it makes sense as teens get ready to leave their birth family to find their own social group and lead more independent lives. This has important implications for the way the teenage brain considers social information and for its impact on their day-to-day behaviour.

There are three ways in which this social reorientation occurs in adolescents:

- the brain is wired to spot *any* social information in their environment
- social information is given high importance
- how the brain processes social information changes during adolescence.

The science bit: Brain and behaviour

Peer influence and peer acceptance are likely to underpin many decisions and actions

Everyone is influenced by other people's opinions. We are all social animals, but adolescents especially so. Many studies show peers' views have exceptionally high value in adolescence and thus, particularly in early adolescence, young people are more influenced by their peers' opinions. Moreover, acceptance by the group is a very powerful motivator. Social rewards, such as teens being esteemed by their peers, cause the brain's reward centres to fire on all cylinders. Important information – which for teens is peer acceptance – needs to scream loudly so that teens can learn the signals for social integration. Just as we make important information in the environment highly visible – think about fire exit signage – so the brain makes important information for teen developmental tasks highly visible (peer attention). It makes sense, then, that concern about peer acceptance will shape social interactions and decision making.

Peer presence can cause a degree of stress

Simply being in the company of peers in adolescence is unique. There is a change in the stress hormone (cortisol) and brain activity that is **specific to teens** if they simply believe their peers are watching them. They don't even need to see, hear or talk to their peers, just hold in mind the idea of their peers watching. This makes sense as it is a time when social comparisons might be made by their peers whose thoughts and acceptance matter so much. As we will see in the chapter on stress (Chapter 15: Good Stress, Bad Stress), a degree of stress is not in itself damaging – the message from this finding is more about the importance of peers to teens.

Social processing takes conscious thought in adolescence – but it is automatic by adulthood

The social brain network consists of regions in the thinking part of the brain (the frontal cortex) and some in the back of the brain where less conscious thought is involved. Activity in the social brain develops from being 'front brain dominant' in adolescence to 'back brain dominant' in adulthood, which is likely to reflect important changes in how young people learn to process social information.

During adolescence, social information processing in the teenage brain is still getting stronger and more effective. Decision making therefore requires more conscious thought and self-reflection for a teenager. By adulthood, this process becomes more automated in the brain and requires less conscious thought. As Sarah-Jayne Blakemore suggests in her 2018 book *Inventing Ourselves*, this theory is supported by the finding that adults are more able to multitask while reasoning about social information than teens, probably because it causes less interference with other forms of processing.

 ## Translating your teen

Teens become more socially interested and more socially aware

As anyone involved with a teenager knows, there is an almost overnight change when a teen becomes more aware of their friends, more interested in their opinions and more prone to social embarrassment. This social integration is a key developmental task of the teen years. Don't be freaked out. This is a passing, although extended, phase. It's important because young people need to pay attention to social information to prepare them for finding where they will belong in adulthood.

The effects of exclusion are more potent in adolescence

You will remember from Chapter 5 (The Teen Brain Loves Other People) that the same neural circuits service physical and social pain. Adolescents differ to children and adults in the way they understand social information. One of these differences is that the effects of social pain are more significant during the adolescent period. Studies find a greater drop in mood and heightened anxiety for adolescents when they are left out of a virtual ball game (see Figure 8.2). Ostracism by the group can be powerful in altering an adolescent's state of mind and potentially affecting their well-being. Fear of exclusion may even mean that the young person compromises their choices or activities, as in the case study featuring Tammy later in this chapter. Try to bear this in mind when you are interpreting teen behaviour. The young person may well prioritise friendships over revision for a test or music practice and it is not because they are irrational human beings who don't care. Peer approval is their priority for good reason.

Figure 8.2: Exclusion is particularly painful for teens

With a growth mindset, social rejection is less painful

We talked about the importance of mindsets in Chapter 3: The Teen Brain Learns and Believes. Remember the benefits of a growth mindset when young people learn? It turns out that a growth mindset is also useful when it comes to friendships and the social world. Young people with a fixed mindset about personality believe social traits are fixed and unchangeable. These teens experience any rejection from their peer group – such as not being invited to a party – as more stressful because they think this is fixed and they will always be left out from parties or their friends will always think them boring. However, someone with a growth mindset sees personality as more malleable, and therefore that missed party invite won't be considered quite as significant. Growth mindset people can dismiss this event as a 'one-off'; they may believe the person had specific reasons for not inviting them this time or that people can change and they might be invited next time.

The good news is that mindsets can be taught, so you can help a young person minimise upset and rejection after one missed party invitation. Moreover, nurturing a flexible mindset has other potential benefits: it helps make social transitions such as moving school less stressful. While moving schools may not seem a big deal to us, given teens' need for social integration, it's a highly vulnerable time for them. Establishing their social status is likely to be more important than doing their homework at that crucial time, and so it would be natural for there to be a shift in attention to social inclusion, possibly at the cost of academic focus. If this does happen, try not to consider this a fixed trait of the young person: 'they will never pass their exams, go to university or get a good job' (can you hear yourself thinking that?).

Reining in our own catastrophic thinking and the way we respond to a young person managing these transitions is very important. Growth mindsets are important for us too; more about this later. Remember that for teens to be in their positive cycle of learning they need to remove social and emotional distractions. For a teen, joining a new group is without a doubt a social distraction which needs attention and support before other types of learning can really take off.

What does that mean day to day?

Social content takes priority over other information – it still takes brain power

When we see this basic shift in reference towards social priorities in teens, it means they may experience acute self-consciousness and embarrassment in social contexts. It is as if the volume on a teen's social awareness is turned up a little too high. Indeed, adolescents experience greater self-consciousness on a day-to-day basis, according to their own reports. The case study with Jack below describes how, even very early on in adolescence, we might see these changes and the potential impact on other family members. Young people are tuning into the minds of other people, especially peers, and considering what *they* might be thinking about, but this takes some effort – it's not quite automatic yet.

Social isolation is particularly damaging for teenagers

The fundamental teen need for social integration means that social instability and isolation are particularly damaging for teenagers. It is not ethical or desirable to study social isolation in people, but studies using adolescent rats have found that being separated from peers results in structural differences in the frontal regions of the brain. Isolation was not so potent at other times in life. Moreover, following a period of isolation, these adolescent animals were inclined to play less with their peers. As they played less, they lost out on opportunities for brain learning and to develop resilience amongst their peers. The initial 'insult' of stress was having a domino effect on their development with long-term implications.

Social interaction happens on the phone

The image of a teenager being permanently attached to their phone is a common one. If we think about the social brain, we can begin to see the natural appeal of the phone. The teenage brain isn't driven towards phones, but it is driven towards friends, and there is probably a virtual social hang-out happening on your teen's phone right now. That is why it can feel to a teen as if you have taken away their *life* when you take away their phone. We cover technology and social media in Chapter 16:

#Social Media and Technology. But bear in mind that young people are not addicted to their phone. They are addicted to their friends.

What does that mean for learning?

Emotional information can distract young people from learning

We have established that adolescents are highly sensitive to social information and this means that they pick up on facial expressions, tone of voice and so on with their sensitive social antennae. Teens are proficient learners, but if social stimuli are emotionally charged their capacity to learn will be decreased. If they have fallen out with a friend who is sitting next to them, their teacher is cross with them or they feel threatened socially, their learning may be affected. Social exclusion is a very unsafe place for a young person to be. Remember, the brain must attend to safety before it can get into the positive cycle of learning.

Asking a question in class might be a great social risk to a teen

Anyone who has taught a new group of teenagers, unfamiliar with one another, will have felt palpable anxiety in the room. Each young person is wary of being judged by the others. Putting up your hand in class and asking a question might be one of the greatest risks to social standing a teen can take because of the potential to be judged by their classmates – their peers. It can be a really useful exercise for teachers to consider, subject by subject, what the particular social risks are for that subject. For example, speaking out loud in a foreign language may be a big social risk for a teen given the fact we often use accents in humorous sketches. In PE there may be a risk to wearing potentially tight or revealing clothes, and in English, creative writing might reveal an inner thought or idea that requires a degree of vulnerability. By reducing teen social risk you might find a much more amenable group of students.

If losing social standing or being punished are consequences, the former will win

Schools use a variety of techniques in class to help students listen and learn. Teachers might notice that different strategies are effective with young people at different ages. For example, if a teen is told by the teacher, 'Do that again and you will get a detention', and peers exchange glances or smile at the student in response, the student may well opt to take the detention. Their teenage brain might consider detention a fair price to pay in order to gain social standing. Adolescent brains are, after all, telling them that integration with peers is their most important task at this time in their lives.

So, what now?

The development of the social brain and social attention and salience is at an all-time high during adolescence. You can show your understanding of the importance of social relationships to a young person, rather than dismissing this area as soft skills that might distract from exams or similar. Strong relationships, developmentally relevant social interactions and robust friendships are the key to building a resilient, confident teenager and by happy coincidence may also underpin some splendidly well-encoded academic learning too.

Look after your teen when they are in social pain and help them to have a growth mindset if they are left out of an event. As adults we are in a position to facilitate and protect social connections for the teens in our care. Further, we can underline the importance of social connection by giving it equal (or one might argue more) value to other areas of success, such as academic achievement or a path into a well-paid career, in day-to-day conversations and actions.

Case study: Sean

Sean had always been a happy go lucky boy who didn't care one iota what he was wearing, whether his hair was brushed or what he looked like. He was into his football and loved playing it, dealing football cards with his friends and playing it on the Playstation. His biological mother, Caoimhe, had always taken him to school. They would walk along together, chatting in an animated way, sometimes joined by a friend of his and sometimes alone. Just after his 11th birthday, Sean said that he wanted to walk on his own to school. He didn't mind if his mother was walking behind him, but he asked if he could be a few steps ahead of her.

Sean had become increasingly aware of what his friends thought of him at about 11 years of age. His friend, Piers, had an older sibling and they were supposed to get the bus together, but mostly Piers came into school alone. He had a certain confidence about him that Sean noticed. Nothing had been said, but Sean noticed a small smirk on Piers' face when Sean gave Caoimhe a kiss goodbye at the gate. He would not have noticed before, but suddenly this made Sean feel embarrassed and ashamed. He wanted to be independent like his friend, and asking his mother to step back was the only way to achieve this.

This had come as a shock to Caoimhe. Sean was growing up but was still small in stature and she had greatly valued that morning chat in her day. She felt somewhat rejected and sad. This feeling of rejection brought with it a sense of irritation with her son that she hadn't experienced before. 'How can he be so cruel?' she thought. 'Is he trying to hurt me?'

A good resolution

It took a few hours, but eventually she contacted Sean's other mum, her partner Naomi, and asked if they could spend time together talking that evening. Naomi cancelled her swim class and they decided to organise a sitter to stay with Sean. The couple discussed the situation. They both discussed the changes that they had seen in Sean during the recent months, physically and emotionally. They talked about their decision to have Sean together and all of the work that had been put into that. They started to map out how together they would work to understand the changes that he would go through and how they would support him in the coming years.

In this case, the support and reassurance that Caoimhe needed was available from Naomi, but she had to ask for it. A small event with Sean had made her feel insecure and worried about her son's love and future, but together the couple could look at the incident through the lens of Sean's development.

Not burdening Sean with this realisation and upset was helpful as there would be little he could do to change it or protect his parents.

What might get in the way?

Caoimhe could have acted on her initial emotional response which was to feel angry with her son and hurt by him. This could have caused Sean confusion about how to reconcile his drives and developmental needs with his mother's needs. Moreover, it could have damaged their relationships, so he avoided telling his parents how he felt about other things. This could have closed a window of support needed in the future as he went through the often turbulent social experience of adolescence.

Case study: Tammy

Tammy was a 16-year-old girl who had always been good at dance. From nursery, she had a sense of rhythm better developed than any of her peers. Tammy's mother was a ballet dancer in the 1980s and had taken great delight in watching her daughter achieve certificates and accolades. Tammy's commitment to dance had been a big part of her life. She had been consistent in her training and practice and appeared to love the challenge.

Recently, Tammy had been dating Ben, who lived on the other side of town. They both went to the same school and saw each other most days. Ben belonged to a large group of teenagers who did everything together. Tammy and Ben had become inseparable from one another in the past school term.

Tammy came to talk with her mum and said she was thinking of giving up two of her three dance practice classes. She felt that the dance practice was making her stand out and she felt self-conscious about it. She said that she was too tired to study and that it meant she couldn't see Ben as often as she'd like. She was very calm and had clearly thought the whole situation through. She explained it would enable her to balance her studies and seeing Ben and his friends more.

Her mum felt shocked, let down and confused. At the same time, mum could see that Tammy's ability to express her conflict and underlying feelings was so mature and heartfelt. She saw her enormous talent and potential but knew that if her daughter gave up dance now it would be very hard to regain the strength to do it as well later, and she wanted to convey this potential sacrifice to her without telling her what to do.

A good resolution

It was a good time for Tammy's mum to think about what was important for her in this situation and how this might impact the advice she gave to Tammy, but also to think carefully about the way she conveyed emotions when speaking about this tricky situation. Teenagers experience far bigger reactions and may be less well able to control their response to facial emotions than younger children and so her mother might expect an emotional response from her teenage daughter. Mum might also have re-experienced disappointment in giving up her own dance career and Tammy would be acutely aware of that emotion. A good resolution would be for mum to tell her she supported her decision and understood that Tammy had made her own evaluation of the risk of giving up dance. In addition she might have wanted to agree several 'check-ins' to review how Tammy was feeling about the decision with a plan to guide her so that she had a way back to dance if she decided she wished to take up her dance practice again.

What might get in the way?

If the experience of the adult, parent, teacher and relative is too strong to enable them to gain perspective of the teenager's experience, then this can lead to difficulties. If the important adult did not have the opportunity to develop this level of emotional regulation themselves in life, then support from a third party might be needed. Putting on your teen lens to understand what is driving the teen behaviour while also remembering that young people should be able to make their own decisions is important here.

Action point: Prioritise your teen's social relationships and ensure they have opportunities for social integration

Ensure your teen has opportunities for integrating with their peers so they can develop the important and complex life skills of managing peer relationships.

Action point: Beware of competing rewards, because peer social reward will likely win

Many adults, in both home and school settings, try to shape adolescents' behaviour using external rewards such as money or certificates. While these might work in isolation, if a task you set your teen is in direct competition with a behaviour that might gain them social status, the latter is likely to win. Your teen is not being rude or disrespectful – they can feel the full force of the brain's reward centres when they are acknowledged and viewed positively by their peer group. Nature has made that hard to resist.

Action point: Always reinforce a growth mindset to build resilience against social rejection

Reinforce a growth mindset about peer relationships with the language you use. This will offer some protection against the fear of missing out (FOMO) that is inevitably a part of teen life. Try 'Oh, you weren't invited this time. Let's have a look at who's going. Look, he invited all the families that live over on that side of town. It's not personal', to teach a growth mindset. If your teen joins a new peer group, expect them to focus on peer integration *first*. Only when they feel safe and comfortable amongst their peers will they be able to focus on other tasks such as academic work. This hierarchy is part of nature. Try to work with it.

Action point: Use your teen lens to empathise with key social risks

The importance of the social world means that risks associated with possible social exclusion are far greater for a teen than we can imagine. To a teen, putting up their hand and answering a question where they are uncertain may be a big social risk. Phoning a friend to ask something might bring up all kinds of fears to a teen. Try to take their perspective and come alongside them to give support as they work to overcome these fears. It's always important to respect and listen to them.

Action point: Pay attention to your facial expression, body language and tone of voice when with teens to avoid distraction

Consider your facial expression or tone of voice while you are in the company of an adolescent, particularly if you want them to learn. Your feelings and the implied social meaning is likely to be what the young person will notice most. Sarcasm, diminishing tones or looks of disappointment will, in practical terms, interfere with the content of what you are saying in day-to-day parenting or teaching.

The moral of the story is...

Teens are highly attuned to social information and motivated by social acceptance. We can harness that drive towards social factors to help shape a wide variety of learning experiences. Your actions really matter to help facilitate this complex process.

Downloads: Cracking the Social Code

Social motivation changes over our lifetime. While younger children focus on caregivers, teenagers turn their attention towards their friends. Teenagers are programmed to orientate towards their peers, learning as much as possible before independence and adulthood. This means that peer influence is considered crucial by the teenage brain and peer acceptance is likely to underpin many decisions and actions.

Exercise
Note three instances that illustrate how much your teen is focused on peers.

Instance 1

. . . .

. . . .

Instance 2

. . . .

. . . .

Instance 3

. . . .

. . . .

Judging by their reaction to social invitations – or exclusion from them – do you think your teen has a fixed or growth mindset about their own or their peers' social standing?

....

....

....

....

....

....

What do you do to facilitate your teen's social experience and ensure they are working to strengthen peer relationships?

....

....

....

....

....

....

....

When this happens...	Instead of this...	Try this...
Your teen knows there is a party tonight from Snapchat. They don't get an invite.	Oh no, you didn't get invited to the party. That's terrible. Those boys are really horrible people – stay away from people like that.	Sorry to hear you didn't get invited this time. I'm sure there was a good reason – maybe there was a limit on numbers? Why don't you invite a friend for a sleepover?
		Support a growth mindset around social standing
Your teen doesn't want to stand up in class and talk in a group exercise.	Everyone else has done it in the class. Why not you? If I make exceptions for one, it will invite chaos. Everyone has to stand up and talk.	If you would rather not give your answer verbally, just stand up and write it down on a piece of paper. We will work towards you giving verbal answers in the future.
		Protect them from unnecessary social pain and embarrassment
Your teen is cheeky and answers back to you when his friends are round. His friends laugh at his jokes but you feel embarrassed.	My son is embarrassing me in front of his friends. He isn't usually like this and I don't like it. I am not going to let him get away with this, even if my shouting at him embarrasses him.	My son is never cheeky like this usually. I won't confront him while his friends are here as it might embarrass him but I will make sure to speak to him about it later, as that is not OK.
		Don't confront a teen when their social status is on the line as peer admiration is hard to resist

Chapter 9

Risk Taking and Resilience Making

Long story, short

- Risk taking can result in a good or bad outcome.
- Teens are biologically driven to take risks – it's not simply a lack of control.
- The presence of peers increases risky behaviour as teenage brain functioning is highly sensitive to context.
- Risk taking is important – it affords learning opportunities and builds resilience.
- What teens perceive as risky is different to what we perceive as risky in adulthood.
- Empower your teen to take positive risks by being by their side.

Introduction

Risks are simply uncertain outcomes

What comes to mind when you think of risks in relation to your teen – what would you say? Alcohol? Drugs? Unprotected sex?

The words 'teen' and 'risk' conjure up danger, but in fact risk simply means the outcome is uncertain – it can be positive or negative. Uncertainty is a familiar feeling when parenting or caring for a teenager.

You might take a risk and leave your old job to start a new one. You might love the new role (positive outcome) or you might wish you had never left that previous job (negative outcome) – changing your job is risky behaviour. Bias in seeing risk as inherently negative might mean we consider risk taking as problematic, but it also has important advantages.

Sensation seeking is heightened in adolescents across the world

Teens are more likely than any other age group to take risks. The reasons for that are complex, but it boils down to a drive to seek out new sensations, because their brain is sending out reward signals when they act in that way. It is a consistent finding and one that is found in many different cultures – it is not just a Western phenomenon. As psychologist Laurence Steinberg and colleagues recently showed, the desire to take risks increases during the teenage years in a variety of different cultures, peaking around the age of 19 (Steinberg *et al.* 2017). The teen drive towards risk taking is seen in animals too: adolescent mice take more risks than adults, for example. These cross-cultural and pan-species data strongly imply that taking risks in the teenage years is a fundamental biological drive.

The science bit: Brain and behaviour

Peers influence risk taking behaviour, especially in males

We know teens are drawn towards risk, but research suggests that the increase in risk taking is context specific. Teens take more risks when their peers are around. One well-replicated study designed by Laurence Steinberg (2007) involves playing a driving video game while in an MRI scanner. Players take a risk at each set of traffic lights: to drive on (winning more points but possibly crashing) or stop (avoiding a crash but earning fewer points). It's a question of balancing the risk with the reward. Risk taking in four groups is recorded – adults who believe other adults are watching them, adolescents who believe other adolescents are watching and adults or adolescents who believe they are playing alone. Who takes the most risks? Adolescents watched by peers are the greatest risk takers. Interestingly, this is not about driving skills because adolescents who are alone take a similar number of risks to adults (alone or being watched).

The powerful influence of peers has been described and demonstrated in many settings. Consistent findings using pseudo-gambling games show that teens will take a short-term small reward with peers present rather than wait and play the long game so that they can reap larger rewards (so-called delayed gratification). In the real world this might translate into spending all their allowance the day they get it (short-term reward) rather than saving it to get trainers next month (the larger reward in the future). This effect is seen in animals too: adolescent mice will drink more alcohol in the presence of peers, but similar amounts to adults when they are alone. The same is not true for adult mice, who drink a similar amount when alone or with their peers. While we are pretty certain human teens act in this way too, ethics committees quite rightly won't give permission for alcohol consumption to be tested in teenagers.

Gender is part of the story too as teenage boys are generally more willing to take risks and are more sensitive to peer influence than similar-aged girls, although these differences tend to get smaller with age. The point is clear: risk taking for teens is heightened when other adolescents are around.

It is not peer pressure or distraction – it's just peer presence

You might be imagining that peer influence on behaviour comes from them being egged on by peers ('Go on, you can make the lights'), but the increased risky behaviour is not related to peer pressure or the need to impress peers. We know this because simply telling a teen that their friends or classmates are watching them – even when they aren't – produces the same effect. For example, the peers in the driving experiments are virtual – the player can't see them and no words are exchanged. As Laurence Steinberg has shown in his extensive research, behaviour becomes riskier with peer presence. But interestingly, there is also some evidence that when mothers, older teens and romantic partners are added to the group, teen risks diminish. Teens' behaviour is, indeed, highly context dependent (Steinberg 2014).

Steinberg's group have explored the effect of changes in the presence of other figures in a teen's life. One study found that when mothers were present during this task the teens took fewer risks. Another that they take fewer risks when a young adult is in the group, and another that they take fewer risks when with a romantic partner. The quality of the relationship seems to be important in moderating risk. Parents and carers who respect their teens' feelings, whose teens spontaneously disclose and who have fewer arguments have teens who take fewer risks. These studies need replication to confirm the findings, but it suggests that the role of the people present, and trusting relationships specifically, influences adolescents' risky choices.

Figure 9.1: Teen risk-taking behaviour is highly context dependent

Teens can size up risk accurately – they choose when to take chances

We have established that teens are driven to take risks and are particularly likely to do so in the presence of peers, but there is a subtle caveat – they are discerning in their risky choices. If teens think the odds are stacked against them or the reward unappealing, then they won't take the risk. However, if there is a good chance of success, they will go for it. Adults are more risk averse. Maybe teens are smarter in this way than we are.

Neuroscience suggests that life is just more rewarding for teens

The way we make decisions depends on which of the emotional brain and the thinking brain gains the upper hand in the process (see Chapter 2: The Teen Brain Thinks and Feels). Adolescents in the driving experiment showed specific patterns of brain function, different from both younger children and adults. In line with their driving behaviour, their brains functioned differently in the presence of peers. But contrary to expectation, it wasn't that their thinking brain was poor, it was that the reward-sensitive areas of the emotional brain (ventral striatum) were lighting up like a Christmas tree.

Adriana Galvan's elegant studies (e.g. Galvan 2013) show that, compared with at other times in the lifespan, adolescents are most influenced by incentives and rewards. The reward regions of the brain are highly sensitive at this time – they respond to the probability of getting a reward, the size of the reward or even when just thinking about rewards.

When in rewarding situations, the teen thinking brain can't always keep up

Laurence Steinberg's classic Dual-Systems theory (2007) suggests that during the teen years the emotional and thinking brains are developing at different rates. In *social* situations, the thinking brain hasn't quite developed enough muscle power to make a timely reasoned response, and cannot over-ride the strong motivations and drives of the emotional brain, which is firing on all cylinders. The most important point is that the two parts of the brain are not working at equivalent levels until about 20 years of age. This means that while younger teens can make extremely good rational decisions, in certain emotive situations (being with friends being a key one), the emotional brain wins.

Maybe emotionally charged and motivated behaviour is a necessary step towards adult–level regulation

The Dual-Systems theory was highly influential and ground breaking in many respects but it feeds into the negative or 'deficit' view of the teenage brain. Recently, psychologists have wondered if this period of increased risk taking might be an important learning step that should not be quashed. This proposes that there is an ordered hierarchy in brain development and every stage is important for the final outcome.

First, the reward and emotional parts of the brain become strongly connected to each other, thereby increasing teenagers' impulsive action in response to emotional cues. The emotional brain's strong signals at this time help teenagers learn what they find rewarding and motivating, which is important for their long-term self-knowledge. Only after this connection is well established does the emotional/ impulsive brain link more strongly with the thinking brain – enabling, in the long run, greater cognitive control over a well-interconnected emotional-reward system and a cohesive brain system. Rather than seeing emotionally charged and motivated behaviour as a deficit, we need to see it as critical for the development of teenage self-knowledge and an important step towards appropriate regulation in the future adult for emotionally charged situations. The implication is that we should expect and perhaps embrace this period of risk taking, while protecting young people from the potential downsides. Trying to short-circuit the process might have negative long-term consequences for the individual.

Translating your teen

Time for a reframe – risk taking has advantages

Teens' brains are telling them, in no uncertain terms, that risk taking is a valuable activity. It figures, because the recent brain studies are strongly pointing towards the idea that risk taking is actually an *essential* stage of development. If we skip this part of development, yes, we might avoid negative outcomes, but we also lose advantages in learning and brain growth. More than this, there is an evolutionary advantage to seeking new opportunities and experiences. If you are taking risks, you are acting flexibly and learning efficiently in a variety of contexts. A period of highly motivated risk taking and socially attuned behaviour that allows for trial and error has beneficial effects to the individual and society. Greater flexibility in the world will push the boundaries of our learning and development. Risk = exploration for teens.

Teens are 'fast-adopters of social change' according to Eveline

Crone and Ron Dahl (2012) – just think of the language innovations that adolescents develop which are now 'totes a meme' and in regular parlance, lol. This inventiveness and creativity are reflected in their flexible learning style and with the risks they are prepared to take – they can instigate social change and innovations.

Risk takers might be admired

Our brain grows when we do new things, challenge our cognitive skills and experience variety, and so risk taking needs to be supported and encouraged. A risk-averse individual is limiting themselves to some degree in terms of their cognitive growth, while a risk taker pushes the boundaries of their learning. Risk taking is essential to a teenager; it is driven by biology. Attempts to dull these urges will likely be met with resistance. The answer then is to be smart and to work *with* nature.

If a teenager is a frequent risk taker then channel these tendencies into positive, prosocial risks, rather than quashing them. For example, engineer high-arousal stimulating experiences such as taking them zip-wiring or climbing, encourage them to try out for a new play or sports team or to go on a march in support of something they are passionate about. At the same time, as adults we cannot take our hands off the steering wheel completely when it comes to supporting an adolescent who is taking risks and trying new experiences. Adolescents need guidance, of course. Too big a push from the emotional brain could mean that the young person gets into a potentially seriously dangerous situation.

Those who don't take risks may not develop resilience or experience safe limits

There are large individual differences between teens, and while many teens look for opportunities to take risks, others avoid them. Neither extreme is helpful. A degree of stress on our physical system is crucial in order to develop a strong immune system. Medical doctor Mel Greaves (2018) notes that the risk of childhood leukaemia increases without a degree of exposure to germs in childhood. For our body to develop to full capacity, it needs to learn to cope and protect itself from harm. The same is true for developing resilience through life experience (see Figure 9.2).

Figure 9.2: Teens develop resilience by learning to manage 'stress' in the context of safe and strong relationships

Think of the Zone of Proximal Development (see Chapter 2: The Teen Brain Thinks and Feels). Staying within our comfort zone does not allow for growth. Young people need to be stretched, and take challenges to develop resilience for the future. Actively encourage risk taking in those who are reticent by setting up safe challenges such as giving them responsibilities (finding their way to a new place independently), encouraging them to take part in a competition or enrolling in a challenging class that they may not do so well in. While they may find it hard, they will get through it with a supportive adult at their side (that means you) and they will learn about themselves, learn that they can survive when it's tough and then attempt hard things in the future. When the going gets tough, don't be tempted to over-protect them or 'save' them from the natural consequences of life. If you advise them to avoid taking a chance on a school debate, they may never learn they can survive hard experiences and they won't embrace challenges in the future.

Remember, circuits in the brain don't develop unless we *do* things. Avoidance is never a good strategy as skills can't grow. As the old saying goes: 'Prepare the child for the road, not the road for the child' (Folk wisdom, origin unknown). You cannot protect young people from every difficult challenge in their life, and nor should you. You can give them the gift of experience within a caring structure to enable them to develop resilience for their life to come.

Your teen's brain functions differently when the teen is alone with their peers

Teenagers find their friends' presence highly stimulating and rewarding (see Chapter 8: Cracking the Social Code). Just being with their friends tips the brain balance so that rewarding behaviours dominate and considered, reasoning thoughts take a back seat. Their brains literally behave differently when they are alone with their peers. This does not mean they are irrational or their brains are broken, it means their behaviour changes depending on the setting.

Parents and teachers can use this information to think carefully about environments in which a teen might be at risk. Have you ever heard a teen talk about their friends having a 'free yard'? Just to translate for those not in the know, that means their parents are out. In the early teen years this is likely to be a high-risk environment for a teen. Their brains will be on a high reward setting and they might make a bad decision. We can reduce the risk by, first, helping them understand their own brains. Help them to think of ways to support each other when with a group. Can they look out for each other at a party? Second, we can reduce the risk by having an adult around in the vicinity, not in the room but in the house so that their presence is felt. This is not about stopping teenagers going to a party. We want teenagers to have fun, but we also want them to be safe.

Teens drinking too much and being unwell is unpleasant and increases the likelihood of falling into other situations such as taking sexual risks. It is impossible to completely protect teenagers from risk taking behaviour, so it is important to talk to them about managing situations and minimising risk. Of course, there are extreme outcomes that are hard to even contemplate – these occur in a small minority of cases, but they are the ones we all want to protect all teens from.

What does that mean day to day?

Teens really do have more road traffic accidents with peers in the car

You might be wondering whether the research experiments we describe here reflect real life – do adolescents really behave differently when with their peers and take more risks? The short answer is yes: adolescents are more likely to crash a car when they are with their friends than when alone (or with their parents in the car). This finding is so well established that, in parts of Canada and New Zealand, teens cannot have more than one passenger of the same age in the car with them apart from family members. Similarly, teens are more likely to commit a crime when in groups than when alone.

Teens are wired to find it out for themselves

There is a large body of research showing that adults prefer following instructions (even if they are incorrect), rather than learning through experience. On the other hand, adolescents' brains tell them to find things out for themselves and take a risk. The brain's preferred way of learning changes in adolescence. One of the authors put a piping hot lasagne dish on the dining table saying 'that's *so* hot'. What proportion of the teens sitting round the table put a hand out to touch the dish to confirm this? 100 per cent. Remember, this behaviour may exist for good reasons – it may lead to innovation.

Risks can have positive outcomes – especially prosocial risks

Recent work, including that by American neuroscientist Natasha Duell (2018), focuses on 'positive risks', which are socially desirable, and constructive risks, such as enrolling for a new course or auditioning for a play. These types of risks are highly admired in most cultures and offer enormous prestige.

Prosocial risks which benefit others, such as standing up for a friend, are in particular linked to positive self-identity, good mental health and academic performance. This means that the very same teens that are most susceptible to social influence from peers may have a more positive and healthy adolescent development. Peer influence has upsides.

Interestingly, emerging data show that individuals who take negative risks are the same individuals who tend to take positive risks. This goes against assumptions that teenagers who take risks are on a negative track of development, but rather suggests that this quality in a person – the desire and courage to take risks – is an individual characteristic that can convey positive outcomes for people and society. The case study below describes how it is possible to capitalise on risk taking at school to build other skills.

What does that mean for learning?

Rewards, taking risks and peer learning are likely to be highly effective learning strategies for teens

These striking findings about risk are exciting for educationalists. It means that learning strategies which use rewards and incentives, allow risk taking and employ peer teaching are likely to have a positive impact on these incredible teenage brains. In working with educationalists, we have piloted programmes with teenagers and preteens with great success.

Anecdotally, teenagers respond enthusiastically. Schools are highly structured and governed by rules. Risk takers are difficult to accommodate when a thousand teenagers are watching from the wings. But selecting positive risks, such as speaking out for strong beliefs, may be extremely helpful at school and could help to shape an environment in which the teenagers are happy and successful.

Learning is a risk, and learning with peers increases risk

At the same time, learning is a highly risky activity. When we learn, by definition we lack knowledge, and this may mean being vulnerable in front of peers. There is therefore an inherent vulnerability in risk taking – it is not just a hedonic action. The value of peer presence is an important context to understand *why* risk taking is more likely to happen in the company of peers. Raising a hand in class is highly significant to an adolescent because the outcome could be positive (peer approval) or negative (peer derision). There is a fine line to tread between taking a risk so that one stands out positively in the peer group, but not standing out so far that one risks being rejected by the peer group. The greatest risks of all to a teen are likely to be threats to their social standing or self-concept. Rejection and social pain is truly painful (as we learnt in Chapter 5: The Teen Brain Loves Other People), alienating and can lead to long-term difficulties in adulthood.

So, what now?

Teenage brain development means teens are naturally drawn to experiences of risk and high sensation-seeking. Nature pushes this agenda at a time when teens need to try new experiences to develop life skills. Teens are courageous creatures who need adults to think carefully about their environment and context, to protect them, and conscious goals to stretch them.

Case study: Lara

Lara, aged 15, was a girl who loved life. She was usually the first to volunteer for any activity. She had been happy at her old school, but her parents had recently divorced, which meant a house move and a new school. It was at a time when there were important school exams, which was challenging, but she thought she was managing OK so far. Her biggest worry was how she would find friends. It was hard to become a part of an established group, and to begin with she couldn't find anyone who might become a close friend.

Daisy from her class invited Lara to a party at her house the following week. Lara was pleased, although nervous as she didn't know Daisy well. The next day Lara's dad, Simon, saw a text pop up on her phone from Daisy saying her older brother had promised to get some alcohol for the party. His first instinct was to ban Lara from seeing Daisy ever again. Communication was difficult between her parents in the light of the recent divorce but he took a breath and talked about it with Lara's mum. Lara's parents recognised that exploring alcohol and drugs is extremely common in mid-teens – the question was how to tackle it. They tried to leave to one side that drinking alcohol was bad news at 15 and tried to re-frame it as another type of risk taking, which helped them consider solutions to the situation.

A good resolution

First, Lara's parents had to remind themselves that Lara hadn't actually drunk alcohol but had been invited to. Second, they realised that as she was new to the group, and so vulnerable, she might be more tempted to go with it to fit in than if she had an established place in the peer group. Finally, the *mere presence* of the peer group meant that Lara was much more likely to take part in experimentation of this kind when with her peers than when alone.

They were, however, quite right to manage this situation carefully. The first step was to talk about the text with Lara. Simon asked what she thought about it, as calmly and openly as possible, without judgement. It's very difficult to take a matter of fact tone when it comes to young people putting themselves in potentially harmful situations (particularly if it is your child, because parents' instinct is to protect), but anxious yelling – letting the emotional brain take charge – is unlikely to allow a good resolution. Aiming for an adult to adult conversation feeds teens' yearning for status and is much more likely to be productive. Lara's parents were somewhat reassured to hear Lara say she wasn't keen to drink but she also said joining in might be the only way to become part of the group. Her parents took this worry seriously as a valid concern – and discussed ways of being part of a group and making choices that were right for Lara.

Lara's parents did agree to her going to the party but after some careful thought and reflection. By seeing drinking alcohol as 'just' a type of risk, Lara's parents could think about substituting this sensation-seeking drive with another more positive risk (such as joining an improvisation drama class) – and ideally with a peer group which might form some new social bonds. Second, they recognised the importance of fitting in with the group, so asking her to withdraw completely from seeing

Daisy was neither practical nor would it allow any brain growth so that she could build resilience in other peer contexts, and find a way of managing similar situations in the future.

What might get in the way?

Parents may have different viewpoints on how to manage risk. It's important to find common ground before you negotiate with your teen. It might mean compromise on both sides. Young people aren't always keen to talk things through with parents, particularly if they think it might result in them being given a boundary they don't like (e.g. you can't go to the party). The tone of the conversation is crucial to get right. It can't be a 'telling off'. The listening phase of the conversation must come first (see Chapter 17: May The Force Be With You, Luke) and only then, when they feel heard, is a teen likely to be able to truly reflect. Remember higher and lower brain functioning – if a child feels backed into a corner, judged or angry, they will not have good access to their thinking brain. Adults do ultimately get to decide what happens, but finding a way to come to a more collaborative decision is the best option in the teen years.

Case study: Modelling risk in schools

When a high school teacher joined his new school he was keen to teach the young people in his care about brain development and to encourage positive risk taking. He began a series of seminars and workshops which were optional for students but would involve commitment to a long-term project. The programme centred around topics chosen by the students and involved public speaking, which many students were initially reluctant to do, but the teacher knew the importance of stretching students in this way to grow circuits and develop skills and resilience for the future.

In order to incentivise the students and get their buy-in, the teacher asked what the students would like to learn about and how they would like to set up the workshops. Several students came forward with ideas which included fashion, car racing, make-up and film editing. These were not topics typically taught in school, but the focus of this project was on the processes of learning and risk taking, so student choice was pivotal. It was meant to be a collaborative project that the young people could mould to their interests, tapping into teen motivation and its superpower.

High expectations were set (the teacher conveyed that he believed all of the students had the potential to meet the standard, which would be world-class) and the students were told that taking part in this project would involve taking risks. If the students felt nervous or uncertain, that could be a good thing. They were taught about the benefits of a degree of 'stress' as a form of motivation in the body (see Chapter 15: Good Stress, Bad Stress). It was made clear that if mistakes were made, it would be considered part of the learning process, and a problem solving forum was set up to discuss strategies to manage the more challenging aspects of the project. The students had never been encouraged to reveal their mistakes before or to problem solve strategies in quite such an explicit way, so this intrigued a few.

Rules and boundaries of the project were established and agreed, and students were asked to make a firm commitment in terms of time and goals. The school funded a neuropsychologist to consult to the project, which benefited both staff and students in terms of learning about the brain and how it works, and also increased the credence of the project. The school was also taking a risk with this project, which they advertised.

The programme was delivered over the period of a half term and was a huge success, with more than 70 per cent of students taking part. The project was a source of pride for the school and there was the added benefit that students learnt about themselves as individuals, both their strengths and weaknesses which they could embrace within the safe context of the project. Many students referred to this experience on their university application forms as it stood out as such a valuable learning experience.

What might get in the way?

Without the necessary thought and preparation, this could have been too risky for the teenagers and the school. It needed a strong lead (the headteacher) to back it practically (making time in the school day) and emotionally (believing in the process when others doubted it). Without the collaborative nature of the project, students may have received it as just another school task to take up their time. Allowing their input not only made them excited about it but gave them some ownership and tapped into their motivation. Trust between students and teachers can build through this type of off-curriculum activity, where both learn so much about each other by working together out of their typical role.

Action point: Consider context to determine risk

Teenage brains are highly sensitive to context and behave differently when with peers, particularly without adults around. Talk to teens about context and teach them how to manage their brain. Be very cautious about leaving a group of teens unsupervised.

Action point: Set positive challenges to satisfy a teen's need for risk taking and stretch their development

As adults we can consciously foster positive risk taking and invite a young person into an optimum learning situation. Make sure you consider all sorts of domains – academic (such as taking part in a debate), social (taking the bus for the first time), culinary (making dinner) and physical (training for a cross–country competition). Think of the Zone of Proximal Development. If the challenge is too great it may be such a negative experience it will prevent them wanting to try again. If it is too much within their comfort zone it won't stretch them to grow and develop resilience. Work out where they are and support them to reach the next step.

Action point: Incentivise desirable behaviour

The reward centres in the brain are on fire for teens, so consider ways – in collaboration with your teen if you can – to incentivise desirable behaviour. Think about long-term goals and consider small rewards along the way to maintain interest and motivation. These rewards needn't be material – think about using status and esteem as incentives: earning their own set of house keys, for example, might be a highly motivating reward, or later earning the right to come home late or have their own bank account.

Action point: Respond thoughtfully – with your thinking brain – if you discover a teen taking a negative risk

Calm conversation with careful planning and discussion is the only way to manage an adolescent's poor choices in risk taking, though you may feel like flipping your lid at first. As the adult you have the ultimate say and can and should enforce a boundary, but doing this after listening to the young person's need, perhaps with some compromise, will ensure greater compliance and honesty in the future. Teens are going to take risks. You, as the important adult in their lives, want to be part of that conversation.

Action point: Encourage prosocial behaviour, particularly for struggling teens

Encourage young people to get involved in activities where they take a risk to help others. This is particularly effective for young people who are struggling, as they then benefit from seeing the good they can do for others. It gives them a feeling of responsibility and honour, and the reward centres in their brain will go wild.

Action point: If young people take no risks, purposefully set some up

If you are supporting a young person who has perfectionist tendencies and is overly anxious to do well or fears any kind of negative experience, help them to go out of their comfort zone now and then. Only by experiencing 'failure' can we learn to deal with it, and when we survive it, we fear it less. In an attempt to protect vulnerable young people we sometimes avert a disaster (they missed the bus and so will be late for school) by saving them (giving them a lift), but this does not help them develop resilience in the long term.

The moral of the story is...

We need risk to thrive as individuals and as a species. Risks can mean opportunity. Support your adolescent to encourage positive prosocial risk taking, which is likely to offer well-being advantages. Step back from micro-managing or 'saving' them from every tiny fall to support effective learning patterns and build resilience.

Downloads: Risk Taking and Resilience Making

Teens are biologically driven to take risks. It's not simply a lack of control – their brains are optimised for risk taking because the outcome may be a significant gain. Teens take the greatest risks in the presence of peers.

Risks afford learning opportunities and build resilience. Helping your teen to engage with positive risk is an important part of their development.

Exercise

Note three negative and three positive risks your teen has taken in the last few months.

Negative risk 1

. . . .

. . . .

Negative risk 2

. . . .

. . . .

Negative risk 3

. . . .

. . . .

Positive risk 1

. . . .

. . . .

Positive risk 2

. . . .

. . . .

Positive risk 3

. . . .

. . . .

What types of positive risk could you encourage your teen to take?

. . . .

. . . .

. . . .

What makes your teen more likely to take on negative risks? Who? Where? When? How could you change the context to mitigate the risk while still supporting them to explore and have fun?

. . . .

. . . .

. . . .

When this happens...	Instead of this...	Try this...
Your teen wants to run for the school pupil president representative.	What if you don't get it? The past president is running again and they did so well last year. If you don't win, you would feel rejected afterwards. Don't risk it.	You might not get elected, and don't worry if you don't this time. It gives you experience for next time. It's good practice.
		Encourage positive risks
Your teen has been invited to a friend's house. There will be adults around for some of the day but they will be out all evening. Some older peers will join later in the evening.	He is not going to anyone's house unless the parents are there at all times. Who knows what they will get up to?	He and one friend at home when adults are in and out of the house periodically is OK. Late evening, in a larger group and parents out for several hours is a high-risk situation and unacceptable for young teens.
		Think carefully about context when assessing risk
The formal exams are coming up. In the mock tests your teen knows this topic very well and you have covered it several times previously.	I want you to get full marks in this test. We covered it last week, and if you don't do well I know you weren't listening.	We've worked hard on this topic, but the point of a mock test is to figure out areas that might have been missed or need review. Mistakes will give us information, so just give it a go.
		Cultivate a safe environment to allow for vulnerability in a learning task

Chapter 10

Powerful Feelings and Mighty Motivations

Long story, short

- Feelings help us learn about events.
- The teen years are full of intense, passionate, emotional highs and lows.
- Teens are strongly motivated to learn about things they care about.
- Feelings are valid expressions of what is going on for the young person, not 'just hormones'.
- The intensity of feelings is adaptive – the teenage brain wants to notice emotions to learn.

Introduction

Emotions are strongly felt in the teenage years

The teenage years are dominated by strong feelings – highs and lows, passions and motivations. It is a time when we fall in love with something or someone, when experiences are felt more intensely perhaps than at any other time in life, and those emotional memories stay with us for life. Have you ever noticed how you feel when you hear a song that you listened to in your teenage years? Have you found that it brings back an intense feeling from the past? Economist and writer Seth Stephens-Davidowitz noticed this and decided to do some research (2018). He and his brother disagreed about whether a track was 'good' or not, and as all good analysts do, he took to the data to settle the debate and plotted Spotify downloads to investigate adult musical preferences. He plotted the population's year of birth and the songs' release year and found people listen to songs that were most popular during their teenage years more than any others. It is as if those songs made an emotional imprint on the brain that stays with a person for life. As we understand more about adolescence and how the brain develops, we are beginning to see that there is an emotional sensitivity and 'openness' to experiences that is specific to this time in life.

Feelings are important signals in the brain that we need for survival

Feelings are there for a reason. They rise from complicated processes that go on in our body and they help us decide how to act in the world and they protect us. As we talked about in Chapter 2: The Teen Brain Thinks and Feels, the brain's survival instinct means we feel *before* we think. Feelings alert us to what we need from the environment. Hunger and thirst are essential to ensure physical survival. If our hunger or thirst signals did not work, it wouldn't be long before we would die. We need to feel fear in order to keep ourselves safe and pain in order to prevent physical hurt or treat an injury. And remember that the social pain network is the same as the physical pain network in the brain, so the brain registers social exclusion as similarly threatening to our survival – particularly for adolescents given their drive for social integration.

Feelings also motivate us to act

Feelings are not only internal experiences that protect us, they also cause us to act. If we are anxious we are motivated to avoid a situation. If we are in pain we are motivated to tend to our hurt. If we enjoy something we are motivated to do more of it, or if we love someone we are motivated to spend time with them. So feelings are strongly linked to motivation to act. We can over-ride our feelings by using our higher, thinking brain ('Even though I'm scared of giving a speech I need to do it for my course'), but we cannot, nor should we aim to, *get rid* of feelings.

Adolescents feel intensely for a reason – they are highly driven to learn about the world

This quote from Stephen Fry's letter to his 16-year-old self illustrates beautifully how the teen years are about falling in love:

> *How passionately storm-drenched was your adolescence. How filled with true feeling, fury, despair, joy, anxiety, shame, pride and above all, supremely above all, how overpowered it was by love. (Stephen Fry, letter to his 16-year-old self, 2009)*

Ron Dahl coined the term 'heartfelt goals' (Dahl *et al.* 2018) to describe situations where teens are internally driven towards a goal, much as we are driven to drink when thirsty. It has that survival quality. Consider the passion that teens feel when they fall in love, not only with another person, but with a band, a fashion trend, a political cause, animal rights, human rights, the list goes on. But why is this necessary and what adaptive purpose might it have? How does a heightened period of emotionality impact on an individual?

Many leading neuroscientists, such as B.J. Casey (Casey *et al.* 2017), say the intensity of feelings are an indicator of their significance to adaptive survival (rather than an overreaction). It is developmentally important that they have that feeling with that great an intensity so that it doesn't get missed. Feeling-based motivation is a good way to be alerted to the environment as feelings are quick signals from the brain that can efficiently give us information about the 'here and now'. Young people need to learn about the world, and learn quickly if they are to survive independently – these signals need to be strongest during adolescence when they are learning about themselves, what they love, how they fit in, who they want to be and where is their place in the world. We believe that teenagers aren't just being moody to annoy us and they aren't simply 'overreacting', but their brains are in a different mode of functioning to ours – a different algorithm – enabling them to learn quickly.

The science bit: Brain and behaviour

The emotional and motivational brain is highly reactive during adolescence

So what is happening in the brain? You will remember from Chapter 2: The Teen Brain Thinks and Feels that lower brain regions are drivers and regulators of behaviour. That is where emotions and motivations are housed. Research has shown that these lower brain regions become highly activated early in puberty, so when we scan the brains of teenagers in an emotive situation, their brains light up significantly more than children and adults. This is thought to be the reason teens experience feelings so intensely and have a natural proclivity towards motivated behaviour. This also coincides with a significant increase in hormones, and researchers believe the hormone influx may cause the brain sensitivity. Isn't it nice when brain science coincides with what we see in young people? It helps us to understand that young teens will not have experienced these patterns of activation in the brain with such intensity before, and the result is that it triggers emotional reactions more quickly and powerfully than their usual experience and makes their behaviour more driven by their motivations.

The feeling brain wins when we feel something strongly

Remember also from Chapter 3: The Teen Brain Learns and Believes that we have a thinking brain in the front part of the cortex that helps us make good, rational decisions. Doesn't it sometimes feel like teenage thinking brains just aren't working? It has been one of the long-standing theories of adolescent brain development that their prefrontal cortex is not yet fully formed, but this view is now outdated. The prefrontal cortex does not get *worse*, or regress in its skills during the teenage years. There is no brain degeneration. Rather, emotions and motivations are greater during adolescence, making it harder for the thinking brain to be in charge and make a good decision in that moment. This happens to all of us sometimes. Think of a time when you 'lost it' at someone because you felt so angry, and then afterwards reflected on what happened saying, 'I can't believe I behaved like that.' Your emotional brain was in charge in that moment. The same thing is happening with teenagers, just possibly more frequently because they have stronger feelings and motivations than us.

Putting feelings into words is a helpful strategy

One amazing finding from brain science is that simply naming an emotion reduces its effect. Matthew Lieberman calls this 'affect labelling' (Torre and Lieberman 2018). Studies have found that people shown faces expressing strong emotions when in an MRI scanner show activity in the emotion centre of the brain as expected. When asked to label that emotion just by saying 'that is an angry face', the activity in the emotion centre of the brain reduces and the activity in the thinking brain increases. It is as if the labelling gives the person distance from the experience, thereby reducing its subjective effect. This is perhaps one of the benefits of talking therapies and mindfulness. Just by labelling people's emotional experiences you are helping them with their emotional regulation.

Translating your teen

Emotions will rise but stay close while you watch the snowflakes settle

Anyone who has ever been a teenager or has day-to-day contact with someone of that age will recognise the high emotions. The smallest event can prompt a highly volatile emotional reaction, leaving you bemused and overwhelmed. That may be the sole reason you are reading this book, to work out *why* they do this (and how you can stop it). If you knew there are good adaptive reasons why young people are on an emotional hair trigger, would it make it easier to manage the avalanche of feelings?

Research in brain science is telling us that when we understand why, we respond more effectively. Lisa Damour, author of the book *Untangled* (2017), has written about the low-tech intervention taught to her by a secondary school teacher that we will call the 'snow globe intervention'. When a teenager falls apart and is a bundle of emotions this teacher takes a home-made snow globe, shakes it and puts it on the table. As they watch the swirling chaos of the glitter falling she tells the girl that is what is going on in her brain right now. Before talking they need to wait for the glitter to settle. Lisa now uses this as a concrete intervention with families she sees. It helps the adults know to 'be patient and communicate your confidence that emotions almost always rise, swirl and settle all by themselves' (Damour 2019).

Adults with a central role in a teen's life are the best people to teach emotional regulation

Christine Rogers and colleagues (2019) found that mothers' presence enabled teens to regulate emotions more effectively than if they were alone. Consider the implications of saying to a young teen 'I don't want to look at you right now, go to your room' when they have lost control. How are they to learn to understand the torrent of their emotions in isolation? The research is rather biased as it focuses on maternal relationships, but it is highly likely that any trusted adult, such as a teacher, could provide the safe space to learn emotional regulation. The brain is primed to learn this key skill and does this most efficiently with a supporting adult alongside. Don't abandon them or send them away but help them understand so they learn to regulate their emotions better next time.

Remember your teen is changing and choices now don't necessarily reflect enduring personality characteristics

Remember that teenagers are working out their identities and trying to balance the development of their different selves – academic, physical and social. Their motivations and drives will change and are continually changing and the person before you is not the person they will necessarily be as an adult. Don't read behaviour you don't like as a permanent personality characteristic. Just because they haven't shown an interest in academic studies by the age of 14 does not mean they never will. Model the behaviour you want to see and set up the culture that values the behaviour you want to see in the young person and, believe us, they will follow. You are there to guide young people towards goals that will set them up for success as an adult and that is of crucial importance. Have clear rules and boundaries, but be prepared to listen and take note of their perspective, remembering their behaviour is motivationally led. Just like we can't get rid of feelings, we can't get rid of their internal motivations.

It's not helpful to just blame their hormones – we need to listen

It's tempting and indeed has become common parlance to say teenagers are just being 'hormonal' when they are emotional. While it is correct that there are big hormonal changes going on affecting brain drives, putting emotionally charged interactions down to 'hormones' is likely to belittle the teen's experience and undervalue the function of these behaviours. It invites the idea that an emotional outburst is 'irrational behaviour' when, in fact, the young person's strength of feeling is for a real reason, meaningful to them in that moment. Remember, brain drives cause teens to focus on certain aspects of their experience (social integration, self-identity) more than others and these things have high salience for them for good reason. What their best friend said or their football team's result may seem trivial to us, but they are the sort of events that matter to a teen and which could evoke a strong reaction. For them, in that moment, those things *are* very important and we need to respect that.

Teens' emotional behaviour is driven by strong motivations which are rational to them, in that moment

Remember that feelings motivate us to act, and so if we feel more intensely, our motivations will be stronger. As teen behaviour is more driven by their emotional brains, motivations can be very powerful. But why are they drawn to make 'bad' decisions so frequently? Why do they want to go to a party the week before important exams in their lives? Are they behaving irrationally or 'throwing away the good money I've spent on their education'? The answer is no. They are not crazy, lazy or irrational human beings. Their behaviour is just strongly driven by what is important to them at that time.

Take a situation where a young person, Troy, has been invited to a party. He also has a test he should be revising for the next day. He wants to do well in his test but recently he has really begun to enjoy hanging out with his friends and, having felt somewhat socially isolated in the past, his motivation to build his social status is strong at this time. He does well academically, and so in weighing up the decision between academic value and social value in that moment for him, the latter wins. Does this make him crazy or lazy or someone who doesn't care about their academic work? No, it makes him someone who values and is motivated towards strengthening their social value at this time.

So, should you just let your teenager party all the time and throw their lives away? No, we are not suggesting you let teenage drives and motivations take full control. Remember the co-pilot analogy in Chapter 1: The Incredible Teen Brain – Time to Upgrade. They are not in charge, but nor are you completely in charge. You can put your metaphorical foot down and in some cases you would do so (and boundaries are essential), but being able to understand their perspective and motivations will help you to empathise with them and problem solve together. If going to the party tonight really would have a big impact on their academic success (and so the answer is that they cannot go), maybe you can think of when they can next spend time with those friends, given the importance to them of their social standing at that time.

What does that mean day to day?

Strong emotional feelings should be expected

As the young person in your care hits the teenage years you may well see a step change in how emotional they are. In mental health services we talk about 'externalising' behaviours (emotions shown very clearly in their behaviour such as shouting and hitting, aka 'naughty' kids) and 'internalising' behaviours (emotions kept inside and not talked about, aka 'anxious' kids), which describes how young people express emotions differently. Actions too far in one extreme are not adaptive. Helping young people to emotionally regulate and manage their behaviour is one key task at this time in their lives, when their brains are highly plastic and ready to learn. But remember that learning about emotions does not equate with squashing emotions. We can't make emotions go away, we need to help them manage them. Use the 'snow globe intervention' while you stay alongside your teen, metaphorically holding their hand, while their emotional brain settles. See Chapter 17: May The Force Be With You, Luke for a guide about what to do next.

New passions and motivations are likely

Young people are driven to find things they love. Their brains are telling them to find what they are passionate about, just like their brains were the driving force as they learnt to walk when they were toddlers. The problem is, they may not fall in love with the thing you *want* them to fall in love with, so what should you do? Alison Gopnik (2016), a developmental psychologist, talks about the carpenter and the gardener when it comes to parenting. Carpenters try to mould a child into what they want them to be, chiselling away at the sides and trying to shape them. Gardeners toil the soil to make it as lush and ripe for growth as they can and let them flourish while accepting their own limited ability to control the outcome. If you support their newfound direction in life (while maintaining dual control), you will make the most out of these incredible teen years and help them blossom.

Teens can fall in love with a cause

Adolescents, particularly older teenagers and young adults, often become engaged in debates, political movements, or other forms of activism. They fiercely stand up for human rights and animal rights sometimes to the point of obsession. If we think about what is going on in their brains this makes sense. It as if they not only feel their own pain more intensely but they are highly tuned into other people's pain. They also have a fundamental drive to develop meaning in their lives, and as we will discover in a later chapter (Chapter 12: Ready to Launch (with Your Support)), they have a fundamental need to have a role and status in society. These strong motivational drives can support them to take 'positive risks' (see Chapter 9: Risk Taking and Resilience Making) and you have a chance to support these actions and behaviours. It also may be true that youngsters who stray into negative life choices and subsequent downward life trajectories in adolescence often do so because an alternative positive path was not available for them. This is what Ron Dahl calls an 'inflection point' (Dahl *et al.* 2018). We would encourage you to think hard about how you can help young people find a positive role and purpose in their lives and tap into positive motivational outlets at this important time in their lives.

Sometimes emotions can provide false signals about the world

In most situations emotions serve to give us valuable information about the world and help us figure out our next actions. In rare instances, emotions mislead us and give us a false idea about the world. Take a fairground ride – our emotions might tell us it is scary and should be avoided, although it is actually safe. At the same time, it can be hard to implement rationality in some instances: we know logically that even though eating chocolate feels good, we should not go on doing it, yet sometimes we keep unwrapping those bad boys, one after another. This point is particularly important in adolescence as we know that teens are such sensitive learners, acutely sensitive to signals in their environment. False information from a positive or negative emotion following an event could, in certain circumstances, become a habitual response: at worst there may be risks of mental health issues such as phobias or substance addiction. For example, if a young person experiences reduced anxiety at a party after drinking alcohol, they will reach for alcohol before the next party. If a young person is allowed what they want every time they get angry with adults around them, they learn that getting angry is the way to get what they want and that becomes a habit. It is likely that the instinctual brain is doing its work here in keeping the teenager safe but results in a maladaptive response, which may have been useful 10,000 years ago when risks were far less well controlled.

What does that mean for learning?

If a teen is motivated to learn something, the differences in their energy are palpable

Many educational curriculums are fairly prescribed, resulting in a lack of choice, but if you can offer choice and tailor learning around a teen interest, the teenage brain will fire on all four cylinders. This is not because they are difficult young people, it is because their brains are wired to use motivations in a positive way to learn quickly about the world. Their behaviour is just much more context-driven than that of children or adults. To continue the car analogy, if the motivation comes from them, they are in top gear, alert and engaged. If they are not motivated it's like the brakes are on and they are dragging themselves up the hill. Imagine how much easier it is to reach those 10,000 hours of repetition if a young person actually *wants* to do it. Wait for the fire to light and watch their brains grow at lightning speed. Help them along the way if they aren't motivated. Don't tell them off. Maybe give them an incentive. Empathise first ('I know you don't feel like doing geography today') and then incentivise. This way round will always get a better response (see Chapter 15: Good Stress, Bad Stress).

Learning can be an emotional experience

When young people come to a difficult task their emotional experience can overwhelm and distract them. Remember from Chapter 2: The Teen Brain Thinks and Feels that the feelings brain dominates in the hierarchy of the brain. Challenging learning tasks can trigger feelings of anxiety, frustration or sadness. Be prepared to come alongside them at these times. Don't berate them for 'not trying' but support them to work through the moment. Guide them to realise that the hardest moments in a learning task are the times when the *most* learning is taking place. That is when real brain growth happens. Name their feeling, validate their experience and support them to work through and embrace those moments of struggle. It's not easy but it will serve the young person well now and in years to come.

Should we be re-thinking the shape of our education system?

This science can help us to reflect for a moment on the education system found in much of the Western world. Adolescence is a time of emotional intensity, sensitivity and vulnerability in life and a time when teenage brains are drawn to other kinds of social and self-learning tasks. This has prompted some people to ask whether this is the right time in the life cycle to timetable high stakes and stressful exams in the form of public examinations. There is a growing conversation about whether there needs to be a revolution in education given all we are learning about the adolescent brain.

So, what now?

Teenagers are going through a period of high emotionality, falling in love with things and ideas and people. They have motivations and drives which are new and they are learning how to manage them. They also may experience difficult emotions and need adults alongside them to help. Chapter 17: May The Force Be With You, Luke gives a lot of ideas for how to do this with teens, but for now use this new lens to understand their behaviour.

Case study: Juan

Juan was a social, popular, outgoing kid of 15 years old. He had recently started going to a film club after school; it sometimes went on for two hours or so. One evening, he arrived home in tears. His mother opened the door, wondering what on earth had happened. He was in such a state she wondered if he had been badly hurt. She couldn't get any sense out of him and began to imagine all sorts of dreadful scenarios. He pulled out his phone and sat at the table, then cried even more desperately. He started to say that there had been a hang-out party after school at the house of a kid who had a new gaming system, but he'd missed the invite because he was at film club. He could see all the photos from Instagram. 'Everyone' was there and he had missed it. As each new Instagram post popped up, his howls got louder.

His dad came into the room and said 'Oh come on mate, don't be daft, it's not the end of the world.' He was perplexed to hear such a scene. Why such a big reaction? But for Juan, in that moment, missing a hang-out with many of his fellow students really did feel like the end of the world. For a teen who is wired to want to be included by his peers, where his social identity was highly valued, missing a high-profile social gathering with a stream of photographic evidence to boot was really truly distressing. Putting it in perspective as something that was not a major event in the world scheme of things, while a well-intentioned attempt to help and, of course, objectively true, didn't acknowledge the degree of significance it had for Juan.

A good resolution

In this situation, the most important response was recognising how important that event was. It was a true threat to Juan's sense of social self. His parents remembered this and were able to listen, empathise and reflect back that he was upset and worried he wouldn't get another invite to a hang-out again. Once Juan was calmer, he was able to discuss the true likelihood of there never being another hang-out and he arranged to watch a movie with some of his friends at his house the following weekend.

What might get in the way?

When a teen is crying or in distress it can be hard to come along-side and not act. When we are upset or angry *we* are motivated to act – we want to make things better. This is particularly the case for parents, who love their child more than anything in the world. It is important that the adult doesn't jump in with a judgement or try to resolve the situation ('Come on, I'll take you in the car and you can catch the end of the event') or to get upset with them ('Oh my god, that is terrible!') or to get angry ('Well, I did tell you that you were doing too many after-school activities. You won't listen to me'). All are forms of invalidating the young person's experience. Be patient and try to manage your own emotional reaction. If you can't cope with their emotion, you can be 100 per cent sure they won't be able to. They *will* feel better if you can come alongside them in the moment and you will know that you are doing the best job for them.

Case study: Leon

Leon, aged 17, had worked very hard on his robotics project all year. He didn't have a great relationship with his technology teacher but his passion for robotics and future aspirations to work in engineering had motivated him. He spent long days in the robotics studio and often missed out on other activities that his friends were involved in. Leon had put his heart and soul into this project.

One month before the submission date, probably later than

might have been ideal, Leon shared his project with his technology teacher. The teacher was quite off-hand initially and then became critical, identifying minor weakness after weakness in the model. The teacher was clearly irritated at having been consulted so late in the project and blamed Leon for not sharing the work earlier. Leon was devastated. He went home, got his bike and cycled to the beach, where he cried. He was desperate, felt like leaving school, questioned the university courses that he had applied for and generally felt very unappreciated. Later that evening he sat down with his parents, who listened carefully to him, reflected back his angry and difficult emotions and helped him make a plan. He was keen to manage the situation by himself.

A good resolution

Leon looked at the International Federation of Robotics Charter again. He had consulted the website and guidance early on in the project for ideas. With the help of his mother, he made a list of the strengths and weaknesses of the project based on formal resources. The critique was detailed and very honest. He took a deep breath and sent an email to his tech teacher to request a meeting. The technology teacher had felt bad about the interaction and was aware that he had not approached it in the best way. He had thought that he would approach Leon at school and speak with him about the incident. He was also aware that he should have approached Leon earlier in the year. Leon presented his independent evaluation of his project based on the guidelines that he had sourced. The teacher and Leon had a good discussion and were able to lay out their respective concerns. The teacher tried to be respectful and highlight many of the positive attributes of Leon's work. He recalled the importance of status for teenagers and asked Leon if, once the exams were complete, he could help put together an instruction for the prospective robotic students coming into high school so that they would have insights into the demands of the course and the timeline. The teacher found a small fund from which to pay for Leon's time. In addition, he suggested that Leon write an article for the school magazine about robotics and his project and experience in doing the course in particular. Leon was delighted and accepted his teacher's offer.

What might get in the way?

When students become passionate about a subject they can want to do everything all on their own. Their internal brain drives can take over and in their emotional state they may forget the proper order of things. Leon's teacher could have pulled his authority card on Leon and told him to start again with the right advice, but that would have quashed Leon's passion and motivation. Instead, he found a way to build Leon up and support his interests, giving him new roles and responsibilities that made Leon feel valued and respected. Who knows where his passion in this subject could take him in the future?

Action point: Talk to your teens about emotions

Talk about emotions in everyday life. Pretending that emotions are not there and brushing over emotional moments is not going to be effective in the long run. That doesn't mean the whole world stops when the young person you care for feels an emotion, but do acknowledge their feelings and make time to speak later. You don't get to choose *when* they are ready to talk, so don't demand conversation, but wait until they are ready.

Action point: Help teens work through the emotional struggles of learning

Learning is emotional, and deep learning can generate strong feelings, making a person want to run away. Find ways to support young people to work through the heightened emotions associated with learning. Remember, emotions are a part of learning, and the times of greatest frustration in learning are when their brains are growing the most. Those are the times to keep going as amazing circuits are being built.

Action point: It's **not just hormones** – acknowledge emotional events as important, consider your teen's motivation

If your teen has a strong emotional reaction to an event, it is not a sign that they can never cope. Teenagers may well feel overwhelmed at times because of how their brains are functioning. But the feeling is real. We cannot dismiss those feelings and we should help the young person understand them.

Action point: Understand that their values influence their decision making

It may seem that heart more than head is used to inform your teen's decision making. This is probably an accurate observation, although it may seem less than optimal when the teenager has what feels like life-long decisions to make. They are weighing up what is most important to them and their decision making may seem highly variable. Guide them and put down clear boundaries if necessary, but try to take time to understand. Their brains are the driving forces behind their behaviour.

Action point: Help teens connect with something bigger than themselves

The teenage years are a time of motivated action when young people develop 'heartfelt goals'. Think about how you can harness the power of this emotional and motivational power for good – for them and for society. Teens can often tune into their sense of injustice about things. Help them to connect to something bigger and become active citizens. It can also address their need for taking risks and trying new things.

The moral of the story is...

Emotions are intense for good reason in adolescence. You can help set teens on a path of life-long emotional well-being by acknowledging and labelling any kind of emotion and helping them to listen to their emotions, share their emotional experiences and learn how to manage them.

Downloads: Powerful Feelings and Mighty Motivations

The teen years are full of intense, passionate, emotional highs and lows. Feelings help us learn about events and are intense for good reason in the teen years. Healthy emotional regulation can help set teens on a path of life-long well-being. Now is the time to help them understand their emotions by acknowledging, listening and helping them label their emotions so they can manage them and use them to achieve their passions and talents.

Exercise
Note two 'heartfelt' interests your teen has (e.g. a cause such as animal welfare, a hobby such as dance or bicycle design).

Interest 1

. . . .

. . . .

Interest 2

. . . .

. . . .

How do you respond in those moments when your teen is feeling strongly emotional, and support emotional regulation? What do you say? What do you do? What are you thinking?

. . . .

. . . .

. . . .

. . . .

. . . .

. . . .

What do you say or do to let them know you understand their emotional experience (even if you feel their emotions outweigh the significance of the event)?

. . . .

. . . .

. . . .

. . . .

. . . .

. . . .

What do you say or do to show that you accept all sorts of emotions whether they are good or bad?

. . . .

. . . .

. . . .

. . . .

. . . .

. . . .

When this happens...	Instead of this...	Try this...
Your teen has become vegan.	Veganism is ridiculous and you are putting your health at risk. Please stop it now before you become ill.	I can see how passionately you feel about the environment and that is admirable. We must also make sure your health doesn't suffer for the cause.
		Accept their passions and don't judge them
Your teen spends three times as long on her art homework as she does on her geography homework.	How come you can be so focused when you are doing art? Why won't you put the same effort into a 'real' science subject like geography?	Your focus on your art is amazing. It's a real passion. I wonder how you could tap into those skills in other subjects too to support your all-round learning.
		Understand that a motivated brain fires on all cylinders
Your teen asks if you ever get angry after he has had a major meltdown.	I don't think I ever get angry. I have learnt that there is no point.	I get angry sometimes but I have worked hard over the years to try to find ways so I don't explode and do or say things that I will later regret.
		Talk to your teens about all their emotions and yours

Chapter 11

Self-reflection

Long story, short

- Self-reflection is a crucial aspect of development.
- Teens' abilities to reflect get more complex and may fluctuate from limited to strong insight.
- Teen self-image is acutely sensitive to all feedback from others – aim for empowerment.
- Remember, self-image extremes are often momentary – but consistent negative experiences may have a lasting impact.
- You can help your teen recalibrate a self-image crisis by listening, sorting through the recent events, and co-creating meaningful, positive alternative explanations.

Introduction

The ability to reflect on ourselves makes us uniquely human
Our ability to reflect on ourselves and think about who we are and how we are different to others is a uniquely human characteristic. These reflections involve evaluation – I am a *good* musician or a *weak* mathematician or a *kind* sister. This is a highly complex process, based on the vast array of roles we have in society and characteristics we show in life.

Self-concept becomes more complex, abstract and domain-specific from child to adulthood

This differentiated sense of self is slowly constructed throughout childhood and is shaped by experience and increased cognitive capacity. Young children describe concrete and observable behaviours or characteristics, such as 'I am a boy'. They become more complex and include social comparisons ('I am better than my friend at drumming') later in childhood. During adolescence there is an increasing interest in, and capacity to, reflect upon one's self, using abstract concepts such as 'I am moody, tolerant, an introvert'. There is a focus on the inner world of feelings, thoughts and personality. Roles also become differentiated with separate reflections of oneself in relation to academia, physical characteristics and the social world. This is part of a process, which is to develop a complex and robust self-concept, with knowledge about one's own person in relation to others. It is a time devoted to working out our role in society and our relationship to the world. Young people may doubt what family or other key adult figures have taught them as they carve out their identity and separate from them. This is referred to as a period of identity formation and identity development.

Identity formation is an iterative process leaving teens vulnerable – handle with care

Psychological models describe how adolescents construct and revise their identity over time. These models emphasise the dynamic process by which adolescents form, evaluate and revise their identity. Elisabetta Crocetti, Monica Rubini and Wim Meeus (2008) suggest we go through three phases while forming self-identity. The first – a commitment to a self-concept – is a stable phase which promotes well-being; as we adapt to new identities there can be a period of in-depth exploration of that identity, characterised by gathering information, thinking, talking about and reflecting on that identity. This confers openness to new experience (typical of adolescence), but too much deep exploration can lead to emotional instability. If unsatisfied with this identity there is a period of reconsideration which tends to be an unstable or crisis-like phase when the person is vulnerable to low mood and anxiety.

This iterative process, moving between certainty and uncertainty, is characteristic of adolescence, with often short periods of stability and frequent modifications. The good news is that if your teen is exploring extraordinarily radical hair styles or fashion, it is likely to be part of an exploration that may be re-evaluated shortly. The serious point is that the period between discarding one look and exploring another is a time of significant teen vulnerability. We see how important it is to avoid negative commentary to your teen. Handle them with care.

Parenting style is associated with the time teens spend in each phase, with stronger commitment being associated with warm and trusting parent–teen relationships and greater reconsideration found in families with poor relationships including high parental control and low trust. This highlights what we keep coming back to, which is how important your relationship is with your teen at this sensitive period of development in their life.

Figure 11.1: Teens are vulnerable to the impact of negative comments about themselves

Identities are explored and reconsidered, but with more in-depth exploration and fewer revisions, in later adolescence

Adolescents 'try on' different identities. An individual enters adolescence with a set of identities in terms of their interpersonal lives and ideological lives, influenced most particularly by family values. These are challenged as the young person begins to separate from their parents around the time of puberty (sometimes called **individuation**).

The reconsideration phase dominates between 12 and 16 years of age, when there is a tendency to try out different identities, reflecting instability at this time. Older adolescents carry out more of an in-depth exploration. Identity formation continues into young adulthood, with progressive stability. Not all adolescents show the same pattern of development, but there is compelling evidence that a considerable proportion of adolescents show uncertainty in their identity development over this period of their lives.

How teens move through these phases of identity formation is influenced by close relationships

Parents and siblings are role models for identity formation. Parents whose identities are more strongly 'committed' – i.e. they have a clear and stable self-concept – tend to have children with a stronger association to their identity. An older sibling with a strong self-concept is also influential.

Peer relationships play a role, for example conflict with friends is associated with a weak self-concept. If a teen has high levels of commitment and a healthy degree of exploration, they seem to be protected against peer pressure towards more undesirable behaviours. Our role modelling as parents and teachers is important to help young people navigate this potentially turbulent period when they are asking 'Who am I?'

Self-concept reaches extremes as teenagers are acutely sensitive to feedback

Adolescence is a phase in life when we are much more unstable and uncertain about our identity, with sometimes daily fluctuation and reconsideration. This, as we saw from Figure 11.2, can be linked to heightened stress, anxiety and low mood. As we move towards a stable identity, the system calibrates and, like anything trying to find the right balance, it can overshoot or undershoot. We know that young people are acutely sensitive to social signals from others. This sensitivity to feedback may be the reason that a teen might describe a total lack of positive self-perception on one day and seem to have a heightened sense of worth the next. Your teen's self-identity is chameleon-like while it is forming. It rapidly changes in response to the environment, from one extreme to another. When the environmental signals are conflicting, chameleons will appear half one colour and half another (they really do), providing a perfect analogy for the confusing experience of identity formation during adolescence.

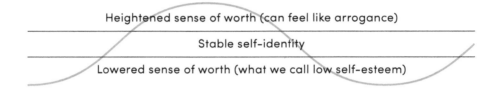

Heightened sense of worth (can feel like arrogance)

Stable self-identity

Lowered sense of worth (what we call low self-esteem)

Figure 11.2: Extreme variation is possible as teens work towards a stable identity

What we tell teens about themselves may become a self-fulfilling prophecy

There is lots of evidence that teenagers live up to the stereotypes we assign them. Teens who hold a negative stereotype about teenage behaviour such as 'teens are irrational and behave in a dangerous manner' are more likely to show this behaviour, whereas teens who hold a more positive belief foster more constructive behaviour. We need to think carefully about how we inform teens about what is typical of their age and stage of development because it does have an impact.

Three sensitive domains of self-concept

Three key aspects of self-identity commonly studied are: physical (what we look like), academic (how academically able we are) and social (social relationships) domains. While physical and social domains tend to remain at the same level over the adolescent period, teens rate their academic self-concept lower overall and their academic traits decline in middle adolescence. Why does their academic self-concept reduce over this time period? Is it because they are acutely sensitive to the demands of education at a time when they are receiving daily feedback about their academic output? Is it because they are under academic pressure and compare themselves with peers, causing negative evaluation? We need to consider how this might be linked to mental health and well-being in the longer term.

The science bit: Brain and behaviour

The prefrontal cortex is associated with self-reflection

Neuroimaging studies show us that there is a network in the brain, dominated by frontal regions, that consistently 'lights up' when we think about ourselves and our personality, whatever our age. Indeed, we know quite a lot about which parts of the brain are involved in which aspects of self-reflection. The system is complex, with many different parts that come online over an extended period of development and particularly during the teen years. It seems the brain has adapted, in evolutionary terms, to consider many subtle aspects of self-reflection and ourselves in relation to others. These skills are clearly important to our survival.

The areas of the brain linked to self-concept are more active in adolescence than in childhood or adulthood

We know from MRI data that the brain areas associated with self-concept are highly active in adolescence. Why is this? It could be that ideas about self-concept are more dominant during adolescence *or* that teens need to put significant effort into thinking about themselves as their self-concept is undergoing transition. Or it could be both.

Translating your teen

Your teen is developmentally programmed to be somewhat self-absorbed as they form their self-identity

Brain and behaviour changes seen at this time show that adolescence is a critical time for developing identity. If you have a teen who seems self-absorbed or a little egocentric at times, seems to spend an inordinate amount of time taking photos of themselves on their phone, looking at themselves in the mirror and tending to their hair and make-up, or seems to need to talk endlessly about 'who-said-what' at school and what it might mean about them, your teen is doing exactly what is required for their stage in development. Remember, forming a strong self-identity takes time and resources. The fact that they are focused on self-identity issues more than other competing topics and therefore they don't have spare head-space for other concerns that are on *your* mind is developmentally appropriate.

As they work out who they are, teens may be a little tetchy about personal comments

Among the behavioural changes parents and teachers notice in teenagers is a heightened sensitivity or degree of 'tetchiness'. It can feel like you suddenly can't say anything or even make a joke involving personal information – it's as if teen skin is thin and easily bruised. This is because teens have heightened attention to personally relevant information and personal comments could tip them below the line of a stable self-identity more easily than at other times in life.

 # What does that mean day to day?

Comments to an adolescent are powerful

We can all remember a comment made to us, such as 'that's very unlike you', and wonder what someone meant by that. The same comment made to a child or adult may not have the degree of impact that it would on a teen. Adolescents are in their sensitive period of identity development and therefore will likely place a significant amount of credence on these opinions, more so than younger children or adults. This sensitivity means teens are highly tuned into interactions and communication cues including facial expression, implied meaning or feedback about things that they have produced, including academic work. So, while it is important to carefully consider making a personal statement to or about an individual at any age, the potency of such comments is greatest during the adolescent years. They are tuned into the smallest incidents which, in isolation or over time, contribute significantly to their concept of self. At worst, a put-down from an adult can cause extreme humiliation and perhaps even long-lasting shame.

Teens are sensitive to feedback – use it well

This sensitivity also offers great opportunity to initiate positive cycles. Teens can be boosted enormously by positive value. They are highly motivated to earn prestige and to be valued by society. Given all we know about child–adult relationships from many years of research, it is perhaps not surprising that adults might be considered to have superpowers in their ability to enable the teenage self to grow in a positive trajectory. Many will recall from their past a teacher or mentor who played a key role in their learning something of great interest. We may think that we were interested in a subject first and then a good teacher encouraged us, but often it can be the other way around. A teacher's positive comment can be so highly valuable to an individual that it can engage them in that subject and set them on a path of interest and development for many years to come.

Don't be fooled. An 'I don't care' response is self-protective

Your comments always matter. Imagine a situation in which an adult makes a disparaging comment to a young person – they may say, 'Well, they didn't seem to mind, they were rude back and walked off giggling with their friends. I don't think my comment made the slightest bit of difference to them.' Given teenagers' acute sensitivity to feedback, they are continually protecting their sense of self, and so showing vulnerability to others is a highly dangerous endeavour at this time in life. There may well be a mismatch between an adolescent's outward response and their underlying feelings, particularly in a situation where they are put down. Don't be fooled. They do care what you think of them and have an acute awareness of how you view and value them as individuals. In fact, when a teenager is having a difficult time, this is exactly when they do need your help to reframe and work out how they are going to cope with a situation. See the case study about Zac below, where we give an example of this.

What does that mean for learning?

Actions speak louder than words – do you mean what you say?

Being highly tuned into what another person thinks of us means we will have an acute sensitivity to all kinds of communication. We communicate what we mean with words, but research shows that adolescents often *discern* what another person means by what they say. In other words, they are watching closely to work out what we *really mean*. For example, if a young person makes a mistake and their teacher intervenes to correct it, the young person may discern that the teacher does not believe they were capable of doing it on their own. This is true even if the teacher says, 'I know you can do this', but corrects the mistake even so. The teacher's words in this situation would be less meaningful than their behaviour. This of course would apply to parents helping with school work, or indeed many other situations in which a teen needs adult feedback.

Consider the message of what you say – what is the implied meaning?

Bearing in mind a student's sensitivity to feedback, how can we enable the teen to feel competent by offering our help or support? Just offering help to them might be *discerned* as criticism or an implication that the adult thinks they are not capable of succeeding on their own. Have you ever had the experience of saying to a teenager 'When are you going to do your homework?' and received an emotionally charged 'I *am* going to do my homework. You do nothing but nag me about my homework'? You may have been simply asking for information, but a highly sensitive teen may read this question as a suggestion that they weren't planning to do homework. What is the result? You are left confused, they are upset, possibly feeling undermined and certainly emotional (not a good state to embark on homework), and your chance to help and to connect with the young person is lost. The point here is that the *message* of actions or words needs very careful thought, much more so at this stage than any other stage in life.

So, what now?

As the teenage brain is strengthening in areas devoted to self-identity, a teen is likely to become somewhat self-absorbed and sensitive to personal comments. Now is the time to lay off personal comments ('You've lost weight', 'Your legs are so long'), even if you think you are being positive, as such comments have a superpower at this time.

Case study: Zac

Zac, an 18-year-old, had an evening hanging out with some friends. It was at the time when they were doing university applications and everyone was on edge. Zac had different groups of friends and the three teenagers he was with this evening all happened to be academically ambitious and capable friends, with a slight competitive edge to them. Zac liked these friends, but together he found them a little overwhelming and had a tendency to feel inferior. Discussions about politics and history could become quite heated and edgy, with facts thrown at each other in a kind of one-upmanship manner. Nevertheless, the evening was fun. His friends had gone to a party late, but Zac stayed home as he was part of a music college that met on a Saturday morning. The next day Zac was going to his music class. He played the piano in a jazz group which he enjoyed, but at times it could make him feel somewhat insecure. On this occasion the teacher directed an activity that didn't play to Zac's strengths. By lunchtime Zac was overcome with negative thoughts. His brain was telling him he wasn't very clever, he wasn't a good musician and he wasn't very popular. In fact, he rationalised that he wasn't *really* good at anything. His mood dropped and he felt quite anxious.

A good resolution
Zac was in the phase of his life where he was developing his sense of self. This means that he was highly tuned into how interactions, conversations and events reflected on him as

a person. His sense of self was also vulnerable to fluctuation, and even though there were no direct negative comments or feedback on his performance, he inferred his value to be less than his peers in two somewhat high-pressured and competitive situations. Fortunately, Zac had a good relationship with his mother, who was able to listen and hear his concerns, not invalidate them or overreact to them, but act as a container for his emotions in that moment. He called and said, 'Mum, we need to talk. I'm feeling like I'm just not very good at anything.' He told his mother about feeling out of his depth in the jazz group. He talked about his university application and worries that he may not get a place at his chosen university. He said he was worried his friends found him boring as he didn't always want to party as hard as them. As he talked and his mother listened, his emotions calmed. His mother helped him piece together the events that had led up to him feeling this way and gently pointed out a few positives that might challenge his negative thoughts. Gradually Zac was able to get some perspective and his self-identity regained some of its positivity. While still clearly vulnerable, with the help of his mother, Zac had ridden the wave of self-uncertainty.

What might get in the way?
Eighteen-year-olds don't always reach out to parents when they are struggling, perhaps because that is their character or perhaps because of past experiences of not being heard. Try to look for clues that might indicate a young person is struggling. They might be quieter than usual, be grumpier than usual or act differently, such as not going to see friends when they usually would. At these times straightforward questions (e.g. 'What's wrong?') may not work, but try to start talking about something else to engage them in conversation and then gradually ask if everything is OK. If they don't want to open up straight away, tell them you are always ready to listen if they are struggling with anything or have some 'tricky' thoughts. If they know the door is open they will talk when they are ready to.

Case study: A flashbulb moment for a teacher

Katie is a devoted teacher, having taught for several years. She loves young people and thrives on their 'aliveness'. After hearing a talk about the teenage brain, Katie had a moment of realisation, particularly about her 'superpower' as a teacher of teens. The science of how important teacher feedback is to a student's self-identity really sunk in when she thought of feedback she had given to a student on a piece of work which read: 'This is not your strongest work Najma, I expect more of you.' Perhaps surprisingly, Najma said to her teacher that this comment had really boosted her confidence as she didn't realise her teacher thought that much of her. What power indeed.

Katie reflected on how many comments, both verbal and written, she makes each day to students, not necessarily considering the impact it might have: 'I say things to them all the time without even thinking. Every word matters. I am going to make them count.'

Action point: Manage your expectations

Expect some fluctuation in self-identity in a teen's life. Don't over-react to a new image or if they use new slang. They are trying on new identities. It may not last and, moreover, if you react strongly against it, the result may have the reverse effect of making it stay longer than ever intended. Expect them to be somewhat self-absorbed during this time. Be careful what you make of this, and if you catch yourself making a character interpretation ('Oh my God, I have the most self-absorbed, egocentric child in the world'), stop and remember this is an important part of their development.

Action point: Listen, reflect and offer positive alternatives

Expect there to be fluctuations in a teen's sense of self. It is normal and natural for young people to question their identity, including focusing on what they look like. Our job as a parent or teacher is to be able to 'hold' those thoughts and be alongside young people while they pass. Always be a listening ear for your teen to talk to. They are working out what others think of them and how they fit in. The way they do this is to think deeply about what has been said and what it meant and talk it through with someone. You may hear reflections of low self-worth or a heightened sense of worth at times. Try to stay close, reflect back what they are saying to show you have heard, offer new perspectives and work towards more objective positive alternatives.

Action point: Be careful what you say to a teen

Remember, your superpower can boost the positive self-view of a teenager or puncture it. Use your words wisely around teenagers and be careful what you say in relation to them. A quick quip or aside might stay with them and affect their self-image without you even realising. If you do say something you later regret, don't be afraid to apologise later. This might be very important for the young person you are supporting.

Action point: Make sure comments are about what the person did, not who they are

Small words make a huge difference. It is very different to tell a young person they *are* lazy (character trait) rather than tell them they *are being* lazy (situational trait). Pay attention to these details as young people are storing them up and basing their identity on them. If they are told they are lazy repeatedly, they might just believe it and it may become a self-fulfilling prophecy.

Action point: Be aware of your role modelling around your teen

As adults, we all have insecurities and days when we feel unsure of ourselves. Try to be aware of how you behave and what you say around your teenager. Remember, one of the most powerful ways teens learn is through watching significant adults in their lives. If you spend your day lamenting the chocolate brownie you ate and berating yourself as a weak person, your child is likely to similarly berate themselves whenever they treat themselves.

Action point: Always work towards having a warm and trusting relationship without over-controlling your teen

We know warmth and trust in the parent–child relationship is associated with greater commitment to self-identity and optimal exploration and ultimately robust mental health and well-being. Try to remember the importance of this in your interactions with your teen and resist the temptation to over-control. This is so vital to all aspects of a teen's development that we will be saying it over and over again.

Action point: Look after yourself

If you're struggling with your teen's self-identity development, give yourself some space. Practise positive self-care. Talk to someone, go for a walk, try yoga, eat a delicious peach and take a breath. Try and see this stage as a necessary part of development, of which you are a necessary piece.

The moral of the story is...

Self-image is developed on the basis of feedback from day-to-day experiences: your words and actions make a difference to your teen. Use this period of sensitivity as an opportunity to support them to develop a positive, balanced self-image for adulthood.

Downloads: Self-reflection

Teenagers are developing a complex self-concept, and while they work out who they are and how they fit into the world, they are highly sensitive to personal comments made by significant adults in their lives. Even in a short space of time their identity can be pushed high or low, neither of which is helpful.

Critical feedback could cause long-lasting damage and may cut off possibilities. Positive feedback opens people up and expands possibilities.

Exercise
Note the kind of feedback you give to young people. Do you give negative feedback ('you never clean up properly', 'you don't try hard with your studies', 'you aren't a good mathematician') that could be damaging to them, believing it will motivate them?

. . . .

. . . .

. . . .

. . . .

. . . .

. . . .

. . . .

. . . .

. . . .

Write down five feedback statements you have given your teen lately. If they are negative, try and rephrase them so that they are positive. Tell the teen what you want to aim for, rather than your concern.

Feedback statement 1

. . . .

. . . .

Feedback statement 2

. . . .

. . . .

Feedback statement 3

. . . .

. . . .

Feedback statement 4

. . . .

. . . .

Feedback statement 5

. . . .

. . . .

When this happens...	Instead of this...	Try this...
Your teen has left tea cups in his room. There is mould growing in some of them because they have been left so long.	You never clean up properly. How are you going to live with a partner if you leave a mess like this?	Cleaning up is dull but it's got to be done. What's your idea for a system so it is done and over with quickly? Now put the cups in the dishwasher.
		Build them up, don't knock them down
Your teen is sitting looking sullen at a family lunch party.	I'm such a bad parent. No other teen is as rude as mine. I must have done something wrong.	I feel really irritated. He's usually a social kid but it's not going to be perfect every day and we all have off days. I must look after myself and stay calm so I can help him figure out what's going on and avoid this sort of difficulty in the future.
		Look after yourself as you adjust to your teen's needs
Your teen has spent all morning playing a video game.	You do nothing but go on your video game and have no motivation in life. How are you going to get a job playing video games? Wasters play video games all day.	You love that video game so much. I get that it's hard to stop doing something you love. It's important to do other things as well, so let's make a plan for the day.
		Link behaviour to emotional experiences, not a character trait that is set in stone

Chapter 12

Ready to Launch (with Your Support)

Long story, short

- Parents' and carers' relationships with teens need to change from pilot to co-pilot.
- Adults need to make changes in how they relate and talk to teens as their role transitions.
- Telling them what to do without respect for their opinion is unlikely to be effective at changing behaviour at this age.
- Teens who help in the home are happier, kinder to others and find their contribution rewarding.
- Isolation is toxic in adolescence; having a role is essential.

Introduction

Transitioning from co-pilot to lift-off

As Ronald Dahl says, 'it [adolescence] encompasses the transition from the social status of a child (who requires adult monitoring) to that of an adult (who is him or herself responsible for behaviour)' (2004, p.9).

Adolescence is a period of around 10–15 years, post-childhood, which nature has devoted to preparing the young person for adulthood. All of the brain adaptations we have discussed get the young person ready for an integrated life with their peers, living independently of their parents, in which they understand better who they are and what motivates them. That is quite a long time of preparation, but living life is a challenging task and there is a lot to learn.

As a parent, carer or teacher, your role is different at this time in their lives compared to your role in a child's life. You are needed to keep teenagers safe, but your role is moving from being in the driving seat to being more of a co-pilot, as we discussed in Chapter 1: The Incredible Teen Brain – Time to Upgrade. You are very definitely alongside and ultimately can metaphorically 'put your foot down' if there is danger, but the young person is trying to take charge and learn how to drive in a way that will be safe without your presence by their side in the future.

Teens need parents and teachers all their lives, but their roles change with time

Teens relate in a particular way to adults in their lives. That is just a fact. They are biologically driven to question what you say, they begin to realise you are fallible (sorry) and, with their new-found self-consciousness, you may well do or say something that will embarrass them. It can feel like they are pushing you away and you are no longer needed. But don't be fooled. Parents, teachers and mentors are essential throughout life and particularly during these often-turbulent teenage years. Your role is changing, requiring you to make some changes to how you relate to teens and talk to them. We are struck by the challenge faced by parents and teachers to get the balance right between allowing for autonomy, exploration and learning, while also staying close enough to offer sufficient protection.

Remember that autonomy is not the opposite of relatedness. Both are essential for healthy development. Indeed, teenagers may need the relatedness of the most important adults in their lives more than ever at this age given their vulnerability. They just have a funny way of showing it sometimes. You may feel a sense of loss – loss of the child you once had, loss of the power you once had over them – but flexibility and reflection will get you through. That is, indeed, why you are reading this book. The secret of the teenage years is that if you can get this part of your relationship right, there are plentiful rewards for the rest of your lives.

The science bit: Brain and behaviour

Teens have a fundamental need for status and respect

Teens want to be respected. They are suddenly much more sensitive and aware of their status in their social environment than when they were younger, noticing things that passed them by before. Research suggests that this is related to an increase in testosterone (a hormone) in both boys and girls at this time in life, causing the individual to be more attentive and reactive to respect from others and more likely to adhere to instructions given in respectful language. A simple shift in phrasing from 'It might be a good idea to take this medicine' to 'Just take the medicine' reduced adherence in teenagers high in testosterone in one study. Moreover, when compared to younger children, adolescents perceive adult attempts to influence their behaviour as a sign they are being disrespected. This might explain their sudden sensitivity to how they are spoken to and tendency to take offence. But it is also important to help us understand how best to influence teens' behaviour to get changes in behaviour we might want to see.

Changing teen behaviour requires a different approach

One of the oldest theories in psychology has been influential in how we typically change behaviour. It is called the behavioural decision-making theory and is based on the idea that telling people about the risks of a behaviour will lead to a positive behaviour change. For example, if we want people to smoke less, a campaign that informs people of the health risks of smoking will reduce the number of smokers. The same approach has been used with children and often forms the basis of school anti-bullying campaigns or campaigns to encourage healthy eating in schools. However, research has consistently found that these interventions are less effective or even completely ineffective during the adolescent years. This is true for studies on anti-obesity and depression prevention and is also true for many of the hundreds of studies that target social-emotional skills training. One study even found a negative effect following an anti-obesity programme for adolescents – obesity increased following the campaign.

David Yeager and colleagues (2018) believe that traditional

programmes of behavioural change with teens are ineffective because teenagers are highly sensitive to being treated with respect and accorded high status. Research is still relatively new in this area but there is some research giving some important pointers about ways to influence adolescent behaviour.

A 2016 study by Christopher Bryan and colleagues compared ways to promote healthy eating to teenagers to see which was most effective. There were two schools who took part. School 1 used a traditional intervention of giving young people knowledge about how the body processes unhealthy food, warning about the long-term risks of unhealthy eating and including activities in the school day and homework that reinforced the same messages (the behavioural decision-making approach). School 2 harnessed the desire for status and respect that is so inherent to adolescent functioning by using journalistic-style accounts of how the junk food industry is tricking and harming young people for the sake of profit and marketing food so children become addicted. It focused on how the food industry was disrespecting young people. School 2 therefore had the effect of the forming of a social movement to stand up to the hypocritical adults and, more importantly, they did not *tell* the adolescents what to do. Rather, teens were invited to discover the meaning of the message – thereby their need to be treated according to their age and not in a child-like manner was met.

The key outcome in this study was the amount of sugar content students from each school selected the next day (from the choice of a healthy vs. unhealthy snack). School 2 selected significantly less sugar, supporting their hypothesis. This illustrates one way that harnessing adolescents' need for respect and status can be used for positive change. Rather than telling them what to do, School 2 appealed to the young people's desire to be part of something larger than themselves, encouraged them to stand up to injustice and was teen led. Tapping into these teen drives seems a more effective way to galvanise a group of adolescents to action.

Teens respond best when spoken to with respect

Anyone with a teen in their care will have experienced the need to say things over and over again to the point of *telling* them what to do. However, heavy-handed methods of instruction where messages are repeated over and over again and young people are told what to do are likely to result in reduced compliance (be honest, we knew that already, but why do we keep doing it?). This is probably because they experience this kind of communication as disrespectful and infantilising. One study scanned the brains of teens while receiving maternal criticism (or 'nagging') and found that teenagers had increased activity in the emotional parts of their brain (particularly anger) and decreased activity in the control regions of the brain (thinking brain) and in the social-cognitive networks (suggesting greater difficulty understanding another person's point of view – unhelpful in the circumstances) when parents nagged them compared to other types of more neutral communication. This suggests that nagging causes more of an emotional (lower brain) reaction in a teen and reduces their ability to think clearly in the moment.

While all parents and teachers will tell teens what to do with good intentions – after all, they care deeply about the young person they are talking to – top-down, heavy-handed or threatening instructions may be *reducing* the likelihood of the teenager complying with their message. We need to think more carefully about how we communicate with youngsters at this age.

When teens help others they gain respect and feel good

You will have heard the saying 'with great power comes great responsibility'. If teenagers want independence and autonomy, how do they cope with the responsibility that goes along with that? Research has looked at whether the act of helping others in a meaningful way has positive or negative effects on teen development. Much of the research in this area has considered the burden of children helping in families, in contexts where the parents have a debilitating psychological or physical illness. However, if the burden does not take away from the adolescent's developmental tasks, perhaps it could be beneficial for the teenager. Taking on responsibilities and tasks in the home could not only allow young people to develop important life skills but could also be a way for teenagers to feel respected and make a valuable contribution within the family. And indeed, there are beneficial effects as found by Andrew Fuligni and colleagues (see Fuligni 2018; Fuligni and Telzer 2013). A group of 17–18-year-olds who assisted in the family home reported greater happiness and positivity and had a greater sense of meaning in their lives. They were also more generous when playing an online game and, when their brains were scanned, the reward centres of their brain lit up more when giving to others. As an aside, teens find winning for their mothers as rewarding as winning for their friends according to the way their brains respond at least. While it feels like they'd rather give their last Rolo to their friend, they care deeply about their adult relationships.

Other studies have found that young people with stronger family obligations show greater activation of the frontal region of the brain during cognitive control tasks, in line with better decision-making skills. The 'one point in time' nature of this data makes it hard to say what causes what, but it could be that young people who are used to putting others' needs first by fulfilling family obligations develop more effective cognitive control.

Teens are motivated to earn prestige within their family, cultural group or wider society

An intriguing twist in this part of the research suggests that the teen need for respect and prestige is influenced by cultural values. While you might think that all teens want to be famous or 'cool' or care about physical attraction, it might be the case that whatever is held in high prestige within a culture, implicitly or explicitly, is what adolescents will aim for as a way to gain high status in that culture. Not all cultures value the same characteristics in society – for example, in the Tibetan culture that values compassion and kindness, adolescents will work to earn prestige according to those values,* while a culture that values fame will draw their adolescents to seek fame.

It is interesting to think about the implications of these findings in relation to small cultural groups such as families. Whatever is held in high prestige within that culture, implicitly or explicitly, is likely to be what adolescents will aim for as a way to gain high status

---

* Personal communication by Ron Dahl that came out of a discussion with the Dalai Lama at a conference organised by Richie Davidson and the Mind & Life Institute.

in that culture. We need to think about how our behaviour directly and indirectly influences young people about what is an aspirational characteristic (remember the learning models in Chapter 5: The Teen Brain Loves Other People). Indirect learning may be more powerful for young people. For example, when a teen arrives back from school and the first thing we say when they walk in the door is 'What homework do you have?', our child will discern that homework is most important to us. If we change that to 'How was your day?' or 'What was the most fun you had today?', we imply that we value how they are more. Societal values are hard to change, though we can be part of a conversation of change. You can think about the values you are conveying by what you focus on in conversations and check-ins. These are powerful, and while they will influence values at any time in a child's life, getting this right is particularly important during the adolescent years.

Translating your teen

Teens are sensitive about how they are spoken to

If we want teens to change their behaviour we need to think carefully about how we talk to them. Top-down behavioural control strategies that are effective for younger children may no longer work at this point in their development. 'Nagging' or 'lecturing' them is often met by eye rolling or a stern look, and if we are really honest we know it doesn't work well. Yet we continue to say things in the same way, perhaps because we know no other way. Teenage brain research is helpful in showing us that the devil is in the detail. Communication needs to be respectful, appeal to their senses and not infantilise them or make them feel small or stupid. If you can get them onboard with the goal you are trying to achieve, even better.

Many schools try to teach young people the rules of acceptable behaviour through detentions and even exclusion. Brain research suggests this approach can have a counter-intuitive effect. At this age, it is unlikely to change behaviour and, moreover, punishments can alienate a student who is already feeling disaffected and may even incite the oppositional behaviour that they were meant to prevent.

In addition, at this important inflection point, such a negative experience could propel a young person into a negative spiral that is hard for them to get out of.

Making contributions to others and having a positive 'role' fulfils our fundamental need to belong

Many theories of human development help us understand why making willing contributions to a social group can increase the sense of connection, promote a sense of impact and allow an individual to feel competent and effective. This is perhaps never more evident than during the teenage years when social worlds are expanding and young people have a strong need to belong to the social group and have a positive role among their peers. This social draw, coupled with young people's increasing understanding of the complexities of social situations including fairness and equality, can mean this is a time when young people engage in politics and issues of social inequality with great passion and meaning. These opportunities which offer positive risk are highly valuable to the developing teenage brain.

They may pull away from you and seem to need you less, but don't be fooled or feel rejected

If you respond to adolescents' need to develop autonomy and independence by feeling rejected and pulling away from them, you lose the opportunity to give them much needed guidance. This seems one of the ways in which teens are most vulnerable as they are left alone to work things out, which can mean they travel down dangerous paths. It's important to culture positive nurturing relationships. Recent imaging data with teens and their mothers (Renske Van der Cruijsen *et al.* 2019) show us that if you want your teen to make decisions with you in mind, it's more likely to happen if you have a warm relationship. It is highly likely that this effect is true for fathers, teachers and any adult with a significant role in the teen's life. Remember, they have a fundamental need to be in a close relationship with someone. If you are not there guiding them, you can be darn sure someone else will step in – and maybe it will be the internet or someone who will take advantage of them. If there is one time in life to keep talking to them, it is now.

Figure 12.1: Teens need parental love and attention more than ever, even though they may pull away

What does that mean day to day?

Maintain a growth mindset about teen behaviour

Remember how important mindset is for our behaviour? (See Chapter 3: The Teen Brain Learns and Believes.) Our beliefs about a situation can even have an influence on our *future* behaviour. So just be careful not to get stuck in a fixed belief that the teen years are going to be dreadful; while some families and schools experience conflict and strain during the teenage years, many don't. In the context of relationships that are emotionally open and supportive, adults and teens can manage to negotiate individuality while staying connected without difficulty. Remember that conflict and teen autonomy are not signs of dysfunction – indeed, we might be more concerned about a relationship where there is a lack of autonomy and conflict during adolescence. Conflict is normal in all relationships, and we would encourage you to allow teens to express their opinions even if it leads to disagreement.

Don't let them be rude, but let them be angry

Anger is an interesting emotion that is often associated with adolescent rebelliousness. Anger towards another person can be a way of coercing them to fit with our views, or a way of trying to force the other person into action. Passion and anger can be driving forces which are about breaking through and seeing things in a new way or trying to get others to see something new. Anger is therefore more likely to arise in situations where things matter deeply, and so knowing what we know about the passion and motivations of adolescence, it's not surprising to find anger punctuating many teens' lives. Anger is also inherently about power. It is often triggered when things are not in our control and so often apparent when the power relationship between parent/teacher/adult and young person is being negotiated. While we do not condone rude or aggressive behaviour in any way, allowing teens to express anger in an appropriate manner is probably very important for their long-term development.

Don't try to exert your control where they have the power

Teens are learning to care for themselves, and part of that process is taking control of what they eat, when they sleep and how much they exercise, which we explore in more detail in Part 4. You are their guidance in this plight, but it is unwise to try to wield your power around these areas of their lives and, if you do, it may well backfire. If you are concerned about a young person's health you may well become anxious, which in turn causes you to be heavy handed – but communication in the form of curiosity, discussion and problem solving is the only way. If the issue continues then consult a professional doctor or psychologist.

Communicate to problem solve

The teenage brain is ready for higher order learning. The frontal part of the brain which houses important problem solving skills is ripe and ready for development. This, combined with the teen need for respect, makes it the ideal time to help a young person learn how to problem solve when problems arise. Make time for debate, allow controversy and, while we would never recommend shouting or arguing, disagreements that allow the young person the ability to think for themselves are absolutely recommended. If there is a disagreement, make time to listen whole-heartedly to their side of the story. You don't need to agree with it, but you do need to listen. Then you can tell them that they also need to listen to you and give your point of view. You might not reach a clear agreement, but you are respecting them and teaching them how to manage disagreements. Setting clear, kind but firm boundaries after discussion is the way forward at this time.

What does that mean for learning?

Older teens need more control of their learning in line with their need for autonomy

Clear instructions and boundaries around work topics and homework are essential for young children, but as your teen grows they need to begin to exert more autonomy and personal identity around school work. It can be hard for teachers and parents to let go given the high stakes of academic failure and the desire to help each young person reach their potential. However, trying to control teens with strict rules and harsh boundaries around learning is likely to fail at this age and in the long term could have the side effect of reducing their internal interest and motivation towards learning. It may be harder for older students to be a committed learner unless they are given freedom in how they learn and even to some extent what they learn, given their need for autonomy and personal identity. Modelling good behaviour around learning, showing an interest in their learning and supporting them to work, but letting them begin to make choices about when and where they do their work is the best strategy.

Behaviour that is modelled and held in high esteem will be highly sought after by teens

As teens drive for prestige and status in the culture of a school, be aware of what values are being held in high esteem either implicitly or explicitly. Think carefully about what behaviour you reward. Do you always reward grades and not effort? Do you hold up behaviours such as kindness and compassion as worth aiming for, commenting on them and highlighting them? If we want compassionate young people in a school, we need to model compassion towards all students.

Harness teen motivations to change behaviour in schools

There is good evidence that traditional ways of changing behaviour in schools are less effective for teens. Teens are in a period of their lives when they are moving towards autonomy and independence and it is normal for them to want to think for themselves about their own behaviour. Trying to leverage on peer-delivered interventions that harness teen motivations for good and tap into the power of the social group is likely to be taken on most readily by teenagers. Think of the recent climate change movement led by Greta Thunberg, which is the biggest environmental protest the world has ever seen, dominated by teenagers and young people. Teen power to spread a message among the young population is as yet an untapped resource in many walks of life including health and education.

Teen need for belonging and status can lead them to adopt positive or negative 'roles' in school

Bonell and colleagues (2019) discuss the ways in which a student's need for a positive 'role' and sense of belonging to a group can influence engagement in academic learning in school. All students make choices of roles to maximise their chances of high status and respect. If a more pro-school role (e.g. engaged, compliant, high-achieving student) is not available to them for whatever reason, they may be drawn to a more anti-school role or group such as a disengaged or disruptive student. There are many factors that influence choice of role, to do with the individual factors and the culture within the school environment, but what is clear is that schools with a narrower definition of 'success' in schools (such as schools that only celebrate academic students or those who excel in arts or sports), are more likely to have a higher number of anti-school students who are disengaged, perhaps bent on challenging school rules making them more vulnerable to academic under-achieving and mental health problems.

You can use this framework to find strategies to manage disengaged young people in school or at home by finding ways to help them contribute and have a role. We know that a feeling of belonging in secondary school is predicted by students' beliefs that their ideas are valued by the organisation. Finding ways for disengaged students to be involved in decisions such as student-led learning, classroom practices and being involved in negotiated school rules can help disengaged students feel a part of a community. This can shift their mindset about who they are, so they can begin to see themselves as young people who have value and make contributions, while also giving them a sense of respect and purpose, which is so important at this age.

So, what now?

Teenagers are driven towards more autonomy and independence and it is a developmental task for them to question what the adults in their lives think and believe. Don't be put off by this behaviour, and try to adjust your reactions and instructions to take this need into account. It is likely to be much more effective.

Case study: Tessa

Tessa had recently found guitar practice *so* boring. She had played since she was nine, flown through her grades and shown such promise. Her dad, Michael, a musician himself, was concerned she was losing interest and might, like many of her friends seemed to be doing at the age of 12, begin to talk of 'giving it up'. Tessa's first teacher had been a young woman, Martha, who made the lessons fun, and as far as Tessa was concerned she was cool. She looked forward to her lessons and wanted to impress her teacher. Martha really believed in Tessa, loved teaching her and had high expectations of her. They would find a way to laugh when it was hard and Martha's comments of 'I know this bit is hard but I also know you can do it' worked a treat. The positive cycle of learning was working beautifully for Tessa. Martha had to stop teaching Tessa as she was going abroad to study and so Tessa began lessons with a school guitar teacher who was excited to take on such a promising student. It started well but Michael began to notice she picked up her guitar less and for the first time she resisted practising and it became a point of tension at home.

A good resolution

Michael decided to tackle the conversation when they were out for the day and enjoying each other's company. He knew it was important not to nag or just tell her to practise more or that he was 'paying a lot of money for lessons'. He needed to understand the change in behaviour, so he gently asked her about guitar in school. He found out that Tessa was not enjoying the lessons as much. She liked her teacher, but she had enjoyed her time with Martha. More importantly, the new teacher was forcing her to play in a guitar group which she didn't want to do. All the other children were younger and it took away from her break time and lunch time with her friends who were so important to her. Michael could empathise with her and so offered to talk to the teacher. He felt like it was a temporary phase, and if she was allowed more choice and the group playing was with a more appropriate peer group, it might help her feel more internally motivated to keep playing. Moreover, Martha was returning in a year and could teach Tessa again and so just a short-term solution was needed to get her through. Just having had the conversation and Tessa feeling more in control had shifted something and Tessa realised how important the guitar was to her. She also joined the Spanish guitar group at school, which was a stretch for her, but the kids were pretty cool and her motivation was back.

What might get in the way?

Another parent might have responded with anger and determination to keep going without considering the teen's point of view. The student–teacher relationship had been a key element of her enjoyment of her instrument and her parents needed to find a way to keep her going even when her favourite teacher was missing. Without that approach, Tessa could have responded by digging in her heels more and her guitar playing would have deteriorated. With teens it is important to look at the detail and trust their choices. Relationships with teachers are important, and who they spend time with, even for group ensembles, is an important detail. While it's important not to just allow young people to 'give up', it is also important to make small changes to support their needs at the same time.

Case study: Chip

Chip, aged 11, was driving his teacher Vanessa to distraction. He was a smart boy but he was always late, forgot his books, his work was messy and he would not stop chatting in class. There was a tough curriculum to get through and more needy students in the class. Vanessa tried positive reinforcement by congratulating him when he was on time. She tried consequences for behaviour by threatening detentions if he didn't stop talking. She moved the seating plan round. These approaches helped for a while but not for long. She was at the end of her tether, and one lesson she lost it – with her emotional brain in charge, she shouted at him, 'God, when will you learn? What is wrong with you?' Instantly she regretted what she had said partly because of the shocked look on her students' faces.

A good resolution

Vanessa knew she needed some help. She asked for a meeting with the head of year to help her think it through. Vanessa's colleague gave her time to 'download'. Teaching was stressful and this class was a challenge. With her end of year review in sight she needed to get her class focusing so that she could cover everything in the curriculum. Vanessa needed an empathetic ear and then the two teachers could begin to problem solve. They decided on a three-pronged attack. Vanessa had a short check-in with Chip at the end of every lesson, to tell him what had gone well and strengthen their relationship. She worked on an empathetic approach to behaviour, trying hard to understand what had triggered him. She gave him a 'pro-school' role that allowed him to have status among his peers. He was in charge of 'council' for their class, where students and staff discussed creative ideas for learning and negotiated rules. This played to his quick, creative mind and engaging communication style with his peers. The meetings took place every half term and enabled all students to also feel that they had some autonomy in how their classroom ran, led by Chip. The head of year also had a chat with his parents to consider whether this type of behaviour had been evident in his past and whether an assessment to consider neurodiversity was required.

What might get in the way?

In another situation a teacher may have continued with the same approach, increasing the number of detentions as Chip became more disengaged with learning. It is often hard for teachers to admit they are struggling to control their class. Seeking advice from a colleague cannot be seen as any kind of failure, but rather having the strength to problem solve in order to find a solution for each child. Moreover, without this thoughtful approach, the student–teacher relationship would have deteriorated and Chip would not have had an opportunity to learn from his mistakes.

Case study: Jacob

Jacob was 14 years old, son to Maxine and Ed. He had an elder sister, Phoebe, 17. Phoebe had a turbulent time in her early adolescence when she suffered from chronic fatigue syndrome. At around the same time the family sought consultation with a psychologist about Jacob, who had always struggled with attending and focusing in class and had tended to get in trouble in his junior school. He was given a diagnosis of ADHD and started on medication. The positive impact on his school performance and behaviour was enormous. Jacob and his parents felt like the diagnosis was spot on and the medication was life-changing for him. However, the family had been through quite a challenging time and the years prior to diagnosis with high emotions and behavioural challenges had left a mark on everyone. Maxine felt guilty. She felt she had let her family down in not identifying her son's difficulties earlier and still struggled with exactly what ADHD meant.

Maxine sought support from a parenting specialist to help her work out how to strengthen her relationship with her son. She admitted to trying to micro-manage his homework. He was shutting her out of the conversation completely, and the more she asked him 'What homework do you have?' or commented on his work ethic – 'You have only spent half an hour on homework tonight, that can't be enough' – the more he withdrew, went to his room, shut the door and refused to talk to her. Although his teachers said he was doing fine, she was getting more and more anxious about him not keeping up and ultimately not doing well enough in his exams in two years' time. At the same time, he and his friends were beginning to meet up at night and the party scene was starting to happen. Ed and Maxine had made an effort to engage their son in conversation about drugs and alcohol and their possible damaging effects. However, the ADHD diagnosis confused Maxine. What did it mean for her son? Wasn't he more likely to take risks because of his diagnosis? She was beside herself with anxiety and just wanted to keep him home and lock the door. Maxine said she couldn't just sit and watch him take risks at weekends and throw away his chances academically and she knew her instincts were right.

Jacob retreated from his parents more and more in response to their increasing anxiety and attempts to control him. It felt like all his parents cared about was how he did at school and they had no interest in his social life, which was important to him. His biology meant he was thinking about his friends and how to fit in with them most of the time. He was keeping up with his school work but that was not his driving force. When he got home he took to his room as quickly as possible to get away from the nagging.

A good resolution

The challenge for Jacob's parents was how they could allow him the autonomy he needed for exploration and learning while offering him protection and support. The answer may seem counter-intuitive. While his mum's instincts may have been correct, she could no longer just tell her son what to do in a directive manner and expect him to comply. His biology was telling him to begin to develop his own view and to have some autonomy from his parents. At the same time she couldn't sit back and do nothing. Remember, autonomy is not the opposite of relatedness. The way forward was to be prepared to listen, to have conversations, to set broad boundaries but not to dictate. Some degree of negotiation within limits was needed. Maxine needed to manage her anxiety elsewhere and not let it dominate her interactions with her son. She found a regular slot in the week when she spent time alone with her son. He enjoyed cooking so they decided Wednesday night they would shop for food and cook together. She made sure she steered away from conversation about homework and chores and did not nag. As their relationship grew he was more open to discussing homework strategies and he even asked his mum for help with devising a timetable for his exams. Trust was building.

What might get in the way?

To begin with, conversations might need to be on their terms – when they are ready and at a time when they feel able to. If a parent pushes too hard the young person may retreat more. With a new diagnosis, everyone is trying to work out what it means and this can be a confusing time. It might be a good idea to make use of the excellent books and resources available, or if conversation is still hard, book some time with a professional who might be able to shift things a little so that better conversations can take place.

Action point: Never underestimate the importance of your relationship with your teen

Even though teens push boundaries in their drive for independence, don't ever doubt your importance in their lives as their parent, mentor or teacher. They are pushing away but they don't want you to disappear. Having a close connection with caring adults, even in the early years of university or college, is protective.

Action point: Respect a teen's need for status and independence in the way you talk to them, and don't nag

As the young person grows, their need for autonomy, respect and independence will also grow. Be prepared to reflect on the way in which you interact with your teen. Be respectful and reduce threats which appear to undermine. As the adult in charge, you absolutely have the final say in what happens and the boundaries are yours to set, but expecting blind compliance at this age is unlikely to work. Take the time to problem solve with the teen, ask for their opinions, listen and show an interest in their view even if you disagree. It will get you a long way.

Action point: Offer more control and autonomy to how and what older teens learn

Older students have a developmental need for autonomy and to establish personal identity in their learning. Try to let go of the reins a bit and allow them more freedom. For example, rather than saying, 'Go and do your homework now and come down for dinner at 7pm', try helping them to work out how they will spend their time by saying, 'Have you got a plan for how you will manage your work today? Dinner is at 7pm and we have agreed no school work after 10pm. What is your plan?'.

Action point: Offer diverse activities and roles within a school to engage more students

Schools should consider adopting a broad definition of 'success' so that students have greater choice of pro-school roles available to them. For example, as well as celebrating academic and sporting success, consider roles such as peer educators or mentors. For teens who seem disengaged, find a role or responsibility they can take on where they gain prestige and respect not only among the teachers but with their peers. As they begin to feel good about themselves, watch them grow.

Action point: If you are often confronted with anger, try to give more autonomy

Anger is often a signal that someone's power or control is being threatened. While it's important not to reward inappropriate anger or aggressive behaviour and to manage rebellious behaviour, it is equally important not to react to anger with over-control. Consider stepping back and allowing the young person more autonomy and self-control, where you can.

Action point: Think carefully about what is admired and valued in your community

Take advantage of the fact that young people are highly sensitive to feelings of respect, admiration and being valued, and think about what values are being modelled in the community – the wider community, school or family. If you want teens who work towards being kind and compassionate, you must show that this is valued in your community. If you support a culture of competitiveness and one-upmanship, expect teens to thrive to be the best at beating people. It's worth getting right.

The moral of the story is...

Teenage behaviour can be challenging and adults are the ones in charge, but the way you interact with your teenager does need to change. This is a period of transition, and transitions require adjustments.

Downloads: Ready to Launch (with Your Support)

Adults need to make changes in how they relate and talk to teens as their role transitions from being sole pilot to being co-pilot, travelling alongside their teen.

Teens need parents, teachers and important people to look up to in their lives. Support for teen behaviour requires communication using collaboration, problem solving and discussion, acknowledging their need for respect and status. Even though they will sometimes push you away, they need close adults in their lives now more than ever.

Exercise

Think about you and your teen's top two moments of communication around difficult topics. How did you do that?

Moment 1

. . . .

. . . .

Moment 2

. . . .

. . . .

Note three situations when you and your teen come into conflict and how you tend to resolve the situation.

Situation 1

. . . .

. . . .

Situation 2

. . . .

. . . .

Situation 3

. . . .

. . . .

What are the behaviours, ethics and values that you use in your school or home? These will be your teen's reference point.

. . . .

. . . .

. . . .

. . . .

. . . .

. . . .

. . . .

. . . .

When this happens...	Instead of this...	Try this...
Your teen has hardly said a word to you all week – it's hard to get anything out of her about how she is.	She doesn't need me any more and she doesn't even seem to care about me, she's so cold towards me.	She's not communicating very well but she's under stress. She might not know how she's feeling yet. I am going to check in every day, let her know I am there; even if she doesn't talk I will be there so she knows I'm alongside her at this difficult time.
		Never under-estimate the importance of your relationship with your teen
Your teen loses his football match. He missed the bus and shouts at you that he needs a lift to his friend's house or he'll miss the meet-up.	I won't change my mind however much you shout at me, I am not taking you in the car. You need to learn to talk to me in a civil way. I am not a member of your staff.	Your team lost. I know that is a big deal but it is not OK to speak to me in that tone. I can't take you in the car right now. Let's talk about this later when you are feeling calmer.
		Don't let them be rude, but let them be angry
Your step-daughter is putting her college application together following a discussion and plan. The limit of 500 words means that she has to choose which of her many hobbies and activities she can include and she is getting overwhelmed and upset.	Give it to me and I'll do it. You're too upset to think straight.	This is a toughie. Let's take the dog for a walk and come back with fresh eyes. Then let's brainstorm all your ideas. That will be enough for one day and tomorrow you can have another go at writing it.
		Help them develop strong problem solving skills

PART 4

Care and Self-Care for the Teen Brain

Chapter 13

Sleepy Teens

Long story, short

- Sleep is described as a 'wonder drug'.
- A lack of sleep is endemic among teenagers.
- Teens need sleep for long-term brain development and to manage everyday life.
- Teen biological sleep cycles shift, but the social context is more to blame for a lack of sleep in teens.
- Sufficient and regular sleep aids learning and memory.
- Poor sleep is detrimental to mental health and well-being.

Introduction

As a parent or teacher of a teenager you will know that a lack of sleep is endemic amongst teenagers. Few teens are getting the minimum recommended eight hours a night of sleep and the consequences are significant, both short-term and long-term. Moreover, conflict as a result of lack of sleep – due to teens falling asleep in class, teens being irritable or teens not focusing on what is being said to them – is damaging relationships between teens and the adults in their lives. Rather than just accept it and say, 'Oh, that is part of being a teenager', can we dig deeper and understand what is going on and what we can do about it?

Sleep as a wonder-drug

We spend a lot of time asleep. If we live to 79 years of age, we will have spent 26 years asleep. The question of why we spend so much of our lives asleep has been debated for many years, and while sleep may feel passive and unproductive, neuroscience is showing us that the brain by no means shuts down when we sleep, but is very active and essential for physical and mental well-being. Indeed, Matthew Walker, author of the book *Why We Sleep* (2017), tells us how sleep is a wonder-drug:

> *Scientists have discovered a revolutionary new treatment that makes you live longer. It enhances your memory, makes you more attractive. It keeps you slim and lowers food cravings. It protects you from cancer and dementia. It wards off colds and flu. It lowers your risk of heart attacks and stroke, not to mention diabetes. You'll even feel happier, less depressed, and less anxious. Are you interested? (Walker 2017, p.107)*

'I'll take some!' I hear you say. But how can we get this message across to teenagers? How can we help them to see that insufficient sleep affects motivation, reduces our ability to focus our attention, make us more irritable and reactive, lowers our mood, increases our risk for obesity and makes us more likely to reach for stimulants such as coffee to keep us going? Studies have even found a lack of sleep correlated with suicidal rumination in teenagers, although this will not be a simple relationship.

And those are just the short-term effects. Neuroscience is also beginning to reveal long-term effects on brain structure for teens who lack sleep, with strong indications that sleep in needed more than ever at this time of significant brain plasticity and development. In other words, at the time in their lives when they need the most sleep, teens are not getting enough.

The science bit: Brain and behaviour

The body clock shifts in adolescence

When we talk to teachers and parents about the teenage brain and do a kind of neuroscience 'true-or-false' type quiz, most people know that during the teenage years the circadian rhythm changes, causing teens to naturally fall asleep later. Our circadian rhythm is the sleep and wake cycle that is regulated by an internal body clock of 24 hours. A hormone called melatonin is released in our brain at bedtime which, in the context of darkness, gives our body an internal signal that aids the process of falling asleep. This happens later for teenagers, causing them to have the biological inclination to fall asleep somewhat later than both their younger siblings and their parents.

Scientists have used this as a way to explain why teenagers want to go to bed so late. Moreover, this finding has led to calls for a shift to later school start times for teenagers. The argument is that, by insisting on teenagers getting up early when their body is telling them to go to bed later, we are reducing the amount of sleep they get. Studies in Europe and the United States are being carried out where the school day starts later for teens. The later start allows students to wake up later and seems to be associated with some positive effects in grades and improved attendance. This is an exciting area which needs more research.

But...the social context is more to blame for a lack of sleep

However, Ron Dahl and Daniel Lewin (2002) point out that the change in circadian rhythm in teens is only part of the problem. In fact, they argue that the delay in the release of melatonin accounts for perhaps only 1 per cent of the problem. The other 99 per cent, they say, is due to social context, which is exacerbating a tiny biological effect, so just working on a later start time for schools is not going to work on its own.

The social context includes a number of factors. For example, technology is likely causing later sleep time because the light emitted by computers and handheld devices misleads the brain into thinking it is daytime. Then there is the social draw of technology at this time in life, when the teenage brain is signalling the individual to make contact with peers and feel part of the group, causing them to reach for their phones to check social media. In addition, there is the research finding that rumination and worry at nighttime tends to increase during the adolescent years, also causing teenagers to be awake for longer while they lie in bed contemplating their concerns. All of these factors layer on top of a tiny biological shift to cause greater concern and potential negative impact on the health and well-being of teenagers. It is their sensitivity to the social environment that is having the greatest impact.

Figure 13.1: The social context explains teen sleep patterns

It's not just duration, variability in the timing of sleep is highly problematic

Interestingly, research is showing that just counting the number of hours asleep is not enough to understand the problem. As you will know, one of the most prominent behavioural changes that occurs during adolescence is the shifting of sleep schedules. As they begin to meet up with friends online, go to parties or go on 'sleepovers' (a somewhat misleading name given the amount of 'sleep' that actually takes place), teens tend to shift 'time zones' at weekends and in school holidays, so that they might sleep from 3.30 am to midday at weekends instead of their usual 10.30pm to 7am on weekdays. The *amount* of sleep is the same, but there is a big shift in *when* they get their sleep.

Interestingly, this phenomenon, known as 'social jet lag' (Roenneberg *et al.* 2004), has been found to have a greater detrimental effect on brain development and functioning than loss of sleep hours alone. This is perhaps surprising but is likely related to sleep cycles. Shifting time zones, effectively, shifts our sleep cycles and our bodies become confused and function less well. Imagine flying to the other side of the world every weekend and think of how exhausting that would be.

Translating your teen

Insufficient sleep is highly detrimental for mental health and well-being

Mental health is highly sensitive to a lack of sleep. Rather intriguingly, the 'optimal' amount of sleep for positive mental health is 8 to 10 hours, which is somewhat more than the optimal number of hours associated with getting high scores on standardised tests (7–7½ hours). Moreover, the relationship between mental well-being and sleep is complex and works two ways. While emotional arousal and distress can interfere with sleep, as rumination and worry make a young person alert and prevent them from falling asleep, a negative spiral can quickly ensue as emotions are harder to regulate without sufficient sleep, including low mood, making us less likely to be able to deal with the knocks of everyday life. Add to that the fact that after little sleep we are more irritable and our tolerance of frustration is lowered, which could result in more conflict and negative interactions with others. We quickly see how poor sleep makes our teens vulnerable to dysregulation during the teen years, but also how regular sleep can support a young person who is struggling emotionally. See the case study about Kasia below and the impact of reduced sleep on her well-being.

What does that mean day to day?

A teen with insufficient sleep may be grumpy, as their lower brain is in charge

After a poor night's sleep (or a night out on the town) we all feel more emotional, more likely to say something we regret and more likely to fall into bad habits such as unhealthy eating. This is true for all of us – we are all more likely to 'lose it' when we have had a bad night's sleep, and this is because the emotional brain dominates and higher order parts of the brain struggle to come online quickly enough (remember how our brains work from Chapter 2: The Teen Brain Thinks and Feels?). But this is perhaps even more true for teens because the thinking parts of their brain that regulate emotions and behaviour are not yet fully developed. If your teen has had a poor night's sleep, even if it was because they were out having fun (which irritated you a little), try to give them a little slack the next day and lower expectations of them. Direct conflict will only likely flare up when a brain is firing on less sleep. If there has been a step change in your teen showing any of these emotional or behavioural signs or symptoms, take the time to help them manage their sleep schedule and ensure they are getting sufficient and regular sleep. As Matthew Walker says, sleep is a wonder-drug.

At night time, worries often magnify

We have all had the experience of lying in bed at night, ruminating about something that is hard in our lives – how we will pay the bills, whether we upset our friend, how we are going to get that report written for work. Indeed, we are often ruminating about our teens at night time. But for teens, this rumination can go into overdrive – negative tapes on replay. Anxiety increases the body's fight or flight response, getting it ready for action, and in that mode our body is in no state to fall asleep. A recent study in Ron Dahl's lab showed that, in the context of family stress, parental support was an important predictor of longer and less variable sleep in teens. Your relationship with them matters to their sleep. Talk to your teen about rumination and help them understand what is going on. Remind them that the thoughts in their head aren't always true, particularly at bedtime (why do our thoughts become so self-sabotaging after 10pm?), and give them another time and space in their day where they can discuss difficult things in their lives, freeing up their brains for sleep at night time.

Phones in bedrooms at night are hard for teens to resist

As we have learnt, with their highly attuned social brain, teens are driven to integrate with their peers, and a lot of peer integration in this generation happens…on the phone. Phones in beds late at night are therefore not only a strong social pull for teens, but the blue light emitted by technology gives their brains the signal that it is still wake time (remember, melatonin release is triggered by darkness). A double whammy for the impact of phones on teen sleep. We cover social media in Chapter 16: #Social Media and Technology, but when thinking about sleep and teens the number one rule is 'no phones in bedrooms after bedtime'. If all parents stuck to this one rule, a whole generation of teenagers would benefit.

Small things can make a big difference to quality of sleep

One recent study has revealed a surprising and simple answer. The study led by Adriana Galvan tracked the sleep quality of young people aged 14–18 (2018). Their brain scans after two weeks of tracking revealed greater connectivity in areas of the brain involved in self-control, emotions and reward processing for those who had slept better. A deeper investigation into environmental correlates was surprising. Those who got better sleep weren't those who had less technology in their room, less noise or a darker room – they reported greater satisfaction with their bedding and pillow. This is only one small finding, and quite what constituted a good pillow differed for individuals. Moreover, most young people in the developing world have a sufficiently comfortable pillow. However, the message is clear that good sleep is linked to good brain activity and comfort matters when it comes to sleep.

 ## What does that mean for learning?

Good sleep increases a young person's ability to enter the positive cycle of learning

We described the positive cycle of learning in Chapter 3: The Teen Brain Learns and Believes, where a teenage brain is engaged in a task and thereby brain pathways are strengthened. Poor sleep can act against the positive cycle of learning due to difficulties with sustaining attention and regulating emotions, affecting a young person's ability to cope with a challenging learning task. After a poor night's sleep brains just don't work so well and can't cope with the ups and downs of learning so well. This is true for all of us, as we are sure you know well, but may be even more true for teens given that the systems in their brain for regulating attention and emotions are still under development. Studies have consistently found that sleep duration is linked to academic achievement, so sleep is one of the first 'go-to' places to support young people's academic success.

Good sleep helps encode memories for teens

Sleep has been described as the 'glue of learning', for it is during sleep that the brain encodes recently learnt information. Matthew Walker describes sleep the night after learning as clicking the 'save' button on those newly created files. Fact-based learning that teens are required to do for school is encoded in deep sleep, typically during the early hours of sleep. Support teens to sleep and educate them about the importance of sleep for memory consolidation and learning.

High workloads eat into a teen's free time, with consequences for sleep

As a society we need to think about the high workloads young people have. Even after a full day of learning, many young people are expected to do three to five hours of work in the evening. We are not sure how we would feel if we were given another three hours of work to do after a full day in the office, but this culture is embedded in the education system of many Western societies. This not only increases stress levels and tension in family life, but it also means many young people have no time for relaxation, socialisation or following their own passions. It is quite possible that in their quest to take back time for themselves while fulfilling the demands made of them from homework, teens often stay up late into the night. Perhaps this is the only time they have to do things they love. Many people have written about the chronic lack of sleep in this generation of teens, which is likely impacting on brain development and mental health, but rather than just blaming teens themselves, we perhaps need to take a look at whether we are responsible for over-scheduling them.

So, what now?

Sufficient and regular sleep is essential for teenage brains to work well, yet too many teenagers are not getting enough. As we realise the significant impact of poor sleep on brain functioning and brain development at this crucial time in a person's life, we need to do whatever we can to help teens get more sleep. The social context has a big part to play in this problem, and being aware of the issues is important so you know when to intervene and how to support a teen to get more sleep. Remember, they are learning how to care for themselves and this will take some trial and error. Put on your teen lens to tune into their drives and follow our action points below.

Case study: Kasia

Kasia is a 16-year-old girl about to take her final school exams. She is a hardworking and conscientious girl and always has been. She prides herself in doing her work on time and loves her school books to be neat and tidy. She has always been like this and her parents have admired this quality of hers. Her teachers have always said she is a girl who is going to go far in life. 'University material' has been associated with her name since nursery school.

In the lead-up to the exams there is a lot of homework to do. In Kasia's attempt to be thorough she takes a long time to complete her work. This means that she is often up late at night. Her parents often leave her in her room as she is 'just finishing this essay' when they are exhausted, trusting that she will put her phone away and get into bed when her work is done. They often feel so relieved they don't have a teenager that wants to party and challenge them. She is just such a delightful, hardworking and conscientious girl.

However, they have noticed recently that Kasia has been complaining of headaches and stomach aches. She has always had a tendency to get migraines, but they are becoming more intense and too common an occurrence for their liking. Kasia also says that she is struggling to focus in school. There is a meeting called at school with Kasia, her parents and her teachers to discuss her progress and at that meeting Kasia is brought to tears by the simple, kind question from her teacher: 'How are you coping with the amount of work?' Kasia reveals that in a quest to get her work done to the high standard she likes she often works until 2am or 3am. Her parents are shocked. They had no idea. They all calculate that she is perhaps averaging four to five hours' sleep a night. No wonder she is getting headaches and beginning to feel tearful and anxious.

A good resolution

Kasia's parents need support from her teachers at school to assure them and Kasia that she does not need to be doing all of this homework in order to do well in school. Kasia is an able girl, and ensuring a balance between achievement, health and mental well-being is most important at this stage in her life. Kasia's teachers agree to reduce her workload. Kasia is told that under no circumstances must she work past 10pm and assured that she will not get in trouble for not completing her homework. She is helped to develop a good sleep routine to help her brain relax (bath, book, lights out). Another meeting is arranged for three weeks' time to check in and see how the plan is going and to monitor Kasia's well-being.

What might get in the way?

Parents and teachers can be so keen to ensure young people do well academically because of the doors it opens at the next stage of life that they can be reluctant to reduce workloads. We must remember that life balance is crucial, and we must not only support a teen's well-being, but also model to them how important it is to find that balance in life. Even when we are working hard towards a goal, ensuring good sleeping, eating and exercising is crucially important. Brains work better when they are rested, well-fed and exercised.

Action point: Think what might motivate them to sleep more

When it comes to sleep try to think of ways to use motivational learning to help motivate young people. Telling a young person to go to bed early in order to get better grades so they can get into a good university is not going to compete with a socially salient goal in their lives. When thinking about trying to get them to sleep earlier it might be better to ground them in things that are socially and affectively salient for them. For example, for a young person who values academic achievement but also time with their friends, helping them to see that more sleep will allow them to be more attentive and efficient with their work, thereby allowing them more time for socialising, might be more motivating. A teen who wants their skin to look smooth and fresh in the morning may notice how much better it looks after a good night's sleep. By a process of conversation, problem solving, reflection and trial and error, adults can help teens work out what works best for them.

Action point: Never go to bed on a row

Perhaps unsurprisingly, close family bonds are particularly important for adolescent sleep. Parental support acts as a safe haven or safety signal allowing the adolescent to rest and put their worries to one side. Try to ensure your teen doesn't go to bed with an unresolved row if possible, and when families are going through stressful life events a teen's sleep may well be impacted, so additional night-time support and reassurance may be warranted. Many teens still enjoy a hug at bedtime.

Action point: Be careful how you talk to your teen

Remember, teens need a new kind of interaction that is not so 'top-down' but where discussion and problem solving dominate. We can give them good boundaries (e.g. an appropriate time for bed, which we would recommend) and good sleep routines (e.g. phone downstairs, bath, then book, perhaps chat with mum or dad, then lights out), but ultimately, getting *them* motivated to get enough sleep is far more beneficial and long-serving. Problem solve with them and do some trial and error runs to help them see how they feel after more or less sleep.

Action point: Beware technology in the bedroom

Mobile phones at bedtime are a strong social draw for teens that is hard for them to resist and can be a negative factor in promoting sleep. Similarly, other electrical equipment such as a television or computer can compromise sleep. Although it may not be a popular discussion, speak with your teen who insists on having devices in the room and negotiate storing them elsewhere overnight. Having a discussion around the underlying science of inhibition of melatonin may help their motivation, but given the strong social draw of social media this is not going to be an easy win.

Action point: Try to reduce social jetlag

Teens love to stay up late at weekends, but the effect of social jetlag is far more impactful than just getting too little sleep. While staying up a bit later at weekends and holiday is probably important, try to make sure the shift in time zones from weekday to weekend is not so vast to cause problems, particularly around times of academic importance such as exam time. There is a time and place for sleepovers, but every weekend in term time, particularly around the time of academic stress, is a big no-no.

Action point: Make sure teens have a place to talk

Rumination can take over at night time, particularly for teens. Discuss this with teens and make sure teens have someone they can talk to regularly about things on their mind to reduce night-time rumination.

Action point: Remember, sleep is fundamental for good mental health

If you are really concerned about a young person's mental health (even if they are doing well academically), sleep is the first place to look for improvements. If this means reducing their workload to enable more sleep, so be it. After all, it is no use to a teenager having excellent school grades if they have a debilitating mental health problem.

The moral of the story is...

Many teenagers are not getting enough sleep. While there is a small shift in their biological clock causing them to fall asleep slightly later than children or adults, it is mostly their environment that is driving this behaviour. Given the significance of lack of sleep on young people's brain development and functioning, we need to help them manage this part of their life.

Downloads: Sleepy Teens

Sleep is a wonder-drug for the brain, and a lack of sleep is endemic among teenagers. Teen biological sleep cycles shift, but the social context is primarily responsible for teens' sleep deficit. Sufficient and regular sleep aids learning, whereas poor sleep is detrimental to well-being. Adults need to support young people to have regular and sufficient sleep to help reach their potential.

Exercise

Write down your teen's sleep pattern every day this week, including the amount of time asleep and social jetlag (i.e. shifting time zone by significant margins at weekends or holidays).

Monday

....

....

Tuesday

....

....

Wednesday

....

....

Thursday

....

....

Friday

. . . .

. . . .

Saturday

. . . .

. . . .

Sunday

. . . .

. . . .

Are there particular times when your teen worries? Do you notice that their behaviour becomes harder to manage when they are tired? Do they notice that their thoughts become negative and they ruminate at night time? Keep a diary of sleep hours and ask your teen to keep a diary of their mood, worries and thoughts. Working with them, put the diaries together and look at the patterns.

. . . .

. . . .

. . . .

. . . .

. . . .

. . . .

Does your teen have such a high workload that they have little down-time and this reduces their sleep? What could you do to help them change to find a better balance?

. . . .

. . . .

. . . .

. . . .

. . . .

When this happens...	Instead of this...	Try this...
Your teen rarely puts his light out before 1am.	You are never going to get to university if you go to sleep so late. Your school work will suffer. You will get facial spots. You have got to pass the exams well.	I can see how tempting it is to stay up late but having too little sleep really isn't healthy. How can we ensure you get to talk to your friends and get enough sleep in the week? Try getting eight hours' sleep every night for a week and let's see how differently you feel.
		Help find **internal motivations** for them to sleep more
Your teen uses her phone as her alarm clock but the social media alerts seem to ping all night.	It's too much of a fight to get her phone off her at bedtime. All her friends are on the phone – she's going to miss the chat and be left out.	It is going to be a fight to get her to leave her phone downstairs at bedtime. It is worth it to protect her brain development and mental health. I will keep talking to her about this and need to keep this boundary firm.
		Protect sleep by having **clear rules around technology** at night time
Another sleepover with your teen up all night means the next day is a wash-out. She's monosyllabic, pale and seems to doubt all that she says.	She can have sleepovers at the weekend. She can catch up on Sunday night. She's only tired, it won't kill her. Anyway, I've got to let her have some fun because she works so hard in the week.	I want her to have fun and so a sleepover every now and then is fine. Weekly sleepovers will be to her detriment and it may affect learning and well-being. I need to talk to her and make a plan when we are all in a good place and in our thinking brains.
		Try to **reduce social jetlag**

Chapter 14

Creating Healthy Habits

Long story, short

- The teenage years are important for building patterns of healthy behaviour.
- Poor nutrition may impact on brain development and cognitive skills during the teen years.
- Exercise can be beneficial for learning.
- Food preferences which emerge in adolescence may inform life-long eating practices.
- Eating disorders often emerge in adolescence and are best identified and treated early on.

Introduction

The teenage years are an important time to build good self-care habits around food and exercise

Nutrition and exercise are key environmental factors that influence brain function and behaviour. Your teenager will have observed hundreds of people's eating habits and attitude to exercising by the time they are starting to make up their own mind about their choices. As we know, modelling is a powerful form of learning, and what they see others, including you, doing will be important. Eating and exercise patterns are intimately linked with social interactions and vary by culture at home and within the wider community. What is universal is that the teenage years are an important time for building good habits to support the healthy development of their brain and body.

Teens know what they should eat to be healthy, but their eating habits often don't match

The number of children who are classed as overweight and obese increased dramatically at the latter end of the 20th century. The diets of many adolescents are often low in specific necessary food groups (particularly fruits and vegetables), deficient in nutrients (such as iron, zinc, folate, vitamin A, dietary fibre, etc.), and extremely high in fat, salt and sugar. Adolescents understand what healthy food choices are but their behaviour often does not reflect that knowledge (like many of us) or appear as if they are concerned about future health. Teenage eating habits tend towards frequent snacking, skipping meals, eating 'junk' food and infrequent intake of milk, fruit and vegetables.

Young people can get into a negative cycle of poor diet and lack of exercise which impacts on mental health

The Centers for Disease Control and Prevention in the USA suggests that adolescents should do 60 minutes or more of moderate-to-vigorous physical exercise each day. This is probably fairly easily achieved if your teenager walks, cycles to school or plays a regular sport but may be more difficult for teenagers who rely on public transport (or lifts) or who have more sedentary interests. As technology use has increased in the 21st century, exercise levels have decreased for teenagers more than any other age group, leading many to blame technology. However, although one might think it to be the case, the relationship between being sedentary and not exercising is not strong. Some teenagers do a lot of exercise but then also have a lot of sedentary activity, so we cannot blame the screens. However, what is clear is that a vicious cycle can start to emerge where poor diet and lack of exercise impact on mental health and result in unhelpful coping strategies involving poor food choices. As we talk about more in Chapter 16: #Social Media and Technology, when considering healthy choices in your teen's life, use a holistic approach.

The science bit: Brain and behaviour

Nutrition quality and cognition are linked in brain studies, including teen-specific effects

There are many studies (many from low-income countries) which show a strong link between healthy and balanced diet in the first two years of life and subsequent stronger cognitive function. Although fewer studies exist, we now have data to show that a healthier diet and exercise level in the teenage years promotes the likelihood of stronger thinking skills as adults. These studies reflect this outcome even when the impacts of maternal education, social class and home environment are ruled out.

Perhaps unsurprisingly, nutrition quality is particularly important during the teen years. Antonia Manduca and colleagues (2017) looked at the effect of nutritional depletion during the adolescent years in mice. They fed the mice a balanced diet until early adolescence, when some of the sample were given a diet lacking omega-3 polyunsaturated fatty acids, enabling them to look specifically at the effect of the dietary change during the teen years. Mice who lacked omega-3 showed brain changes in both the emotional brain and thinking brain and also were found to have increased anxiety-like behaviour and worse performance on a memory task. This effect lasted into adulthood and was thought to be due to the low-quality diet impairing the brain's ability to fine-tune connections between neurones in these regions. Of course, we cannot completely generalise from maturing mice brains to human brains, but fish intake (high in omega-3) and cognitive performance were associated in a large study of Swedish male adolescents. Moreover, at least one study in human teenagers found evidence that several nutritional factors, such as increased fast food consumption, low vegetable intake and missing meals, result in lower verbal skills during adulthood. Such studies were designed to rule out the genetic effects.

Breakfast impacts on attention, behaviour and academic performance

It not only matters what they eat, it matters *when* teens eat. Breakfast is often described as the 'most important meal of the day' and there is some science behind that. Studies have shown it has an immediate positive effect on memory and concentration in young people and gives them energy to study, play sport and pursue their passions. Despite this, breakfast is the most commonly missed meal in the day. Those who tend to miss breakfast are often from socio-economically poorer homes. When many studies were systematically assessed by Katie Adolphus and her team in the UK (2016), the evidence showed a positive effect of eating breakfast in students in the classroom. Data showed that regularly eating breakfast at home or in school-based programmes with sufficient variety (including enough energy) had a positive effect on young people's academic performance and behaviour in the classroom. The clearest effects of not eating breakfast were found to be poorer performance in mathematics and arithmetic, which require high levels of concentration and executive function.

Structured and varied extracurricular activity is associated with learning

There is compelling evidence for the positive effect of physical activity on brain function and cognition at all ages. Irene Esteban-Cornejo and colleagues (2015) focused on extracurricular physical activity in teens and found that the structure and number of extracurricular activities were related to cognitive performance. Specifically, their study suggested that adolescents who participated in multiple extracurricular activities had better cognitive performance than those who engaged in a single organised activity or none at all. The exact mechanism by which physical activity impacts on brain functioning long-term and mental health is unclear but it does give food for thought. How much is enough for each teenager though will be dependent on many factors – there is unlikely to be a 'one size fits all' rule.

 ## Translating your teen

With a focus on self-identity, many teens are interested in their body shape

A teenager's body shape (and body image) undergoes big changes. Young people of all genders can feel pressure from peers to look a certain way, which might affect the foods a teenager chooses to eat. With a key development task of the teen years being to focus on self-identity, this is perhaps not surprising. Remember that teens are programmed to spend time working out who they are and how they fit in, and a part of this will be having a fresh look at their body shape. It is normal for young people to have a period of focusing on their body, as is shown in the case study of Hanifa below, but this focus also makes it a time when some teenagers are vulnerable to developing an eating disorder.

A few can develop an eating disorder during the teen years

The peak time of onset for an eating disorder is during adolescence, which can present in several ways. These are scary experiences for the young person with the condition, as well as for their family. People with an eating disorder experience extreme disturbance in their eating behaviour and related thoughts and feelings. They may also significantly increase their level of physical activity. They can have an overwhelming drive to be thin and a morbid fear of gaining weight and losing control over their eating. Eating disorders can be an expression of underlying psychological distress and if it takes hold can also cause serious physical and psychological problems. They often run in families, and some, such as anorexia nervosa, have a strong genetic element, whereas other conditions such as bulimia nervosa and binge eating disorder appear to have stronger influences from experience and the individual's environment. Eating disorders can be effectively treated, and the earlier the treatment is started, the better the likelihood of recovery. As we discuss again and again in this book, always look at behaviour as the tip of the iceberg. What is going on underneath that is causing the young person's distress? If you can manage the underlying worry, they can drop the behaviour.

Teens respond when we ask not tell

As we explored in Chapter 12: Ready to Launch (with Your Support), if we want to change teen behaviour we cannot just *tell* teens what to do. They have an inherent need for status and respect and are driven to find things out for themselves. Psychologists Samia Addis and

Simon Murphy carried out a study of how Welsh high school students perceived new menus and the implications for eating at lunchtime (2019). The study highlighted the importance of the 'meaning' of food for teenagers. Student preference was for portable and snack-style foods and they rejected the idea of a 'main meal', as it reminded them of eating at home. For them lunchtime represented a space where they could relax and be with their friends and, in this context, the top-down approaches to menu planning were seen as them having little opportunity for negotiation. When thinking about influencing teen behaviour it is crucial that we are aware of their need for autonomy and independence and ask them, don't tell them.

Young people may make more emotional food choices

An interesting 2018 study of young adult participants from Scotland and Australia by Eloise Howse and colleagues showed that teens have greater emotional connections with food than adults or children, such as enjoyment and nostalgia. Another important factor in understanding food choices was the balance between time and money. Choices were influenced by how much appeal food had, which is likely influenced by social media and advertising. Feelings related to ethical issues (e.g. veganism associated with animal welfare) and moral dimensions (e.g. boycotting foods from multi-national companies) also played a role. While we may think of food as being a bodily need that requires a rational approach, to teenagers emotions and meaning may play a much larger role.

There are motivators and barriers to exercising in teens

When it comes to exercise, motivational drives play a key role. A 2018 study by Antonio López-Castedo and colleagues found the motivational predictors for exercising in teens were competition, social recognition, challenge, muscular strength and positive health. Barriers included fatigue, body image or physical-social anxiety and lack of time. Unfortunately, teasing and bullying about weight, poor body image and low self-esteem can lead to lower levels of exercise. This illustrates the social vulnerability of young people and how lifestyle-choice decisions can be complicated for teens.

What does that mean day to day?

Eating together as a family has a positive effect on teen mental health and well-being

Studies have consistently found that simply eating meals as a family, particularly dinner, is associated with improved diet and mental health in young people. The positive effect extends to behaviour, emotional well-being in young people and more trusting relationships. This finding holds regardless of gender, age, family affluence or, perhaps surprisingly, level of family functioning. The key factor is not how easily a teen can talk to their parents; in any case, regular meals seem to offer learning opportunities and protection for teen well-being.

Making good food choices alongside teens really matters

Family influence tends to diminish in adolescence and compete with pressure from friends, as teens are influenced by their peers and start to purchase and consume food away from home. However, studies have found that the family context has a key influence on teens' diets and that eating behaviours are greatly influenced and developed by their family's preferences and habits. In a Canadian study by Raewyn Bassett and colleagues (2008), teens from a broad range of ethnic backgrounds often took responsibility and reflected on their behaviours while keeping in mind their parents' advice, even if in some cases they were as yet unable to act upon it. This suggests that food choice is co-constructed by both teens and their parents as each resist and respond to the other.

Modelling behaviour is the most powerful form of learning

We know the power of modelling in relationships, and self-care is no exception. As we also learnt in Chapter 12: Ready to Launch (with Your Support), behaviour that is modelled and held in high esteem will be highly sought after by teens due to their drive for prestige and status in a culture. Consider the messages given to teens about body shape, food and exercise. Do you model to them the importance of regular exercise to keep bodies healthy? Do you show guilt when you eat food that is unhealthy and say, 'I'm going to get so fat!', or do you emphasise the importance of healthy eating choices regardless of body shape? *Sesame Street* coined the terms 'sometimes food' and 'always food', which is a nice way to take the guilt out of eating certain foods while still communicating that there are different food types. Our behaviour and emotional reactions around teens in relation to food and exercise matter and can affect their life-long behavioural patterns.

Stay out of conflict and encourage them to read their own body's signs

It is wise to stay out of conflict in these areas of life such as diet and exercise where the teen ultimately has the power. It is better to model good behaviour and encourage self-reflection. Heavy-handed instructions about what and when your teen should eat and how much exercise they do are likely to backfire at a time in their lives when they are driven to start to make their own decisions. As with sleep and social media, encourage self-reflection. Establish a broad boundary (e.g. you need to do some exercise every week) but allow them choice and autonomy within that. Ask your teen to pay attention to cues that their body sends that they are hungry, tired or need an exercise break. Be curious about how they feel after eating certain foods or exercising and, with open discussion, self-regulation can begin. It is much healthier to do this than to focus on external cues such as clocks, rules, reading some crazy tips online or focusing on other people's body shapes.

Offer opportunities to young adults to develop brain circuits before they leave home

The first year at university in particular has been associated with poor eating practices and weight gain. Time limitations can be a barrier for young adults in making healthier food decisions, and young adults are aggressively targeted for advertising of junk foods via social media. Moreover, young adults are managing budgets for the first time, presenting new and sometimes irresistible choices. Making sure teens get to do some of this learning when they are still at home can be so valuable, such as giving them a budget and asking them to cook a family meal one night. Remember, our brains learn through repetition, and the first time we do anything is probably not going to go so well.

What does that mean for learning?

Brains need food and exercise to support learning

Brains need regular meals and exercise; breakfast is particularly important for supporting teenagers to function well throughout their day and for brain development. Learning is much more effective when a brain is fed and watered and the vascular system is well cared for through exercise. Remember that the brain is built to protect us, and if the brain registers excessive hunger, it is much harder to enter the positive cycle of learning. There will be individual differences, but encourage teens to tune into their own body. Do they focus better when they've eaten or had a stretch or a walk? Do they manage their emotions better after exercise or food? The answer is highly likely to be yes.

Be curious if young people are not eating or resisting exercise

If young people are resisting food or exercise at school, consider what this might mean to them. We know there are emotional factors that impact on food choice and social anxiety on exercise. If you can work out the meaning to them and help them solve that problem, eating and taking part in physical activity can resume.

So, what now?

The teen years are a great opportunity to learn self-care in the form of good diet and exercise habits. Understanding how the teenage brain works can help us know how best to support this, bearing in mind the teen's drives and motivations.

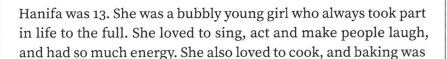

Case study: Hanifa

Hanifa was 13. She was a bubbly young girl who always took part in life to the full. She loved to sing, act and make people laugh, and had so much energy. She also loved to cook, and baking was one of her favourite pastimes as a young girl. Hanifa ate healthily but had always been on the larger side physically compared to her peers. Her body shape had never limited her physical activity and she enjoyed playing netball, swimming and being a part of the hockey team. No-one was concerned about how she looked, including Hanifa. However, at the age of 13 she and her friends began to be more interested in what they looked like and many gave up playing sports all together. There were parties to go to where many of the girls were starting to wear tightly fitting dresses. Boys and girls began to look at each other in a different way and body and shape had a whole new meaning.

Hanifa's happy-go-lucky approach to eating and food changed. She began to say no to sweet food, and sometimes when her mother called everyone for dinner she would reply, 'I'm not hungry.' Her mother's ears pricked up. This was strange behaviour. Was this the beginning of a serious mental health problem?

A good resolution

Hanifa's mother, Joan, who had a history of mild bulimia nervosa from her early 20s, for which she had received excellent treatment, decided that it was important not to overreact. She decided not to give too much attention to the behaviour. She told her daughter that even if she wasn't hungry she had to come and sit with the family for dinner. She didn't focus on making her daughter eat a certain amount but said, 'Just take a little if you aren't so hungry.' She knew that giving the avoidant behaviour too much attention might be reinforcing. She also knew the importance of maintaining a clear boundary (come and eat with the family even if you only take a little). She noticed that her daughter would always eat a little at the table and didn't go to bed hungry. A couple of days later, Hanifa and her mother were out together shopping for a new swimsuit. Joan asked gently about school and friends and asked if anything was on Hanifa's mind. Hanifa said she felt too big next to her skinny friends and wanted to try to lose weight. She had been trying to think about doing more exercise, but mostly she wanted to give it up. Joan listened, empathised about her daughter's feelings and said she would think with Hanifa about how to make their evening meals lighter in calories if this was important to her. Hanifa felt better just talking about things. She felt heard and that her mother was alongside her, taking her concerns seriously. Together the whole family found healthy alternatives to refined sugar and enjoyed making different kinds of food. Hanifa's thoughts about wanting to be thin dominated less and her eating patterns remained healthy.

What might get in the way?

As teenagers become more self-aware and self-conscious, and in a culture where thin bodies are rewarded, we might expect teens to go through a period of reflecting on their own bodies. Try not to overreact if a young person begins to adjust their eating habits, as this can reinforce the power and draw attention to the behaviour. Try to avoid commenting on whether a child has lost weight as this can be very reinforcing of the behaviour. Try not to comment if they have put on weight as this can make them feel bad about themselves. Modelling good habits with regular exercise and healthy eating choices, having clear boundaries and sharing mealtimes together are important. It is important to not ignore signs that a young person is not eating or if you notice significant weight loss. If this is ongoing or you are unable to have a helpful discussion with the young person, seek medical advice.

Action point: Model healthy habits and eat a family meal together

Your teen is watching you and that is a powerful way in which they are learning. Eating a meal together regularly seems to protect against mental health difficulties, as well as provide a good learning opportunity for your teen. Be mindful of how you behave around food and towards exercise because your teen may well copy you.

Action point: Have boundaries but don't tell them what to do

By the teen years you are past the point of being able to tell your teen what to do and food and exercise are dangerous areas to come into conflict about as they have all the power. Model good habits and support good choices while helping them to tune into their own body signs. Some clear boundaries are important. For example, say they have to sit with you at dinner but don't tell them what or how much to eat. Say they have to do *some* form of physical exertion, but don't tell them when and how, as that is likely to backfire. As they grow up their preferences may change and that is their prerogative. Appeal to their need for respect and autonomous choices. If concerns are ongoing, seek medical advice.

Action point: Tap into your teen's motivations to help with self-care

Use whatever interests your teenager has to help them learn self-care. If they are interested in science, use a scientific approach ('what vitamins and minerals do you need?') to discussing their preferences with food. If aesthetics are important, tread carefully and keep away from making any judgement about their body.

Action point: Give them opportunities to build helpful brain circuits

Use the teen years, before they leave home, to encourage your teen to learn about and develop good habits. There is good evidence that revision of food labels helps to encourage healthy eating. Help them to understand why we eat fibre, carbohydrates and healthy fats. Talk about 'energy in and energy out' so they understand the relationship. Give them opportunities to buy food and cook for you at home and make it fun. You are building important circuits. It is important to teens to feel respected and that they are making their own choices.

Action point: Listen and discuss, don't tell them what to do

If your teen is behaving strangely around food or making excuses about doing exercise, be curious. They are emotional creatures who are self-conscious and in need of peer integration, which can be complicated. If you can find out what is underneath their behaviour, you stand a much better chance of changing it.

Action point: Help them see their brains need food and exercise to learn

Remember, brains need fuel, particularly breakfast. If there is one meal that you should encourage your teen to have regularly, it is breakfast. Encourage them to take an interest in the effects of food and exercise so that they see the benefits to their attention, focus and brain functioning. If self-study, such as homework, is not going well, consider whether they need food or an exercise break. It can make all the difference.

Downloads: Creating Healthy Habits

The teenage years are an important time for establishing healthy routines including good eating and regular exercise habits. Poor nutrition can impact on brain development and cognitive skills. Similarly, exercise is highly beneficial for learning. Disrupted eating patterns can emerge in adolescence, so getting it right at this time is likely to protect against future difficulties. As always, your behaviour sets the tone for the teens in your life, so ensure you model behaviour that establishes healthy diet and lifestyle choices.

Exercise
Where is your teen excelling at looking after themselves? Find three areas.

Area 1

. . . .

. . . .

Area 2

. . . .

. . . .

Area 3

. . . .

. . . .

Note down any self-care habits that concern you about your teen. Can you find a time to talk to them about what you notice? Keep the focus on habits rather than personal comments – remember, a teen's self-identity can be influenced by your thoughts.

. . . .

. . . .

. . . .

. . . .

. . . .

. . . .

. . . .

Are there meals your teen avoids regularly or food choices that have changed? What can you do in the home or school setting to model regular healthy eating habits?

. . . .

. . . .

. . . .

. . . .

. . . .

. . . .

. . . .

Does your teen get regular exercise and have a positive body image? If they are not exercising regularly, why is that ? Note down three barriers to exercise. Could you change these?

Barrier 1

. . . .

. . . .

Barrier 2

. . . .

. . . .

Barrier 3

. . . .

. . . .

When this happens...	Instead of this...	Try this...
Your teen is avoiding PE lessons and has stopped her gymnastics class after school.	I know I don't exercise, but I was never built for that, but my daughter really needs to get up and do something or she will never lose that puppy fat.	Exercise has always been hard for me but I need to model some form of exercise if I am to expect my daughter to learn how important fitness is in life. We'll start with a regular evening walk with the dog.
		Model good habit-forming behaviour
The teens in your year group have started a habit of eating the carbs but leaving the vegetables.	You are not leaving the lunch hall until you have eaten all those greens on your plate.	Those greens are full of goodness. It would be great to see you eat at least some of them before you leave the table – either have the broccoli or the cabbage.
		Have boundaries but offer choices where you can
Over the past six months your daughter has started to avoid meals with the family and exercise every evening. She has steadily lost weight and her behaviour seems extreme.	You feel terrified and start to lay down firm boundaries about finishing meals and banning her from exercise.	Your daughter's behaviour is scary but going in too strong with rigid rules may alienate her. Make an appointment with your doctor to get advice this week.
		If you are concerned about your teen's habits, ask for help

Chapter 15

Good Stress, Bad Stress

Long story, short

- Stress is helpful energy that boosts performance, although excess is damaging.
- Short-term stress can be managed, but long-term and excess stress can have major consequences.
- The teenage brain shows an enhanced stress response, which offers potential benefits and vulnerabilities.
- Promoting a stress-is-enhancing mindset affects the brain's reaction to stress, building resilience.
- Stress is going to be a part of every teenager's life – you cannot fully protect them from it.
- Social support from another person is an excellent way of reducing stress.
- Threat-based learning environments reduce thinking and the positive cycle of learning.

Introduction

How stress got a bad name
The word 'stress' has got a bad name. Kelly McGonigal (2015), a psychologist, has studied stress extensively and she tells the intriguing story of Hans Selye, a Hungarian endocrinologist who was trying to

study the effect of hormones on the body in the 1930s. Before going further, a note of warning that this is a rather cruel animal experiment. If you find these types of experiments upsetting, perhaps skip the following paragraph.

Hans subjected rats to injections of hormones and found they had a significant effect on their well-being and even their life expectancy due to damaging their immune system. This seemed to support his hypothesis that hormones damage the immune system in animals. However, he just needed to check that the damage was specifically due to the hormones. To do this he also had a 'control' condition where he injected other substances such as salt water into other rats that contained no toxins. To his surprise he found the salt water had the same effect on the immune system and well-being of the rats, causing significant damage. Taking it further, he subjected them to other non-invasive but potentially distressing events such as extreme noise and forced exercise over time. Again the effect on the rats was the same as the hormone injection – they became unwell, their immune system stopped working properly and their lives were cut short. He concluded that it was the general exposure to high levels of 'stress' that had caused the symptoms in the rats. This is where the term 'stress' was coined, which has lived on today.

Redefining stress as helpful energy that aids performance

Kelly McGonigal points out that the problem is how Selye defined stress. Rather than defining it as a response to an extreme and persistent environment, which would describe the living conditions of the rats he was working with, he said stress was the 'response of the body to any demands made on it'. But this is misleading. While extreme exposure to harsh environments absolutely can damage the body (see below), our bodies and brains thrive when demands are made on them as those demands are translated into an important form of energy that we can use to help us focus and perform. It's better to think of this energy as 'arousal', as shown in Figure 15.1. According to this model, performance is directly related to the degree of arousal (aka 'stress'). Too little and a young person performs weakly due to a lack of energy. Too much and performance is impaired. But you will notice that optimal performance is at its peak with optimal arousal. Strong performance is not about having *no* arousal (or no stress). A degree of arousal or 'stress' is helpful.

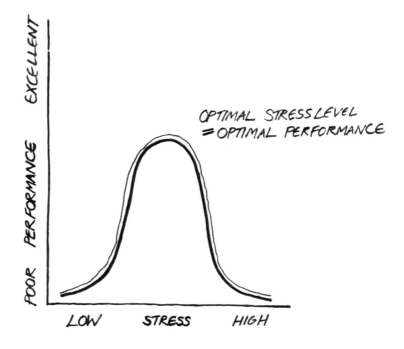

Figure 15.1: A certain amount of arousal ('stress') is needed for optimal performance

The science bit: Brain and behaviour

Long-term high levels of stress are bad and stress response is enhanced in teens

Selye's research was important in showing the impact of extreme levels of stress on the immune system and mental and physical health. As most people know, the impact of extreme stress on humans is similar to that seen in animals. Too much cortisol (a stress hormone released in the brain in extreme conditions) is bad for everyone's brain. More concerning, for our purposes, the hormonal stress response is greater and lasts longer (45–60 minutes longer) in teenage brains than the brains of children or adults, suggesting that the teenage brain has an enhanced stress response. Quite what this means is open to inter-pretation. It could be that we have evolved to have a greater stress response in the teen years to provide greater energy to cope with the stresses of this time. However, chronic excess stress has a negative impact on growth and development, increasing vulnerability to slow brain growth, poor memory functioning and other effects of chronic stress on well-being. There is even early evidence linking aspects of stress-induced brain changes to depression in teenagers, which could be related to early vulnerabilities, but it is concerning.

Maybe we can improve stress without reducing stress – the power of mindset

Mindset research (see Chapter 3: The Teen Brain Learns and Believes) is also highly relevant to the area of stress. A research study carried out in the USA by Abiola Keller and colleagues (2012) tracked 30,000 adults for 80 years. Participants were asked to rate how much stress they had experienced and whether they believed that stress was harmful to their health. People who reported experiencing a lot of stress in the year had a 43 per cent increased risk of premature death. But that was only true for those who *believed stress was harmful*. Those who believed stress was not harmful were the least likely to die young, even if they had a stressful life. The authors interpret this as showing that 'an individual's perception of health plays an important role in determining health outcomes' (p.682). Maybe we just need to help our teens change their minds about how they see stress.

Optimal stress is linked to a hormone response that helps people thrive under stress

Just to look more closely at the impact of stress on brain growth, con-sider the following. There are two stress hormones released by our adrenal glands during stress: cortisol helps turn sugar and fat into en-ergy and improves the ability of your body and brain to use that energy; DHEA (dehydroepiandrosterone) helps your brain grow stronger from stressful experiences by speeding up repair and enhancing immune function. Both hormones are needed, but the ratio of how much is released is important in determining whether the experience is mainly negative or builds resilience. Higher levels of cortisol over time are associated with impaired immune function. Higher levels of DHEA have been linked to a reduced risk of anxiety, neurodegeneration and other diseases. The ratio of DHEA to cortisol is called the growth index of a stress response. A higher growth index helps people thrive under stress and has been shown to predict academic persistence, resilience, etc.

Promoting a 'stress-is-enhancing' mindset promotes a positive response to stress

Alia Crum and colleagues at Stanford University carried out experiments to look at the effect of a stress mindset on the brain's growth index of stress response (2013, 2017). People were hooked up to a machine measuring signs of stress (blood pressure, sweating, checking saliva for stress hormones). They were then given a mock interview. They were told one of two messages. The first group was told: 'Most people think that stress is negative but actually research shows that stress is enhancing.' The interview went on to talk about how stress can improve performance, enhance well-being and help you grow. The other group was told: 'Most people know that stress is negative but research shows that stress is even more debilitating than you expect.' The interview expanded by saying how stress can weaken health, happiness and performance. The intervention had no impact on cortisol, which rose during the interview for both groups, but those who were given the stress-is-enhancing video released more DHEA and had a higher growth index than those who were given the stress-is-debilitating talk. This is again evidence of the power of the mind in determining stress response even at the body level. Mindsets are like filters through which we see things. What we believe, expect and think about stress affects whether stress is enhancing and beneficial and can lead us to develop resilience.

Relationships are the greatest buffers against stress

A series of studies by psychologist Jim Coan and colleagues in the USA (2006, 2015) have shown that the most efficient way we have of regulating stress is being with other people. In their seminal study, participants' brains were scanned in an MRI machine and an electrode attached to their foot. The electrode could and would at times administer an electric shock that by all accounts was painful. There were two conditions. The participants either saw a red circle flash up on the screen which signalled that no shock would come – the safe condition. Or they saw a blue cross flash up on the screen which signalled that there was a 20 per cent chance they would receive a shock. As one might anticipate, when participants saw the blue cross the fear centres in their brain (the lower brain system called the amygdala) lit up. They were scared. This was to be expected. Then a clever adjustment was made. A person with a close relationship to the participant (their partner, for example) was asked to sit and hold the participant's hand during the experiment. In this condition, the participants' amygdala lit up significantly less, indicating reduced stress response. The interpretation is that social support from another person during times of excess stress can substantially reduce the perceived threat. It is important that, at the brain level, the difference between the 'hand holding' and 'alone' conditions wasn't to the degree at which the person regulated their emotions. The difference was that the reaction of the feeling brain (the amygdala) was reduced as if the threat was reduced by the presence of another person.

Many other paradigms have confirmed this finding that the presence of a familiar other person is a stress-reducing resource, helping the environment appear less intimidating and alarming. For example, when standing at the bottom of a steep hill, the hill literally appears less steep when standing next to a friend. Life is easier with a little help from our friends.

We use other people's brains as stress-reducing resources

The implication is that we have evolved to use other people's brains as stress-reducing resources, which helps to shape our perception of risk and threat in a situation. This allows us to economise our own brain resources and exert less effort towards the outside environment. Jim Coan and colleagues argue that having a social resource at our side is the *baseline* assumption of the brain. It is in this situation that the brain is at rest. When that assumption is violated and a person is alone, additional energy is required to function in the world.

Translating your teen

Teens need demands made on them for optimal performance

We learnt in the early chapters of this book that the brain grows in response to the environment and experience. We are also learning that the feeling of mild to moderate stress in the form of demands on a teenager, such as you might feel before getting up to give a speech, can be used as a valuable source of energy. Teens will thrive in a challenging but supportive learning environment where they will be energised to focus and perform, making the most of the enormous potential of their brains. Getting the balance right is essential, but taking away all demands will lead to low performance and brain growth.

Chronic, heightened stress can be highly damaging for their brain growth

Too many demands cause excess chronic and sustained 'stress' and stop a teenage brain's ability to develop, as well as impacting on their immune system, well-being and even mental health. Teens may be more susceptible to chronic stress than either children or adults, making it a crucial time to get this right.

The way a teen perceives stress is an important determinant of their brain's response

You need to be careful about when and how you use the term 'stress' and what mindset you reinforce about stress. If you reinforce a 'stress-is-debilitating' mindset you risk triggering a lower stress index in your teen's brain, which is linked to damage, not resilience. If you reinforce a 'stress-is-enhancing' mindset, by saying that stress can improve performance and help them grow, the body is more likely to respond accordingly, meaning the brain can grow.

You are the most stress-reducing resource in a teen's life

And finally, you need to remember that you are the greatest source of stress reduction you have in your toolkit. Coming alongside your teen when they are stressed will be registered by their brain, which will literally use your brain to reduce their experience of stress. Without saying or doing anything, they will be able to use you as a resource to help them feel better and face the challenges of teenage life.

What does that mean day to day?

For adolescents, social cues and inputs are potentially highly stressful

As we have been learning, the social world is highly important for teenagers. Just being watched by peers increases cortisol levels. During this stage of life young people show increasing neural sensitivity to social cues and social inputs are highly valued. This is a normative shift but creates a developmental context of risk for emerging emotional difficulties. Just as being valued among peers is an enormous boost at this age, the intensity of a humiliation or a social slight at this age can be crushing.

What you say can calm their threat response

If your teen says 'I'm stressed', think carefully about how to respond. Remember the three regulatory systems we discussed in Chapter 2: The Teen Brain Thinks and Feels. If we think stress is harmful, our threat system will dominate, which will draw lower brain functioning and prevent us from being able to think clearly. Try not to just say 'Calm down', which neither empathises nor helps them know what to do. Take time to talk with your teen. Be curious about what they are experiencing and then tell them that their heart pounding is preparing them for action and them breathing more quickly is the body allowing more oxygen into their body. Help them hold a more balanced view of stress – to fear it less, trust they can handle it and use it as a resource for engaging with challenging aspects of life.

Teens are not meant to cope alone

Ask any teenager what they find stressful in their lives and nearly all would say academic work, but as we have seen, there are many potential sources of stress in a teen's life – they are working out their self-identity, they feel things more intensely than others and they are programmed to stand up to adults and question the accepted norm. Brain science is showing us that teens are not meant to cope alone. They need key adults in their life as an important stress-reducing resource. As you read this book you will find tips for how to decode teen behaviour and what to do when emotions rise and everyone is on edge. It's worth working hard to get this right so your teen has your brain resource to tap into at times of stress.

What does that mean for learning?

Mice cannot learn when there is a threatening presence

In a study, mice were given a learning task in different conditions and the speed of learning and number of errors recorded. There were three conditions of the study: the mice were at home, in an unfamiliar chamber or with a cat outside the cage, looking in. The cage was see-through! As expected, the mice learnt the most when at home where the situation was familiar and presumably their lower brain systems were calm and relaxed. When in an unfamiliar chamber they learnt slightly less, but the shocking result was the effect on learning of the presence of a cat, a threatening presence to any mouse. Not only did they stop learning, but they made significantly more errors. Moreover, the effects were shown in the memory centre of the mice (the hippocampus) where the usual connection of neurones and cell changes associated with learning were absent. As with any animal research, we have to be a little cautious in extrapolating from this research to humans, but it does suggest that learning is likely to be impaired in a stressful learning environment.

Figure 15.2: Stressed mice can't learn

Threat-based learning environments are unlikely to reap rewards and may have undesired side-effects

Many adults reading this book might have memories of adults purposefully causing stress or punishment in a learning situation when they were children – this unfortunately even continues to happen today in some places. This punishing style of education is outdated and the vast majority of teachers today understand that making children frightened is no way to get the best out of their brains. The negative presence of an adult in any learning environment may have the effect of triggering a threat-based brain response, blocking access to thinking and learning and reducing the likelihood of them entering the positive cycle of learning. However, threat can be a motivator to act, not as a positive driving force, but as a safety-seeking, protective response. For example, 'scary' teachers can sometimes produce good grades in students. How can this be? In this case, the drive to work hard and focus comes from a place of stress and anxiety.

Research by Paul Gilbert and colleagues (2007) found that when we strive to do well because we fear failure or inferiority, this is often associated with depression, anxiety and stress symptoms. Although the association between learning efficiency and stress is yet to be explored directly in teens, which parent or teacher wants to be the first one to try it when we know that reward-based learning and safe learning environments, which make people feel efficacious and confident, work so effectively?

Academic achievement can be a source of excess stress for teenagers

As teens get ready to leave school, with career choices looming and increasing pressures on young people to achieve highly, school work can cause a stress storm in a teen's life. Who on earth would schedule crucial exams at *exactly* that point when a teenager's brain is undergoing radical changes with heightened sensitivity? Worldwide educational systems, that's who! As a key adult in a teen life, you are always walking the line of providing an environment with enough challenge to motivate your teen but not so much that it overwhelms them. It is not easy and every young person is different, but we hope you will find some tips for how to get this right in this book.

Teens need adults around them who believe in them and have high expectations of them. In one study students who were given notes on an essay in either a 'wise' tone ('I'm giving you these comments because I have very high expectations and I know that you can reach them') as compared to a neutral tone ('I'm giving you these comments so that you'll have feedback on your paper') were more than 50 per cent more likely to review and improve their essay. Moreover, over a year later there were significantly fewer discipline problems for that same group of students.* Changing a few words can impact significantly on the *message* received by adolescents and they will look for clues as to whether you believe they can do it. Stretch them to push the boundaries of their learning to make the most of their incredible brains.

So, what now?

Teenage brains are ready for action but they need adults to monitor the degree of stress they are under. Encourage them to interpret signals from their body and come alongside them when it feels too much. They are not built to cope alone.

Case study: Hanu

Hanu was a 16-year-old with aspirations to become a nurse who had important public exams coming up. His school held 'mock' exams a few months earlier as a dry run for the students. Hanu had turned down his parents' offer of help or advice. His elder

---

*   It should be noted that there was a difference in the findings from this study according to the race of the individuals who took part. The effect was highly significant for African American students, who the authors say are likely to have experienced disrespect or negative stereotypes and was not evident for white students in their study. This needs to be unpicked in future research but highlights what we know about adolescents, which is that there is enormous individual variability and we need to understand each individual student's history and experience to really know how they will respond in any given situation.

sister had done well and she seemed to do it on her own and he was predicted good grades. As the exams approached he began to show some minor signs of stress like having trouble getting to sleep and being irritable with his parents. He said the exams went 'OK' but he didn't reach the pass mark on a biology paper. This was concerning as he needed to pass biology. Moreover, the marks were publicly displayed in the school hall, comparing him to his peers. The day he found out he was devastated and left the school premises without telling anyone or signing out. His parents got a call to say he hadn't come to afternoon registration and his teacher mentioned his results. He was missing for a few hours, wasn't answering his phone and everyone was very concerned. Hanu came home seemingly in a foul mood. He was rude to his parents, ran upstairs and slammed his door.

Hanu's parents were worried and at this point pretty angry. His father felt fed up with what he saw as his son's lack of effort in his schoolwork and his mother was more annoyed that he had left school without telling anyone, leaving her to worry about his safety. This was a time of possible explosion in the household, but his parents realised that it would be more beneficial in the long run to take a step back and think it through.

A good resolution

Hanu's parents took the time to read the clues in his behaviour. While his behaviour suggested anger, they tried to work out what was *really* going on. His mother went up to his room, knocked on the door and sat beside him on his bed, where he was lying with his face down. She gently rubbed his back and said she could see he was struggling. She reassured him that, whatever had happened, it would be OK and said she was ready to listen when he wanted to talk about it and offered to make him a hot chocolate. Reluctantly he came downstairs, and as he felt calmer he began to talk it through, cried a little and revealed his devastation at his mark and more importantly the public humiliation he had felt in front of his classmates. Though tempted to jump in with revision strategies and offer to do a timetable for next time, she knew that metaphorically 'holding his hand' would go a long way to getting him back on an even keel. They cooked dinner together and agreed they would make some positive plans the next day.

In the coming days, Hanu told his parents that his time management had fallen apart in the exam. He had felt overwhelmed with stress and just couldn't think. It was important to reinforce a stress-enhancing mindset with Hanu, reminding him of the positive value of stress in energising the mind and body. They discussed more appropriate ways to manage strong feelings of upset and anger. Disappearing and being rude were not acceptable. They helped him tune into early warning signs of being overwhelmed and made an action plan for how he would manage next time, including reaching out to a trusted adult.

What might get in the way?

Hanu's father had found himself in a career that wasn't his first choice. He saw something of himself in Hanu and was desperate that his son wouldn't make the same mistakes as him. This made it hard for him to control his emotions in the moment. The situation could have spiralled, and not only would their relationship have been damaged, but Hanu would have missed a learning opportunity.

Case study: Franko

Franko was 13 and loved football, his Playstation and his mum. Although a bright boy, he really hated homework and it was a battle every night. He was anxious to do well but he often got overwhelmed and the homework session would end in tears. His mother had started to dread coming home from work. Her heart really went out to him and she knew he was a sensitive boy. He hated getting in trouble with his teachers and so would beg his mother to help with his homework so that he got a good grade. Anxiety often kept him up at night, so he was often tired. His mother wanted to do the best for her son and so helped him and he kept doing well and never missed a homework hand-in.

There had been a few times when he had left his homework at home but he would call his mother and she would jump in the car and take it in, so he never got in trouble. However, gradually over time a pattern emerged where she was taking over his homework more and more.

One week, when Franko was really tired, he realised that he had to finish a long essay that night. He had forgotten! In desperation his mother told him to go to bed and she did it for him. The essay was about the First World War, a topic his mother had studied at college, and she got quite carried away and really enjoyed writing it. A few days later Franko's teacher told the class she was so impressed with Franko's work she would really like him to come to the front of the class and talk about what he had written. Franko froze. He didn't know what he had written because *he hadn't written it.* He broke down and the truth came out.

A good resolution

Franko's mother and teacher had a meeting. His mother admitted that in order to relieve her son of some of his stress she had been increasingly doing more of his homework. It was agreed that this was with the best intention. She also realised she wasn't helping him. By doing his homework and taking things into school when he forgot them, she wasn't helping her son to experience the natural consequences of life and he wasn't developing resilience to the harder parts of life. She also realised she had to do something more about his anxiety. It wasn't going to just go away, so she bought a couple of really good self-help books to help her and Franko understand how his thoughts were tricking him into believing that terrible things might happen if he, for example, didn't hand in his homework or got a lower grade than usual. They committed to working through the anxiety books for a couple of months and if it didn't improve they would get some professional help. Franko took responsibility for his homework and his mother stepped back, sitting with him and encouraging him but not taking over. His teacher checked in with Franko to see how his homework was going and reassured him that he just needed to do his best. When he did forget his homework there was a small consequence, as every student got, but Franko survived it and became more resilient to things not always going right.

What might get in the way?

Franko's mother may have struggled to step back and allow her son to do his homework himself. Parents can sometimes hold anxiety about how well their child will perform at school and find it hard to let their child 'fail'. Allowing children to experience natural consequences is so important for them to learn about life and to learn that it's OK to not always do well, be the best or behave perfectly. In fact, a childhood with no struggles can cause problems later in life. So parents, step back, offer support where needed and teach your child that life can be tough but they can survive.

Action point: Help young people see stress as a form of energy they can use to their advantage

Our mindset about stress predicts how we 'read' stress signals in the body and even how our body reacts to stress. The language we use around young people can be important to help them make a positive interpretation of their experience.

Action point: Support calm, optimal-stress learning environments

Do what you can to reduce the level of threat and emotion for a teen who is studying or learning. Their brain functions best when the lower brain is calm, enabling them to enter the positive cycle of learning. Don't be afraid to invite an extending learning task. It will be a little bit stressful and that's OK.

Action point: Use your relationship to buffer against excess stress

Brain research suggests that teens use social proximity and connectedness to another person to reduce stress reactions. Their brains cope more effectively with a supportive adult alongside, so don't abandon them in their hour of need. If they are rude tell them they can't speak to you like that and be curious about why. Look underneath the behaviour. What's *really* going on?

Action point: Protect against social stress

Social sensitivity during the teen years increases the potential stress of a social slight and the damage of social isolation. Try to remember the teen developmental tasks, take their perspective and offer support while also working hard to support social integration at this time.

Action point: Ensure young people are not exposed to chronic stress

Teens' brains are particularly susceptible to stress, potentially affecting their immune responses, well-being and brain development. If there is any time during development when we need to ensure young people are protected from chronic stress, it is during the teenage years.

Downloads: Good Stress, Bad Stress

Getting just the right amount of stress is important. It can provide energy that aids performance, although too much is damaging and is likely to impact negatively on their learning. Short-term stress can be managed, but long-term stress is usually detrimental.

Stress is part of every teenager's life, but how they understand it and how adults around them support stressed teens makes a difference to how they respond. Having a growth mindset about stress helps teens use stress as a useful energy resource.

Exercise

Note down three situations that your teen finds excessively stressful.

Situation 1

. . . .

. . . .

Situation 2

. . . .

. . . .

Situation 3

. . . .

. . . .

What could you do or say to help your teen read the body signals of high arousal as a form of energy?

. . . .

. . . .

. . . .

. . . .

. . . .

. . . .

How can you come alongside your teen in times of stress?

. . . .

. . . .

. . . .

. . . .

. . . .

. . . .

. . . .

When this happens...	Instead of this...	Try this...
Your teen is applying for an academic scholarship at a prestigious school. She is conscientious and very aware of the financial benefits of getting it. Money is tight in the family. She hasn't been out to see her friends for a month.	Life is competitive. She needs to learn to cope with pressure. I did and that's what made me who I am today.	She is young and her brain is particularly susceptible to excess stress. While it's important for her to take on challenges, achieving this scholarship needs to be put in perspective. The financial worries of the family are not her responsibility. It's important she has a well-rounded balance of activities in her life.
		Protect against chronic stress
The school netball team need to win this match or they will lose the championship by a point. Your teen is the captain. She is tearful before the match.	Calm down. It's not that bad – the worst thing is that you will come second for goodness sake!	I can see you are very wound up about this. What is the thing that worries you the most? What can we do about that? Remember, you can use that amazing energy to help you focus your game.
		Support a growth mindset about stress
A band audition went badly wrong. Your teen is slamming doors and shouting.	Why don't you go to your room until you feel better?	Stay with me, even if you don't feel like talking, and we can watch TV together. When you feel ready we can talk it through.
		Come alongside your teen when they are stressed

Chapter 16

#Social Media and Technology

Long story, short

- Panic surrounds social media and technology use in teenagers.*
- A smartphone is often a social lifeline for a teenager.
- There is little evidence for social media *causing* mental health problems in teenagers.
- Social media use interacts with teen developmental drives, so caution is needed.
- Communication with teens about technology needs careful thought.
- Consider the overall lifestyle of a teen rather than zeroing in on their 'screen time'.
- Have clear technology boundaries within the family, and stick to them yourself.
- The engaging and playful interface can be highly motivating and can help teens enter the positive cycle of learning.

---

* Please note that throughout this chapter we have used the word 'media' to refer to both social media and technology.

Introduction

Daily News – Wednesday June 29, 1938
Too much reading is harmful *by Angelo Patri*

There's Clare with a book. Always reading. I never saw such a child for a book. Didn't she want to go to the party? I thought every child in town was there. They're going to see the picture. They are all simply wild with excitement. Isn't she well, or what? You just can't separate her from a book. She would rather read than do anything else!

There is mass panic around teens and media use

Throughout history, new inventions, particularly ones that engage young people, have been met with fear and trepidation. The above quote describes a societal fear that children who read books were missing out on developmental experiences. This now seems ridiculous to us and, indeed, parents often spend much time persuading their children to read books given the clear link between academic achievement and reading. We are facing a revolution globally in access to technology and social media, and as teens are often the early adopters of technology and the online world is a big part of their lives, many of our fears for what this means are being channelled their way. Not having grown up with technology and given the fast-changing environment in the online world, parents and teachers lack confidence in this area. What we know is that technology can amplify the positive and negative aspects of the non-virtual world.

A small percentage of young people are exposed to risks from online use

Internet use and young people's experiences online change rapidly and up-to-date surveys are needed. At the time of publication for this book, a recent survey conducted by the London School of Economics found that a small percentage of young people are exposed to risk online, but the numbers are not increasing and, moreover, not all risk results in harm. Any harm to young people is too much and needs to be eradicated and there is undoubtedly a need for tougher regulation of social media. However, we do want to offer a balanced review of the evidence for harm from social media and technology, for it allows for a more measured discussion. Technology and social media are here to stay and adults need to catch up fast and work out how to protect young people and enable them to develop resilience and strategies to cope with the negative aspects of the online world, particularly given the enormous benefits and opportunities media use offers to young people.

The science bit: Brain and behaviour

There is no consistent evidence that social media causes mental health problems in teens

Headlines will tell you that excessive technology use in this iGen of young people is *causing* an increase in mental health problems in young people today, but a critical eye on the research evidence gives a different story. Studies have found a small relationship between screen use and mental health, but large-scale studies find the effect to be tiny and certainly not large enough to have implications for policy. At the time of writing, a comprehensive review of associations between adolescent well-being showed many other factors with a larger negative association with well-being, such as bullying, smoking marijuana and not getting enough sleep or regularly eating breakfast. The nature of such associations is hard to capture in research which can produce nonsensical findings such as a greater association between eating potatoes and well-being in teens than social media use and well-being. Moreover, any association is correlational and thus cannot say anything about cause. For example, if high screen use and poor mental health are found in the same person at the same time, we don't know which came first. Only if we measured one first (high screen use) and then the other later (mental health) could we say that screen use caused mental health problems.

Some studies looking at the same person over time, which can infer cause, have found that those with mental health difficulties use social media less and others have found social media use to be a protective factor, resulting in young people having a greater sense of belonging and social support. The evidence does suggest that offline vulnerability predicts online vulnerability, suggesting that the online world can exacerbate problems in young people. Bullying is an example where the 24-hour availability of social media means young people can't escape. There are certainly challenges, but currently there is no clear evidence to support the seeming mass panic around social media and mental health in young people.

Technology has not been shown to affect brain development in teens

Despite many hundreds of studies, no convincing evidence has been published to show that technology or social media use directly affects brain development. Individual variation is the rule when it comes to brain development, and while experience shapes the brain, as you have read in Part 1 of this book, no measurable group differences have been found relating to technology use in young people. We need to take the panic out of the conversation and think carefully about what the risks of media use are to young people in the light of what we know about teenage brain development. We should also consider how our knowledge about the way the teenage brain works might enable us to put technology and social media to good use.

Media use interacts with a teen's need to integrate and find their place in the social group

Social media is a key way that teenagers connect with each other. Young people don't have the dichotomous thinking adults tend to have of having an 'online' world and an 'offline' world. Their worlds blend so that peer integration is taking place *on the phone*. As we learnt in earlier chapters, adolescence is a sensitive period for learning about and engaging with the social world and integrating with peers. There is a magnetic social pull to spend time with peers, helping us to understand why teens are attached to their phones any given chance, and why your suggestion to put their phone away can be met with a look of incredulity and comments like 'I'll die if you take my phone away'. Excusing the extreme turn of phrase, it can feel to a teenager that their world will end if you take their phone away, because their social world is on the phone and their brain is telling them that peer integration is fundamental.

The effects of social media can hurt teens

This sensitive period of development also means teens have an inherent need to belong to and be part of the group. Fear of missing out (FOMO) is something even adults are susceptible to. Remember the Cyberball game (in Chapter 5: The Teen Brain Loves Other People) that shows that the brain registers social pain the same way it registers physical pain and remember that this is more painful for teenagers. We soon see how the online world might cause greater vulnerability for teenagers. We know that social rejection online can be experienced as negatively as face-to-face rejection, and the brains of teenagers respond in a particularly salient manner to such rejection. By the same token, social acceptance is endorsed online through 'likes' and comments, forming a potent source of social rewards for teenagers, at a time when this is a fundamental need for them and when their brains are particularly sensitive to such reinforcers. Understanding this helps us to empathise with our teen who feels devastated by the relatively low number of 'likes' they have received for a picture they posted. It matters because their brain tells them it matters.

Social media can alter a teen's perception of the world

Social media can also alter the way young people perceive the world. The online world is often biased so that only positive posts are made – the best pictures, the most fun parties, the celebratory news. Other factors such as modified images and targeted filters can lead to an altered perception so that it can feel like other people's lives are great, while our 'real' life, with its everyday ups and downs, pales in comparison. We know this is associated with low mood, particularly among young people.

Social media interacts with a teen's need to develop a coherent self-identity

Teens are also in the midst of developing a complex and coherent self-identity. The online world offers both opportunities and vulnerabilities in this respect. For some young people it can be a place where they can bolster their identity and shine amongst their peers, while for others confidence can be easily knocked and self-perception damaged.

Peer feedback online has a powerful influence on adolescents' views about themselves, especially on girls in relation to body image and pressure to be thin. Research also shows that feedback about ideal body image that deviates from normal is associated with greater activity in the emotional centres of the brain for teens, meaning it holds high value and may influence a teen's own body perception. While this could be positive, the potential for danger is clear, making this an area we need to help young teens manage.

The online world can cause intense emotional experiences in teens

We know that emotional brain regions are highly sensitive during the teenage years, making teenagers' emotional experiences intense. This can work in both positive and negative ways. An adolescent guided strongly by emotions may have a stronger draw to video games, making them hard to resist and more painful to put away. We can all picture the teen boy who seems addicted to the Playstation. Knowing that their lower brain is firing on all cylinders while their prefrontal cortex is struggling to keep up helps us see how hard it might be for them to put down the controller and come and eat dinner. It's not an excuse, or a suggestion that gaming should be freely available, but it offers some explanation. It is also true that teenagers find solace and comfort in the online world. Online communities can be the only place a young person can really feel they belong. There can be solidarity with others who are struggling and an increasing amount of body-positive content that others share. Here again we see how, in the context of a teenage brain, online experience is intensified, with the potential to both increase vulnerability and opportunity.

Translating your teen

The online and offline world are the same to your teen

The networks through which people make contact, communicate and share content are online and offline and for teens there is no dichotomy. Nowadays even video games also have social networking facilities and social media is evolving, often with teenagers leading the way. The ever-present and continually changing nature of social media makes it a certain attractor for parental anxiety and frustration, but we need to remember that the online world is a magnet for the teenage brain because developmental tasks are taking place online. Parents and teachers can see this as the young person never being off their phone or off a screen and not living in the real world, whereas to a young person that *is* their connected world.

Risk and opportunity are correlated online

The developmental drives of the teenage brain (such as friends, self-identity and risk) draw teens to the online world. These same brain sensitivities mean the impact on them, both positive and negative, is heightened. The implications are that they are vulnerable and need help to manage their relationship with social media use, but also that unilateral banning of social media is not the way forward because risk and opportunity are correlated in the online world. Young people who use the internet more and strengthen their digital skills also gain great benefits and build resilience for the future.

Young people need to be taught to make good choices, whether or not you are watching

To protect young people, as a key adult in their world, you need to support them to make smart choices for themselves, whether or not you are watching. You cannot be there 24 hours a day in their lives. You need to help them figure out their own boundaries. Evidence shows that the majority of teens are competent and autonomous and can make good choices. The key to developing resilience in young people around media use is to teach them to reflect on their own experience and manage their own media habits. Remember, the brain learns from experience and repetition is the key to success, so this is not going to happen overnight. More importantly, given the way the teenage brain drives interact with media use, teens are going to need help to get this under their belt. Your social media strategy needs to be solid, consistent and long-term, with a large dose of discussion and reflection, some clear boundaries and exemplary modelling. If you do this from an early age, by the time they are adults – remember that is in their mid-20s – they will be fully in control.

The majority of young people act responsibly online

The good news is that research suggests that most teenagers are busy thinking about the difficult issues of how to manage their media use themselves. Research shows that the majority of young people are thoughtful, act in a responsible manner and come up with strategies to protect themselves. They need support and skills and some clear boundaries, but don't get caught up in a fixed mindset yourself. Some parents are highly triggered by seeing their child with a phone and if annoyed about anything will confiscate the phone as a punishment. This is not helping them learn to self-regulate and, indeed, is more likely to push them to a position of denial about the difficulties associated with phone use. All teens have the potential to learn how to manage with your support.

 ## What does that mean day to day?

There is a risk that technology will get in the way of your relationship with your teen

As you struggle to know what to do about technology and fear for the young people you support, your instinct might be to over-control their media use in your quest to protect them. The phrase 'screen time' has become common parlance, and in households all over the world there are battles as parents and teachers try to limit or ban it, while teenagers fight, negotiate and deceive in order to get back to what is for them a lifeline. The risk of this approach is that you will cause a rift in your relationship with your teenager and lose vital trust and channels of communication which are so important to keep them safe in their lives. In order to move the conversation from one of tension and anger you need to start from a place of empathy and perspective-taking. You need to change how you approach this problem, and rather than assuming teenagers can't manage technology, are 'addicted', always will be and are being difficult, you need to help them develop skills so they can manage. Know how they are spending their time and talk to them about it.

Teens need to be metacognitive and reflective about their screen use

Encourage teens to step back from their online experience and reflect on it. Psychologists call this insight into one's own behaviour metacognition. This can only happen successfully if the teen is not feeling backed in a corner or that their phone is going to be taken away from them. Encourage them to notice how they feel when they reach for their phone and how they feel after they have looked at their phone. There is evidence that mood goes down after looking on Facebook as it can provoke a sense of FOMO or a perception that other people's lives are better. Ask them what makes it hard to put their phone down. Is it a concern they will appear rude if they don't answer straight away? Ask them questions such as 'What is energising and what is draining for you on your phone? Do you relax when you play a video game, but are there also negative effects if you stay on too long? When was the last time you were happy online?' Try to resist saying 'I told you so' and listen to what they have to say. Supporting them to reflect is in itself a powerful intervention to help them be more in control.

Teens need to learn to self-regulate

Teenagers are at a point in their lives when they are learning to work things out for themselves. If we have a heavy-handed approach to how they manage their lives they will not only push up against this, but as soon as we take away the restrictions or we aren't looking, they won't know how to manage. Strengthen their self-regulation skills and protect them from potentially greater trouble with more damaging effects later. The area of technology, internet use and social media is one of the most contentious between generations and is an ideal place to begin your relationship of negotiation and joint problem solving. This is not the quick or easy solution, but the alternative just doesn't work. Remember, their brains are ready to learn to problem solve and develop those all-important paths of self-regulation housed in the frontal pathways of the brain. Think of it as a muscle they need to grow. There are some great apps available to help build self-awareness and compartmentalise life. Help them create spaces and think about moderation. Show them the value of digital detox, when everyone has digital free time, and make sure that it is a fun time and a time of connection and enjoyment. And remember the power of modelling behaviour. You have to do it too.

Teens need to develop a critical view of social media content to keep them safe

Have a regular space and time where teens are encouraged to be critical about content and experiences online. This is a great time to take advantage of their growing brain and increasing critical awareness, helping them to navigate the enormous amount of content available to them. Discuss how you know if something is really true. Ask them what feels safe and what feels unsafe to them online or what feels appropriate and inappropriate. You also need to talk through a plan of what they would do or who they would turn to if something doesn't go as planned. It is important that they identify a person who they would feel safe to turn to and they can verbalise any fears they may have about the implications for them and their friends. Ask them 'What would you do if you thought your friend was in trouble online? What would you do if you found content that upset you and you needed to talk about it?' You might even need to talk to them about sexting and pornography and the implications of that for an individual. It is shocking what young people can be exposed to at a young age, and while we work out how to manage that as part of public policy we should be making sure teens have a place to talk about it without negative consequences.

It is most important to take a holistic approach when considering your teen's media use

The other important thing to remember is that 'screen time' is an unhelpful catch-all. It can easily become the thing the parents latch onto and become most worried about, perhaps as it is relatively easy to monitor. However, counting screen time is problematic as there are so many uses of technology, many of which are good (e.g. coding or creating content) or are carried out in the context of a full life (e.g. a child who is fully engaged in life but for whom a video game is where they truly relax). It is more important to ask the harder questions such as what are they doing online. Public health organisations and associations offer guidelines for parents and professionals based on research findings as they are published. These regulations tend to focus on the individual differences, and rather than recommending blank one-size-fits-all recommendations such as a set amount of 'screen time', they suggest a more holistic approach. They focus on ensuring that young people have a balanced life with an emphasis on how they spend their disposable time overall, asking questions that focus on whether it takes time away from sleeping, playing, talking and physical activity. The American Academy of Pediatrics (Yolanda Chassiakos *et al.* 2016) suggests adults ask the following questions of children when considering the impact of technology on their lives:

- Is the young person physically healthy and sleeping enough?
- Is the young person connecting socially with family and friends (in any form)?
- Is the young person engaged with and achieving in school?
- Is the young person pursuing interests and hobbies (in any form)?
- Is the young person having fun and learning in their use of digital media?

The message is not to focus on whether screens are 'good' or 'bad' for young people but to assess whether their social, cognitive and physical activities are at a good level for them.

What does that mean for learning?

Access to knowledge and content in the palm of their hands is a great opportunity for teens

The knowledge and information that is available to teenagers in the palm of their hand is mind-blowing for those of us who grew up before the age of the internet. Two of us were training together in London in the 1990s and have a clear memory of the whole research team crowding round a computer while someone demonstrated the new 'world wide web' that had just been launched. As a search term was entered and the machine chugged away slowly finding information, many of us rolled our eyes and said, 'That's never going to catch on, it's so slow.' Little did we know what was to come. We also remember having to get a bus to the library, walk up the stairs of the library to find a journal, go down stairs to read the journal or line up to photocopy the article we wanted in order to write our dissertations. Now in the palm of our hands we have almost any article we want within about three minutes. This is an enormous privilege and opportunity afforded our young people, which is new for this generation. They have more knowledge and information available to them than we could ever have dreamed of in the 1990s. The opportunities for creative endeavour are similarly massive, with the ability to create high quality presentations, photos, music and films.

Technology can be a force for good or bad in a learning task

There is no doubt that the draw of the smartphone can be a distraction from a learning task, which could get in the way of young people's ability to focus and think and pull them out of their positive cycle of learning. Teachers are working hard to manage this, and many schools now ban smartphones in school. However, this does conflict with the great opportunities technology offers to enhance learning. Online interfaces can be highly engaging and induce positive motivation in young people, supporting them to build neural circuits. Some people argue that schools have a role in supporting pupils to learn to self-regulate their technology use as we have outlined above, but this is not without its challenges.

There needs to be consistency from home and school in rules around technology use

What is clear is that messages about media use need to be consistent from home and school. If a teen is being told by school that they can't have their phone in school but their parents can't manage a day without being in touch, the teen is getting a mixed message. Not only is this unhelpful for them in working out what is best for their learning and development, it also leaves wiggle room where boundaries can be pushed and rules broken.

 ## So, what now?

Teens are drawn to digital media and technology because of their developmental drives. There are risks that need careful consideration, but technology also affords great opportunities to young people. Adults need to think holistically about their teen's lifestyle and find ways to discuss and problem solve issues with their teen to have the greatest success in helping them manage their lives.

Case study: Zainab

Zainab, a 15-year-old girl, was low in mood. She lived with her mother as her parents were separated and had no contact with her father or siblings. She had been struggling with friendships for the past few months and had taken to going to her room after school with her phone. Her mother had been concerned about her and, not wanting to cause her additional stress, had let slip the rule that Zainab could not have her phone in bed at night. Her mother noticed that she was looking very tired and Zainab was often irritable and grumpy, not wanting to take part in activities she previously enjoyed. One weekend, Zainab's mother asked if she was going out with her friends, which she usually would do, to which Zainab answered bluntly, 'No', and went back to her room. Despite efforts to talk, Zainab did not want to spend time with or talk to her mother. One night her mother got up and heard some faint sobbing coming from Zainab's room. She went in to find her daughter crying with her phone in her hands. It was 3am. It was time to do something about it.

In the middle of the night Zainab and her mother went downstairs to get a hot drink. They sat by the fire and Zainab began to talk. After some discussion it emerged that Zainab had fallen out with a group of friends who she had been close to for some time and her friends were now being quite unkind on social media. She was ignored more than taunted at school, but particularly at night time, there were posts and nasty 'in' jokes posted that Zainab was left out of. All alone in her room she did not know where to turn. She was holding onto her phone for dear life hoping things would improve, while actually having 24-hour access to her phone was the thing that was making things worse.

A good resolution

Zainab's mother was able to comfort her daughter in the middle of the night, listen, empathise and help her daughter feel better. She was tempted to pick up the phone to the other girls and scream at them and berate them for being unkind, but she knew this would not help the situation. She helped Zainab to get back to sleep and they agreed to talk it through in the light of day when they had had some sleep and so could think more clearly.

They decided to engage the help of the school counsellor, who was well aware of the dynamic with this group of young people. Zainab needed assurances from both her mother and the school counsellor that they wouldn't talk on her behalf and they wouldn't agree on any strategy before acting. The counsellor was able to offer an intervention that did not cause Zainab to be further ostracised and gradually the friendships returned to normal. The group undertook a whole-class intervention in cyber-bullying which felt inclusive to all and was very helpful. The young people learnt how much social pain can hurt others and how hard it can be to be left out and teased when alone at night time. They all committed to stopping this behaviour.

Zainab agreed with her mother to go back to the house rule of no phones in bed at night. Both she and her mother put their phones on charge at 9pm downstairs and found they could have some special time together after 9pm, watching a box set or talking. Zainab was getting more sleep and as a result was much better able to cope with the stresses and strains of teenage life.

What might get in the way?

Young people need to know that any intervention with friendship issues will be dealt with sensitively. If adults come in too heavy handedly (such as confiscating the phone there and then) they can make the situation harder for the young person. Zainab may not have been ready to open up to her mother, in which case her mother would have had to be patient and offer to find someone else for her to speak to.

Action point: Create structured spaces for discussion and problem solving

We recommend having structured times when you open up a conversation with young people about how best to engage with social media. Invite them into a conversation about how they can manage their online experience. These conversations should be led by the young people to give them a sense of agency and respect for their knowledge. It is as much about listening to them as it is deciding boundaries. Topics for discussion should encourage self-reflection and the answers to questions such as:

- Do they use social media as mood modifiers, turning to their phone when they feel bad?
- How do they feel after they have been on certain apps, e.g. Instagram, Facebook? Does it make them feel good about themselves or bad?
- What are they compensating for with excessive internet use?
- What would they do if they came across content that was upsetting? Who would they talk to? Would they fear getting into trouble?
- Are there things they would say online or in a text that they wouldn't in real life?

Your aim is to enable them to be reflective, develop self-regulation strategies, be critical of content and know what to do if they get in trouble online. Remember with their brain drive for autonomy, any solution that comes from them and is 'owned' by them is more likely to be effective. Listen, be curious, don't lecture.

Action point: Have a holistic approach to judging your child's well-being

It's easy to get stuck on one thing that your teenager does or does not do, particularly if it concerns you. Try to look at how your teenager is doing generally rather than worrying about one particular thing. If they have friends and interests, sleep well, play and are physically active, can communicate with you and manage well in their academic work, then spending time relaxing while surfing the web and playing on their Xbox is unlikely to do them any harm. In fact, it might be the main source of relaxation and their time to themselves. Try not to see all screen use as bad. It is a part of a teen's life.

Action point: Act as a role model

Remember, the most powerful form of learning between adult and adolescent is modelling. Check your own use of phones and tablets and ensure you are modelling balanced media use. Be prepared to reflect on your own struggles. The online world is compelling and we all need to develop strategies and be mindful about our use.

Action point: Have some clear technology boundaries that have been jointly agreed

It is essential that you have clear boundaries for use of screens in the family. Decide on the rules together. Don't call a meeting as a punishment for poor use or the young person will be in a position of fighting to get as much as they can. For example, at home we would recommend a minimum of no screens at the dinner table and all devices removed from bedrooms 30 minutes before bedtime. The rules must apply to *all* members of the community. Try very hard never to break the rules or your teenager will learn that they are negotiable. Make a digital detox a part of everyday life.

Action point: Listen and try to take their perspective

If you are struggling with an area of internet or gaming use, try to be really curious and have empathy before coming up with a strategy to solve the problem. You are much more likely to have a young person onboard with you to work out how to manage that way. For example, if a young person is drawn to Minecraft all the time, try to understand its draw. Perhaps think of how you can link online interests with offline worlds, such as enabling them to join a gaming or Minecraft® club. Some of the more recent games have cleverly included a social element so a young person is locked into a game with their friends, and if they suddenly come off their device, their friends might lose points of status. Be prepared to understand these facets of a game and negotiate around them. Then, together, set a clear boundary.

Action point: Parents and teachers need to work in partnership

It is very hard for young people to straddle two different systems of management. Work with adult partners in the young person's life to try to develop similar systems.

Action point: Protect young people's sleep

As you read in Chapter 13: Sleepy Teens, a young person's sleep is of prime importance. Smartphones are a temptation teenagers' brains are unlikely to be able to resist and we would recommend having a no-phones-in-room policy at night time. Alarm clocks have been around since the 18th century. Your teen could use one of those to wake her up.

Action point: Balance looks different for some young people

Remember that all young people are different in how their brains are wired and in how they experience the world. When it comes to technology, just like any other aspects of life, different teens need different approaches. Consider the individual before deciding on rules around technology, taking a holistic approach for *each teen*.

Downloads: #Social Media and Technology

Panic surrounds social media and technology use in teenagers, but there is little evidence for social media causing mental health problems in teenagers. Access to social media means connecting with peers (which is a developmental drive in teens), so it needs to be managed thoughtfully. The way you communicate with your teen is key. Have clear technology boundaries but also make time for discussion to help them reflect on the pros and cons of social media and technology.

Exercise

Think about the last week. What are your teen's habits with technology? What are the boundaries in your house concerning its use? Are there specific hours of use and areas in the house or school where it is used and where it is not allowed? Where is the phone charger kept? Do you follow the same rules?

. . . .

. . . .

. . . .

. . . .

. . . .

. . . .

. . . .

. . . .

. . . .

What are the pros and cons of social media and technology? Have you discussed these with your teen? What is your reaction if they hold a different view?

. . . .

. . . .

. . . .

. . . .

. . . .

. . . .

How could your teen let you know if they'd made a mistake with social media (such as posting a picture that they regret)? How would you react? What ways do you support your teen to make good choices around their technology use?

. . . .

. . . .

. . . .

. . . .

. . . .

. . . .

. . . .

When this happens...	Instead of this...	Try this...
School camp is coming up and phones are banned. Your teen thinks she'll be homesick without being able to call you.	I don't care if your teachers say don't take your phone on the school trip. I want to be able to contact you, so sneak it in your bag. If you need me, call me and I'll take you home.	I'm going to miss you so much this trip – but I'll get all the news from the teachers every day. You are going to find out some amazing things that you can do by yourself. You'll feel so proud you did it.
		Try to **give consistent messages** to teens in different environments
Your teens are not allowed to use their phones in class. You're in the middle of teaching, but you need to check something quickly.	It's my class and I've got to have different rules because I often need to respond quickly to my messages.	If I want my teen to have good habits, I need to model that behaviour by doing it myself.
		Model good technology use
Your teen gets very wound up when the games console is turned off, even when you've warned him 10 minutes before the time.	You always get angry when you come off your console. If you have a tantrum next time, I'm throwing that thing in the bin.	After he has calmed down, ask: have you noticed you often get angry when it's time to turn off the console? What can we do to change this? Can you come up with a plan? We'll try your idea for two weeks, then review.
		Encourage **reflection, debate and conversation**

PART 5

The Last Word

Chapter 17

May The Force Be With You, Luke

Consider this chapter an executive summary of the principles we have discussed throughout the book, along with some core tips for interacting with teens. Take time to read this chapter because it will improve communication with your teen, and with it, their incredible potential will be unlocked.

As the teenage brain powers up, teens are driven to explore the world, with a propensity to learn that is unique. We can provide the right environment so a teenager is propelled into a positive cycle of extraordinary intellectual, social and emotional learning. They have a once in a lifetime opportunity to shape their brain for the future. Importantly, their vast readiness to learn means that both positive and negative experiences will have a profound impact at this time. Young people need adults alongside them, guiding them and keeping them on a positive track. Teens need stable, connected relationships to keep their learning flowing.

Over the course of this book, we have discussed many elements in a young person's life which contribute to learning in the teenage brain. Genetic and environmental factors work individually and together to grow your teenager's brain to be the most efficient it can be. We believe that a teen's engagement with positive supportive relationships is often the biggest cog in the teen learning machine, though all the components contribute. This is an empowering message – *you* can create positive change in a young person (see Figure 17.1).

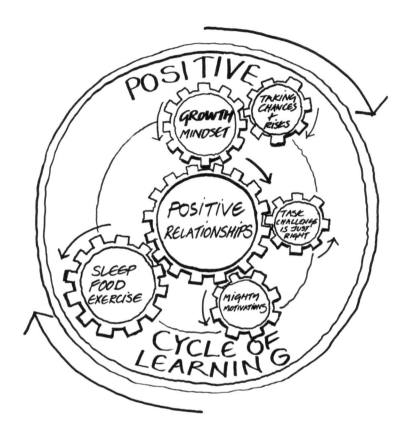

Figure 17.1: Unlocking the teenage brain

Teen brains are under construction; adults are scaffolding while the masterpiece is completed

You might not be surprised to find that science tells us that, really, all we need in life is the knowledge that someone will be there alongside us when the going gets tough. It sounds simple enough, but for teens and those who care for them there are two challenges. Your teen needs you now more than ever, but how do they signal that they need you? And how can you show them you are alongside them without invading their space?

Young children are much easier to read – they put their arms up when they need a hug and you can pick them up and cuddle the worry away. For young children, it's all about getting close to an adult when it gets too much, to be protected and physically shielded, but for teens, it's all about growing towards independence and maintaining status, so the communication and the outcomes are more complex. Luckily, help is at hand.

A seven step plan – May The Force Be With You, Luke

MAYBE THIS SITUATION PUSHED YOUR BUTTONS

THE BEHAVIOUR NEEDS DECODING, WHAT ARE THEY REALLY TELLING YOU?

FORCE YOURSELF TO WAIT WHILE THE EMOTIONS SETTLE

BE ALONGSIDE, BE WITH THEM

WITH HOLD YOUR ADVICE FOR NOW AND JUST LISTEN

YOU DESCRIBE THE EMOTION IF THEY CAN'T

LUKE (LOOK) FOR A SUITABLE TIME TO TALK IT OUT LATER, THINK ABOUT SOLUTIONS AND LEARNING POINTS

Figure 17.2: May The Force Be With You, Luke

Drawing on brain science and psychological research, we have developed a seven step plan which guides you through what to do 'in the moment', when your teen is emotional and you want to provide the best support for them. This is a masterclass in emotional regulation. When emotions run high, neither you nor your teen are likely to be using your thinking brain (see Chapter 2: The Teen Brain Thinks and Feels), and we know in times of high stress we might find it hard to use a new approach (see Chapter 3: The Teen Brain Learns and Believes), so we have developed a mnemonic to help you structure your response in the moment.

We have pegged the guidance steps to a familiar phrase as an aide memoire, but we don't want to be flippant about the message we are conveying. The points we have described are serious and likely to be applied in emotionally taxing or upsetting situations, so we hope you take the idea in the spirit with which it is intended. The goal here is for you to get into your thinking brain so that you can scaffold your teen to get into that zone too.

MAYBE THIS SITUATION PUSHED YOUR BUTTONS?

We'd all like to think we are rational, we are the grown-ups after all, but previous experience can have a significant impact on how we communicate. We carry our personal history in our interactions with the next generation, sometimes consciously but often unconsciously. This is particularly true in situations which may get under our skin and supporting a teen can be demanding and emotive at times.

The first stage is to relax into it and accept we all have patterns and predispositions in relationships; the second is to become *aware* of these inclinations.

Tune into and track your responses to your teen. When you feel an intense emotional reaction to something a young person has said or done, it's likely to be a clue.

If your teen talks through your organic chemistry lesson, does this feed into your lack of confidence at teaching that topic? Does an untidy room wind you up? Is that because your own mother hoards mountains of belongings making her home pretty much uninhabitable?

Notice what your triggers are and reflect on them.

As you tune in, you can gradually learn to change your initial response, and extract the emotional heat that your history brings to a situation, because that will allow you to work out what is best for the young person in front of you.

Don't be too hard on yourself, give it time and it will become easier.

THE BEHAVIOUR NEEDS DECODING, WHAT ARE THEY REALLY
TELLING YOU?

All behaviour is communication, but the language is more complicated in adolescence. Things just aren't always as they appear. If your teen doesn't like their hair that day they might just ooze irritation and fire short-tempered responses at you all morning (personal experience). If we respond directly to the 'top layer' of this behaviour – telling them off for being grumpy – we will miss the opportunity to give them the support they actually need, which in this case might be reassurance about the way they look, or perhaps the confidence to ask that girl out. Adults working with a teenager need to develop the ability to *read the need*.

FORCE YOURSELF TO WAIT WHILE THE EMOTION SETTLES

When teens are experiencing a strong emotion, their emotional brain is in charge. It takes the lion's share of the teen's brain power, which means there is little left for reasoned, logical thinking. It is normal, and indeed an important part of development, to feel intense emotions, when a young person might say extreme things like 'I hate my life'.

Remember the snow globe intervention in Chapter 10: Powerful Feelings and Mighty Motivations? Give them time for the snowflakes to settle before trying any kind of reasoning.

Don't twiddle your thumbs while you wait, you could take time to reflect on your own emotional response (see the first step).

Only when the young person is feeling less emotional and in their thinking brain will they be able to reflect and talk things through.

BE ALONGSIDE, BE WITH YOUR TEEN

Our brains are less stressed in the company of a trusted person – remember the holding hand experiment in Chapter 15: Good Stress, Bad Stress? Just coming alongside your teen will make their experience of the world less threatening. While your teen is unlikely to actually hold your hand, sitting next to them, taking time to listen and empathise with them is likely to have the same effect.

Give young people the message that it's a good idea to share their emotional experiences – good or bad – with another person. This ability to share is important for emotional well-being.

If you aren't the right person to come alongside your teen in a particular situation, help them identify someone who can. Don't be offended if it isn't you, it doesn't mean they don't care for you.

One particular parent, teacher or adult may be more useful than another in certain situations, depending on their skill set and approach. Ideally, gather a range of trusted adults who will offer a safe place to discuss emotional experiences.

We cope better when we are with other people, so teach this to teens.

WITHHOLD YOUR ADVICE FOR NOW AND JUST LISTEN
Listening sounds easy, right? Wrong.

Really stopping, truly deeply listening, without reacting is hard when someone for whom we care is sad or angry. In order to help them manage these strong emotions we have to listen first.

We can work things through more effectively when we say them out loud, and so giving your teen a chance to talk – even if it is garbled and contradictory at first – is important.

If you jump in with your own theory too quickly (*Are you sure you weren't being bossy and that's why they left you out?*), tell them off (*Well I've told you not to spend time with that friend, he's bad news*) or try to save them (*Don't go on the school trip if you're scared*), they won't be able to work things out for themselves.

There might be a time to give your opinion later, but first of all just listen.

If they push you away, tell them you will check back a little later and you are ready to listen whenever they are ready to talk.

You might try and paraphrase back what they said (sometimes called *reflective listening*) as this is a really effective way to let another person know you have heard them. This *alone* will have a positive impact.

YOU DESCRIBE THE EMOTION IF YOUR TEEN CAN'T
Label your teen's emotions – it will help them move into a calmer state.

The thinking brain can start to engage as the brain's response is less intense when emotions are named by another trusted adult.

It is an important way of supporting emotional regulation, but the trick here is in the timing.

Try not to jump in too quickly, remember the steps before this stage, and with time you might comment tentatively: 'It seems like you are really angry with your friend right now.'

If you hear a fierce denial you have probably got the emotion exactly right, but it might also indicate you've gone in too soon and the emotional brain is still in charge, so withdraw the troops, re-group and try again in a while.

LUKE (LOOK) FOR A SUITABLE TIME TO TALK IT OUT LATER, THINK ABOUT SOLUTIONS AND LEARNING POINTS

Strictly speaking this isn't a step to take 'in the moment' but rather some time after it.

Wait hours or even days and look for a calm, uninterrupted time to talk it through.

Respect the pace of their recovery.

Teens want and need our guidance but they want to be a partner in that conversation, so wait until they are in the right place before you start the conversation.

Try to see difficult moments as learning opportunities and come up with a plan for next time.

Don't just hand your teen a fish, teach them to fish.

That situation in the moment may need resolving, but the wider lessons learnt from these experiences are invaluable. Has the young person over-committed by auditioning for a street dance group? How could your teen plan ahead to avoid the consequent drop in their grades? Could they timetable the dance group into a part of the year with fewer academic commitments?

Try and support the young person to articulate solution-focused principles that they can apply for the rest of their lives – don't just save them in the moment.

It is particularly important to talk about situations in which the teen has made poor choices or done something of which they feel ashamed, because these are likely to be important learning opportunities.

Loving, supporting and understanding your teen can be constant even when you cannot condone a particular behaviour or are considering the outcome because they crossed a boundary. Empathy and solid boundaries are not mutually exclusive.

Keep calm and carry on, learning new skills takes time

If it feels hard at first, it's to be expected because you and your teen are learning a new skill – stick with these seven steps and do it regularly.

As you know, it takes time to lay down a new brain circuit.

Keep a growth mindset.

You will get it wrong sometimes, but if you are willing to reflect and perhaps say, 'I don't think I reacted well to the situation this morning', your teen will grow to trust your commitment to them and your relationship will benefit.

Teens might protest initially, but look under the layers of their behaviour and take heart because gradually you will find constructive communication develops and in time they will take a step towards you.

It's over to you. Over and out

Writing this book prompted in us a renewed respect for adolescents, and we hope reading it has done the same for you. Teens are daring, emotional, thoughtful, courageous, sensitive, innovative, pioneering, inspirational, interested and interesting. They experience lifetime firsts at a head-spinning rate while pushing the boundaries of academic and life learning to new highs. Managing one would be impressive, doing both at the same time is phenomenal. Incredible, really.

That's it, it's over to you.

Downloads: May The Force Be With You, Luke

Drawing on brain science and psychological research we have developed a seven step plan which guides you through what to do 'in the moment', when your teen is emotional and you want to provide the best support for them. This is a masterclass in emotional regulation. Here we give you more information and top tips for implementing the plan.

MAYbe this situation pushed your buttons?

Previous experiences have an impact on how we communicate and manage our children's emotions and behaviour, sometimes consciously but often unconsciously. It is important to be aware of your patterns.

Exercise
Note down three occasions when a situation with your teen triggered a strong physical or emotional reaction in you (e.g. when they got angry, when they were left out by their friend, when they didn't study hard).

Occasion 1

. . . .

. . . .

Occasion 2

. . . .

. . . .

Occasion 3

. . . .

. . . .

Can you think of how this might be related to an experience you had in your childhood or the history of your family?

. . . .

. . . .

. . . .

. . . .

. . . .

. . . .

. . . .

When this happens...	Instead of this...	Try this...
Your teen is going out with his friends but you find yourself trying to dissuade him – even though, your friend points out, it is not a risky situation.	Why is he so insistent on going out with his friends? It is affecting the whole family as none of us can sleep until he is home.	I wonder why I have such a strong reaction? My stomach turns at the thought and I can't sleep. There were times at night when I felt unsafe as a child and this might be getting in the way of what my teen needs to grow and develop.
		Tune into situations that push your buttons

THE behaviour needs decoding, what are they really telling you?

All behaviour is communication. The behaviour is the tip of the iceberg – the bit we can see – whilst what is actually going on is hidden underneath. Teen behaviour is often hard to read and needs decoding. If you take the time to decode the behaviour, you have more chance of helping your teen understand what is going on for them and the behaviour can be dropped.

Exercise
Note down three situations this week when your teen acted differently to usual and in an extreme manner. What do you think might have been going on under the behaviour?

Situation 1

. . . .

. . . .

Situation 2

. . . .

. . . .

Situation 3

. . . .

. . . .

Can you think of how you might react next time to help them reflect on their experience?

. . . .

. . . .

. . . .

. . . .

. . . .

When this happens...	Instead of this...	Try this...
Your teen is stroppy and rude, it's unusual.	I'm not putting up with this. I'm giving her a detention or grounding her for rude behaviour.	I wonder what has gone on as this is quite unlike her. I wonder if she's struggling with something. I'll start the conversation so she knows I'm there.
		Read the need

FORCE yourself to wait while the emotion settles

Emotions are felt in the teen years more intensely than at any other time. While the emotional brain is in charge we all find it hard to be reflective and rational. Allow time for the snowflakes to settle while your teen's brain calms. Wait before you talk it through.

Exercise

Note down three situations this week when your teen had an extreme emotional reaction and how long it took before they were ready to talk (it might be minutes, hours or even days sometimes).

Situation 1

. . . .

. . . .

Situation 2

. . . .

. . . .

Situation 3

. . . .

. . . .

When this happens...	Instead of this...	Try this...
Your teen's exam grade was very much lower than she hoped. She's upset and not talking.	I know that's because she didn't work hard enough. She's got to hear that even though it's a hard thing to hear – otherwise how will she learn?	I know that's because she didn't work hard enough but now is *not* the time to talk about that. I might let her sleep on it and discuss it after school tomorrow.
		Allow emotions to settle

BE alongside, be with your teen

Our brains are highly social. We literally use another person's brain to reduce stress because we feel things less intensely when another person is alongside us. Though it may feel like you are doing nothing, just being with your teen, without speaking, will help them cope with stressful experiences.

Exercise
Every teen is different. What does your teen respond to when they are feeling stressed? How can you come alongside them in a way that will offer them support? When everyone is in their thinking brain, can you ask your teen what you could say or do at times of high stress and get some ideas from them about what they would find most helpful?

. . . .

. . . .

. . . .

. . . .

. . . .

. . . .

When this happens...	Instead of this...	Try this...
Your 15-year-old son storms in the door from school. He goes straight to the biscuit tin and shouts at you that there are no Jaffa cakes. Why has his little sister eaten them all?	If you talk to me in that tone of voice again you will be grounded for the week.	I wonder if something has happened in school. It's not about the Jaffa cakes. What's really going on? I'll remind him shouting is not OK, then wait while the snowflakes settle. When he's ready (and his thinking brain is switched on) I'll try to find out what happened to upset him. I'll help him find another way to manage his upset in the moment next time.
		Be with them at times of stress

WITHhold your advice for now and just listen

Truly listening is harder than it sounds, particularly when someone we care for is in pain or very emotional – particularly when we think we know the answer. As teens are working out what they think and care about, they need time to process their emotions and reactions themselves. Stop and listen – don't jump in with what you think too quickly.

Exercise
What are the ways in which you show your teen you are really listening to what they have to say? Focus on what you say and your body language and how you reflect back what they are saying.

. . . .

. . . .

. . . .

. . . .

. . . .

. . . .

When this happens...	Instead of this...	Try this...
Your teen leaves her old friend off her party list after looking at a text she got from her.	I think you've been unkind to your friend by not inviting her. You need to learn to treat your friends better in the future.	I think you are saying that you felt upset by your friend's text and that's why you decided not to invite her to your house, but now you feel bad that you didn't include her. Is that right?
		Listen first, don't jump in with your theory or advice

334

YOU describe the emotion if your teen can't

Neuroscience shows us that the act of simply labelling the emotion has a calming effect on the emotional brain, which may help a person to get into their thinking brain. Don't jump in too quickly (see above), but if they are struggling to work out what is going on you might offer a comment tentatively.

Exercise

Consciously name three emotions every day with your teen around – the good and the bad, as they happen. Try to get as specific as you can. Encourage your teen to do the same, though when emotions are high they may find this hard.

Emotion 1

. . . .

. . . .

Emotion 2

. . . .

. . . .

Emotion 3

. . . .

. . . .

When this happens...	Instead of this...	Try this...
Your teen says he has a stomach ache and so says he's not going over to his friend's house after all.	I don't think you have an illness. Your stomach ache is just because you are scared. There's nothing physically wrong with you.	I wonder what's going on with your stomach. You could have a little bug but I also wonder if it might be a sign that you are worried about going to your friend's house. You didn't enjoy it last time I seem to remember as you felt pressurised into doing things you weren't comfortable with.
		Tentatively name the emotion if they can't – but it's all in the timing

LUKE (LOOK) for a suitable time to talk it out later, think about solutions and learning points

Your teen might take a while before they are ready to talk things through and consider solutions and the learning opportunities from the experience. It is not up to adults to determine when this happens – you will need to read your teen's signs to get the most from the discussion – but it is important that reflection happens at some time after an event. The lessons to learn are invaluable and teens need to take part in a conversation and problem solve together.

Exercise

Think of when you were younger and when you felt most ready to talk through solutions after a difficult emotional time. Was it immediately or after some hours or days? We are all different in this respect. What about your teen? What have you noticed about what works for them?

. . . .

. . . .

. . . .

. . . .

. . . .

. . . .

. . . .

. . . .

. . . .

When you were younger, who were the people who you opened up to the most and how did they enable you to do this? Were they the adults who listened and responded in a timely manner to your needs?

. . . .

. . . .

. . . .

. . . .

. . . .

. . . .

. . . .

. . . .

. . . .

When this happens...	Instead of this...	Try this...
Last week your teen drank too much alcohol with her friends and ended up vomiting on the floor. You had to pick her up and the next morning she was really ashamed. She had written to the friend's parents to apologise but didn't want to talk about it.	It's going to be awful to go back to that night. That conversation is going to be too hard for her. I'll leave it and hope she has learnt her lesson.	That was a tough night and a conversation about it is going to be hard but I must find a time to talk it through. She will be embarrassed and won't be keen. I'll start by giving her a choice about when we talk it through. We need to problem solve together so it doesn't happen again.
		Talk a situation through later

Further Reading

Foreword

Fuhrmann, D., Knoll, L.J. and Blakemore, S-J. (2015) 'Adolescence as a sensitive period of brain development.' *Trends in Cognitive Sciences 19*, 10, 558–566.

Tamnes, C., Herting, M., Goddings, A-L., Meuwese, R. *et al.* (2017) 'Development of the cerebral cortex across adolescence: A multisample study of interrelated longitudinal changes in cortical volume, surface area and thickness.' *Journal of Neuroscience 37*, 12, 3402–12.

Chapter 1: The Incredible Teen Brain — Time to Upgrade

Aslin, R.N. and Banks, M.S. (1978) 'Early Visual Experience in Humans: Evidence for a Critical Period in the Development of Binocular Vision.' In H.L. Pick, H.W. Leibowitz, J.E. Singer, A. Steinschneider and H.W. Stevenson (eds) *Psychology: From Research to Practice.* Boston, MA: Springer.

Barry, S. (2008) *The Secret Scripture.* London: Faber & Faber.

Bryan, C., Yeager, D.S., Hinojosa, C., Chabot, A.M., Bergen, H., Kawamura, M. and Steubing, F. (2016) 'Harnessing adolescent values to motivate healthier eating.' *Proceedings of the National Academy of Sciences of the USA 113*, 29, 10830–10835.

Dahl, R. (2004) 'Adolescent brain development: A period of vulnerabilities and opportunities.' *Annals of New York Academy of Sciences 1021*, 1–22.

Dahl, R.E., Allen, N.B., Wilbrecht, L. and Suleiman, A.B. (2018) 'Importance of investing in adolescence from a developmental science perspective.' *Nature 554*, 7693, 441.

Department for Education, UK (2017) Transforming Children and Young People's Mental Health Provision: A Green Paper (Secretary of State for Health and Secretary of State for Education). Retrieved from https://assets.publishing.service.gov.uk/government/uploads/system/uploads/attachment_data/file/664855/Transforming_children_and_young_people_s_mental_health_provision.pdf, accessed on 08 May 2019.

Foulkes, L. and Blakemore, S-J. (2018) 'Studying individual differences in human adolescent brain development.' *Nature Neuroscience 21*, 3, 315–323.

Fuhrmann, D., Knoll, L.J. and Blakemore, S-J. (2015) 'Adolescence as a sensitive period of brain development.' *Trends in Cognitive Sciences 19*, 10, 558–566.

Giedd, J.N., Blumenthal, J., Jeffries, N.O., Castellanos, F.X. *et al.* (1999) 'Brain development during childhood and adolescence: A longitudinal MRI study.' *Nature Neuroscience 2*, 861–863.

Gogtay, N., Ordonez, A., Herman, D.H., Hayashi, K.M. *et al.* (2007) 'Dynamic mapping of cortical development before and after the onset of pediatric bipolar illness.' *Journal of Child Psychology and Psychiatry 48*, 9, 852–862.

Immordino-Yang, M., Darling-Hammond, L. and Krone, C. (2018) *The Brain Basis for Integrated Social, Emotional and Academic Development: How Emotions and Social Relationships Drive Learning.* Washington, DC: The Aspen Institute.

Kessler, R.C., Berglund, P., Demler, O., Jin, R., Merikangas, K.R. and Walters, E.E. (2005) 'Lifetime prevalence and age-of-onset distributions of DSM-IV disorders in the National Comorbidity Survey Replication.' *Archives of General Psychiatry 62,* 6, 593–602.

Lee, F.S., Heimer, H., Giedd, J.N., Lein, E.S. *et al.* (2014) 'Mental health: Adolescent mental health – opportunity and obligation.' *Science 346*, 547–549.

Special Issue on the Teenage Brain (2013) *Current Directions in Psychological Science.*

Tamnes, C., Herting, M., Goddings, A-L., Meuwese, R. *et al.* (2017) 'Development of the cerebral cortex across adolescence: A multisample study of interrelated longitudinal changes in cortical volume, surface area and thickness.' *Journal of Neuroscience 37*, 12, 3402–3412.

Chapter 2: The Teen Brain Thinks and Feels

Gilbert, P. (2010) *The Compassionate Mind (Compassion Focused Therapy).* London: Constable Books.

MacLean, P.D. (1990) *The Triune Brain in Evolution: Role in Paleocerebral Functions.* New York: Plenum Press.

Senninger, T. (2015) The Learning Zone Model. Retrieved from www.thempra.org.uk/social-pedagogy/key-concepts-in-social-pedagogy/the-learning-zone-model, accessed on 08 May 2019.

Vygotsky, L.S. (1978) *Mind in Society: The Development of Higher Psychological Processes.* Cambridge, MA: Harvard University Press.

Willis, J. (2009) *How Your Child Learns Best: Brain-Friendly Strategies You Can Use to Ignite Your Child's Learning and Increase School Success.* Naperville, IL: Sourcebooks Inc.

Chapter 3: The Teen Brain Learns and Believes

Boaler, J. (2016) *Mathematical Mindsets: Unleashing Students' Potential through Creative Math, Inspiring Messages and Innovative Teaching.* San Francisco, CA: Jossey-Bass.

Dweck, C. (2012) *Mindset: How You Can Fulfil Your Potential.* London: Robinson.

Ericsson, K.A., Krampe, R. and Tesch-Romer, C. (1993) 'The role of deliberate practice in the acquisition of expert performance.' *Psychological Review 100,* 363–406.

Gladwell, M. (2008) *Outliers: The Story of Success.* London: Little, Brown and Company.

Mosner, J.S., Schroder, H.S., Heeter, C., Moran, T.P. and Lee, Y.H. (2011) 'Mind your errors: Evidence for a neural mechanism linking growth mind-set to adaptive post-error adjustments.' *Psychological Science 22,* 12, 1484–1489.

Obama, M. (2014) 'Remarks by the First Lady at San Antonio Signing Day Reach Higher Event.' University of Texas, San Antonio, Texas.

Okonofua, J.A., Paunesku, D. and Walton, G.M. (2016) 'A brief intervention to encourage empathic discipline halves suspension rates among adolescents.' *Proceedings of the National Academy of Sciences.*

Shatz, C.J. (1992) 'The developing brain.' *The Scientific American 267,* 60–67.

Chapter 4: The Teen Brain Connects, Watches and Absorbs

Bandura, A. (1976) *Social Learning Theory.* London: Pearson.

Dawson, P. and Guare, R. (2008) *Smart But Scattered: The Revolutionary 'Executive Skills' Approach to Helping Kids Reach Their Potential.* New York: Guilford Press.

Pavlov, I.P. (2011) *Conditioned Reflexes and Psychiatry – Lectures on Conditioned Reflexes, Vol 2.* New York: Cullen Press.

Skinner, B.F. (1998) *About Behaviourism.* New York: Random House.

Chapter 5: The Teen Brain Loves Other People

BBC (2018) The Anatomy of Loneliness. Retrieved from www.bbc.co.uk/programmes/articles/2yzhfv4DvqVp5nZyxBD8G23/who-feels-lonely-the-results-of-the-world-s-largest-loneliness-study, accessed on 08 May 2019.

Blakemore, S-J. (2012) 'Development of the social brain in adolescence.' *Journal of the Royal Society of Medicine 105*, 111–116.

Casey, B.J., Heller, A.S., Gee, D.G. and Cohen, A.O. (2019) 'Development of the emotional brain.' *Neuroscience Letters 693*, 29–34.

Eisenberger, N.I. (2012) 'The neural bases of social pain: Evidence for shared representations with physical pain.' *Psychosomatic Medicine 74*, 2.

Eisenberger, N.I., Lieberman, M.D. and Williams, K.D. (2003) 'Does rejection hurt? An fMRI study of social exclusion.' *Science 203*, 290–292.

Hamilton, D.I., Katz, L.B. and Leirer, V.O.V. (1980) 'Cognitive representation of personality impressions: Organisational processes in first impression formation.' *Journal of Personality and Social Psychology 39*, 6, 1050.

Harari, Y.N. (2015) *Sapiens: A Brief History of Humankind.* New York: Vintage Press.

Lieberman, M.D. (2012) 'Education and the social brain.' *Trends in Neuroscience and Education 1*, 1, 3–9.

Lieberman, M.D. (2015) *Social: Why Our Brains Are Wired to Connect.* Oxford: Oxford University Press.

Lieberman, M.D. and Eisenberger, N.I. (2009) 'Pains and pleasures of social life.' *Science 323*, 890–891.

Raichle, M., MacLeod, A.M., Snyder, A.Z., Powers, W.J., Gusnard, D.A. and Shulman, G.L. (2001) 'A default mode of brain function.' *Proceedings of the National Acadamy of Sciences of the USA 98*, 676–682.

Rilling, J.K., Gutman, D.A., Zeh, T.R., Pagnoni, G., Berns, G.S. and Kils, C.D. (2002) 'A neural basis for social cooperation.' *Neuron 35*, 2, 395–405.

Sebastian, C., Viding, E., Williams, K. and Blakemore, S-J. (2010) 'Social brain development and the affective consequences of ostracism in adolescence.' *Brain & Cognition 72*, 134–145.

Slavin, E.R., Lake, C., Inns, A., Baye, A., Dachet, D. and Haslam, J. (2019) 'A Quantitative Synthesis of Research on Writing Approaches in Years 3 to 13.' London: Education Endowment Foundation.

Valliant, G.E. (2012) *Triumphs of Experience: The Men of the Harvard Grant Study.* Cambridge, MA: Belknap Press.

Chapter 6: Teen Brains Overwhelmed

Masten, A.S. (2014) *Ordinary Magic: Resilience in Development*. New York: Guilford.

National Institute for Health and Care Excellence (2017) Clinical Guideline 28. Depression in Children and Young People: Identification and Management in Primary, Community and Secondary Care. Retrieved from www.nice.org.uk/guidance/cg28, accessed on 06 June 2019.

Department of Health and NHS England (2017) Mental health of children and young people in England. Retrieved from https://digital.nhs.uk/data-and-information/publications/statistical/mental-health-of-children-and-young-people-in-england/2017/2017, accessed on 08 May 2019.

Volkow, N.D., Koob, G.F., Croyle, R.T., Bianchi, D.W. *et al.* (2018) 'The conception of the ABCD study: From substance use to a broad NIH collaboration.' *Developmental Cognitive Neuroscience 32*, 4–7. Retrieved from www.sciencedirect.com/science/article/pii/S1878929317300725?via%3Dihub, accessed on 08 May 2019.

Chapter 7: Thriving with Neurodiversity

Cancer, A., Manzoli, S. and Antonietti, A. | Besson, M. (Reviewing Editor) (2016) 'The alleged link between creativity and dyslexia: Identifying the specific process in which dyslexic students excel.' *Cogent Psychology 3*, 1.

Geschwind, N. (1982) 'Why Orton was right.' *Annals of Dyslexia 32*, 13–30.

Kapp, S.K., Gillespie-Lynch, K., Sherman, L.E. and Hutman, T. (2013) 'Deficit, difference, or both? Autism and neurodiversity.' *Developmental Psychology 49*, 1, 59–71.

Mandy, W., Murin, M., Baykaner, O., Staunton, S. *et al.* (2016) 'The transition from primary to secondary school in mainstream education for children with autism spectrum disorder.' *Autism 20*, 1, 5–13.

Mannuzza, S. and Klein, R.G. (2000) 'Long-term prognosis in attention-deficit/hyperactivity disorder.' *Child and Adolescent Psychiatric Clinics of North America 9*, 3, 711–726.

Chapter 8: Cracking the Social Code

Blakemore, S-J. (2008) 'The social brain in adolescence.' *Nature Reviews Neuroscience 9*, 267–277.

Blakemore, S-J. (2018) *Inventing Ourselves: The Secret Life of the Teenage Brain.* New York: Doubleday.

Blakemore, S-J. and Mills, K.L. (2014) 'Is adolescence a sensitive period for sociocultural processing?' *Annual Review of Psychology 65*, 187–207.

Bowlby, J. (2005) *Attachment Theory.* Abingdon: Routledge.

Foulkes, L. and Blakemore, S-J. (2016) 'Is there heightened sensitivity to social reward in adolescence?' *Current Opinion in Neurobiology 40*, 81–85.

Gunther Moor, B., van Leijenhorst, L., Rombouts, S., Crone, E. and Van der Molen, M. (2010) 'Do you like me? Neural correlates of social evaluation and developmental trajectories.' *Social Neuroscience 5*, 5–6, 461–482.

Guyer, A.E., Choate, V.R., Pine, D.S. and Nelson, E.E. (2011) 'Neural circuitry underlying affective response to peer feedback in adolescence.' *Social Cognitive and Affective Neuroscience 7*, 1, 81–92.

Maslova, L.N., Bulygina, V.V. and Amstislavskaya, T.G. (2010) 'Prolonged social isolation and social instability in adolescence in rats: Immediate and long-term physiological and behavioral effects.' *Neuroscience and Behavioral Physiology 40*, 9, 955.

Nelson, E.E., Jarcho, J.M. and Guyer, A.E. (2016) 'Social re-orientation and brain development: An expanded and updated view.' *Developmental Cognitive Neuroscience 17*, 118–127.

Ruggieri, S., Bendixen, M., Gabriel, U. and Alsaker, F. (2013) 'Cyberball: The impact of ostracism on the well-being of early adolescents.' *Swiss Journal of Psychology 72*, 2, 103–109.

Sebastian, C., Viding, E., Williams, K. and Blakemore, S-J. (2010) 'Social brain development and the affective consequences of ostracism in adolescence.' *Brain & Cognition 72*, 134–145.

Somerville, L.H. (2013) 'The teenage brain: Sensitivity to social evaluation.' *Current Directions in Psychological Science 22*, 2, 121–127.

Somerville, L.H., Jones, R.M., Ruberry, E.J., Dyke, J.P., Glover, G. and Casey, B.J. (2013) 'The medial prefrontal cortex and the emergence of self-conscious emotion in adolescence.' *Psychological Science 24*, 8, 1554–1562.

Yeager, D.S. and Dweck, C.S. (2012) 'Mindsets that promote resilience: When students believe that personal characteristics can be developed.' *Educational Psychologist 47*, 4, 302–314.

Chapter 9: Risk Taking and Resilience Making

Byrnes, J.P., Miller, D.C. and Schafer, W.D. (1999) 'Gender differences in risk taking: A meta-analysis.' *Psychological Bulletin 125*, 3, 367–383.

Casey, B.J., Heller, A.S., Gee, D.G. and Cohen, A.O. (2019) 'Development of the emotional brain.' *Neuroscience Letters 693*, 29–34.

Chein, J., Albert, D., O'Brien, L., Uckert, K. and Steinberg, L. (2011) 'Peers increase adolescent risk taking by enhancing activity in the brain's reward circuitry.' *Developmental Science 14*, 2, F1–F10.

Crone, E. and Dahl, R. (2012) 'Understanding adolescence as a period of social-affective engagement and goal flexibility.' *Nature Reviews Neuroscience 13*, 9, 636–650.

Decker, J.H., Lourenco, F.S., Doll, B.B. and Hartley, C.A. (2015) 'Experiential reward learning outweighs instruction prior to adulthood.' *Cognitive, Affective and Behavioral Neuroscience 15*, 2, 310–320.

Do, K.T., Guassi Moreira, J.F. and Telzer, E.H. (2016) 'But is helping you worth the risk? Defining prosocial risk taking in adolescence.' *Developmental Cognitive Neuroscience 25*, 260–271.

Duell, N. (2018) 'Positive risk taking in adolescence.' Dissertation submitted to Temple University Graduate Board for Doctor of Philosophy.

Galvan, A. (2013) 'The teenage brain: Sensitivity to reward.' *Current Directions in Psychological Science 22*, 2, 88–93.

Greaves, M. (2018) 'A causal mechanism for childhood acute lymphoblastic leukaemia.' *Nature Reviews Cancer 18*, 8, 471–484.

Logue, S., Chein, J., Gould, T., Holliday, E. and Steinberg, L. (2014) 'Adolescent mice, unlike adults, consume more alcohol in the presence of peers than alone.' *Developmental Science 17*, 1, 79–85.

Pfeifer, J.H., Masten, C.L., Moore, W.E., Oswald, T.M. *et al.* (2011) 'Entering adolescence: Resistance to peer influence, risky behavior, and neural changes in emotion reactivity.' *Neuron 69*, 5, 1029–1036.

Silva, K., Chein, J. and Steinberg, L. (2016) 'Adolescents in peer groups make more prudent decisions when a slightly older adult is present.' *Psychological Science 27*, 3, 322–330.

Silva, K., Shulman, E.P., Chein, J. and Steinberg, L. (2015) 'Peers increase late adolescents' exploratory behavior and sensitivity to positive and negative feedback.' *Journal of Research on Adolescence 26*, 4, 696–705.

Steinberg, L. (2007) 'A social neuroscience perspective on adolescent risk-taking.' *Developmental Review 28*, 78–106.

Steinberg, L. (2014) *The Age of Opportunity: Lessons from the New Science of Adolescence*. New York: Houghton Mifflin Harcourt Publishing.

Steinberg, L., Icenogle, G., Shulman, E.P., Breiner, K. *et al.* (2017) 'Around the world, adolescence is a time of heightened sensation seeking and immature self-regulation.' *Developmental Science 21*, 1, 1–13.

Telzer, E., Ichien, N. and Qu, Y. (2015) 'Mothers know best: Redirecting adolescent reward sensitivity toward safe behavior during risk taking.' *Social Cognitive and Affective Neuroscience 10*, 10, 1383–1391.

van Hoorn, J., Fuligni, A.J., Crone, E.A. and Galvan, A. (2016) 'Peer influence effects on risk-taking and prosocial decision-making in adolescence: Insights from neuroimaging studies.' *Current Opinion in Behavioral Sciences 10*, 59–64.

Weigard, A., Chein, J., Albert, D., Smith, A. and Steinberg, L. (2014) 'Effects of anonymous peer observation on adolescents' preference for immediate rewards.' *Developmental Science 17*, 71–78.

Chapter 10: Powerful Feelings and Mighty Motivations

Bryan, C.J., Yeager, D.S., Hinojosa, C.P., Chabot, A. *et al.* (2016) 'Harnessing adolescent values to motivate healthier eating.' *Proceedings of the National Academy of Sciences of the USA 113*, 39, 10830–5.

Casey, B.J., Heller, A.S., Gee, D.G. and Cohen, A.O. (2017) 'Development of the emotional brain.' *Neuroscience Letters 693*, 29–34.

Dahl, R.E., Allen, N.B., Wilbrecht, L. and Suleiman, A.B. (2018) 'Importance of investing in adolescence from a developmental science perspective.' *Nature 554*, 7693, 441.

Damour, L. (2017) *Untangled: Guiding Teenage Girls through the Seven Transitions into Adulthood*. New York: Ballantine Books.

Damour, L. (2019) 'How to help teens weather their emotional storms.' *New York Times*, February 12. Retrieved from www.nytimes.com/2019/02/12/well/family/how-to-help-teens-weather-their-emotional-storms.html, accessed on 08 May 2019.

Fry, S. (2009) 'Stephen Fry's letter to himself: Dearest absurd child.' *The Guardian*, April 30. Retrieved from www.theguardian.com/media/2009/apr/30/stephen-fry-letter-gay-rights, accessed on 08 May 2019.

Gopnik, A. (2016) *The Gardener and the Carpenter*. New York: Farrar, Straus & Giroux.

Peper, J.S. and Dahl, R.E. (2013) 'Surging hormones: Brain-behavior interactions during puberty.' *Current Directions in Psychological Science 22*, 2, 134–139.

Rogers, C.R., Perino, M.R. and Telzer, E.H. (2019) 'Maternal buffering of adolescent dysregulation in socially appetitive contexts: From behaviour to the brain.' *Journal of Research on Adolescence*. DOI: 10.1111/jora.12500

Silvers, J.A., McRae, K., Gabrieli, J.D., Gross, J.J., Remy, K.A. and Ochsner, K.N. (2012) 'Age-related differences in emotional reactivity, regulation, and rejection sensitivity in adolescence.' *Emotion 12*, 1235–1247.

Stephens-Davidowitz, S. (2018) 'The songs that bind us.' *New York Times*, February 10. Retrieved from www.nytimes.com/2018/02/10/opinion/sunday/favorite-songs. html, accessed on 08 May 2019.

Torre, J.B. and Lieberman, M.D. (2018) 'Putting feelings into words: Affect labelling as implicit emotion regulation.' *Emotion Review 10*, 2, 116–124.

Chapter 11: Self-reflection

Altikulaç, S., Lee, N.C., van der Veen, C., Benneker, I., Krabbendam, L. and van Atteveldt, N. (2019) 'The teenage brain: Public perceptions of neurocognitive development during adolescence.' *Journal of Cognitive Neuroscience 31*, 3, 339–359.

Becht, A.I., Nelemans, S.A., Branje, S.J.T., Vollebergh, W.A.M. *et al.* (2016) 'The quest for identity in adolescence: Heterogeneity in daily identity formation and psychosocial adjustment across 5 years.' *Developmental Psychology 52*, 12, 2010–2021.

Crocetti, E., Rubini, M. and Meeus, W. (2008) 'Capturing the dynamics of identity formation in various ethnic groups: Development and validation of a three-dimensional model.' *Journal of Adolescence 31*, 207–222.

Klimstra, T.A. and van Doeselaar, L. (2017) '18-Identity Formation in Adolescence and Young Adulthood.' In J. Specht (ed.) *Personality Development across the Lifespan*. London: Elsevier.

Pfeifer, J.H. and Berkman, E.T. (2018) 'The development of self and identity in adolescence: Neural evidence and implications for a value-based choice perspective on motivated behavior.' *Child Development Perspectives 12*, 3, 158–164.

van der Cruijsen, R., Peters, S., van den Aar, L.P.E. and Crone, E.A. (2018) 'The neural signature of self-concept development in adolescence: The role of domain and valence distinctions.' *Developmental Cognitive Neuroscience 30*, 1–12.

Yeager, D., Dahl, R. and Dweck, C. (2018) 'Why interventions to influence adolescent behaviour often fail but could succeed.' *Perspectives on Psychological Science 13*, 1, 101–122.

Chapter 12: Ready to Launch (with Your Support)

Bonell, C., Blakemore, S-J., Flatcher, A. and Patton, G. (2019) 'Role theory of schools and adolescent health.' *Lancet Child and Adolescent Health*, 1–7. DOI: https://doi.org/10.1016/S2352-4642(19)30183-X

Bryan, C., Yeager, D.S., Hinojosa, C., Chabot, A.M. *et al.* (2016) 'Harnessing adolescent values to reduce unhealthy snacking.' *Proceedings of the National Academy of Sciences of the USA 113*, 39, 10830–10835.

Dahl, R. (2004) 'Adolescent brain development: A period of vulnerabilities and opportunities. Keynote address.' *Annals of the New York Academy of Science 1021*, 1, 1–22.

Decker, J.H., Lourenco, F.S., Doll, B.B. and Hartley, C.A. (2015) 'Experiential reward learning outweighs instruction prior to adulthood.' *Cognitive, Affective, and Behavioral Neuroscience 15*, 2, 310–320.

Fuligni, A.J. (2018) 'The need to contribute during adolescence.' *Perspectives in Psychological Science 14*, 3. DOI: https://doi.org/10.1177/1745691618805437

Fuligni, A.J. and Telzer, E.H. (2013) 'Another way family can get in the head and under the skin: The neurobiology of helping the family.' *Child Development Perspectives 7*, 3, 148–152.

Lee, K.H., Siegle, G.J., Dahl, R.E., Hooley, J. and Silk, J.S. (2014) 'Neural responses to maternal criticism in healthy youth.' *Social Cognitive and Affective Neuroscience 10*, 7, 902–912.

Van der Cruijsen, R., Buisman, R., Green, K., Peters, S. and Crone, E. (2019) 'Neural responses for evaluating self and mother traits in adolescence depend on mother-adolescent relationships.' *Social Cognitive and Affective Neuroscience 14*, 5, 481–492.

Yeager, D.S., Dahl, R.E. and Dweck, C.S. (2018) 'Why interventions to influence adolescent behavior often fail but could succeed.' *Perspectives on Psychological Science 13*, 1, 101–122.

Chapter 13: Sleepy Teens

Dahl, R.E. and Lewin, D.S. (2002) 'Pathways to adolescent health sleep regulation and behavior.' *Journal of Adolescent Health 31*, 6, 175–184.

Dunster, G.P., Iglesia, L., Ben-Hamo, M., Nave, C. *et al.* (2018) 'Sleepmore in Seattle: Later school start times are associated with more sleep and better performance in high school students.' *Science Advances 4*, 12. DOI: 10.1126/sciadv.aau6200

Fuligni, A.J., Arruda, E.H., Krull, J.L. and Gonzales, N.A. (2018) 'Sleep duration, variability, and peak levels of achievement and mental health.' *Child Development 89*, e18–e28.

Fuligni, A.J., Bai, S., Krull, J.L. and Gonzales, N.A. (2017) 'Individual differences in optimum sleep for daily mood during adolescence.' *Journal of Clinical Child & Adolescent Psychology 48*, 3, 469–479.

Galvan, A. (2018) 'How can we improve a teen's brain? One sleep study may have a simple answer – good pillows.' *The Washington Post*, November 24.

Hagenauer, M.H., Perryman, J.I., Lee, T.M. and Carskadon, M.A. (2009) 'Adolescent changes in the homeostatic and circadian regulation of sleep.' *Developmental Neuroscience 31*, 4, 276–284.

Lee, Y.J., Cho, S.J., Cho, I.H. and Kim, S.J. (2012) 'Insufficient sleep and suicidality in adolescents.' *Sleep 35*, 4, 455–460.

Roenneberg, T., Kuehnle, T., Pramstaller, P.P., Ricken, J. *et al.* (2004) 'A marker for the end of adolescence.' *Current Biology 14*, 24, 1038–9.

Tashjian, S., Goldenberg, D. and Galvan, A. (2017) 'Neural connectivity moderates the association between sleep and impulsivity in adolescents.' *Developmental Cognitive Neuroscience 27*, 35–44.

Telzer, E.H., Goldenberg, D., Fuligni, A.J., Lieberman, M.D. and Galvan, A. (2015) 'Sleep variability in adolescence is associated with altered brain development.' *Developmental Cognitive Neuroscience 14*, 16–22.

Tsai, K.M., Dahl, R.E., Irwin, M.R., Bower, J.E. *et al.* (2018) 'The roles of parental support and family stress in adolescent sleep.' *Child Development 5*, 1577–1588.

Walker, M. (2017) *Why We Sleep: The New Science of Sleep and Dreams*. London: Penguin.

Chapter 14: Creating Healthy Habits

Aberg, M.A., Aberg, N., Brisman, J., Sundberg, R., Winkvist, A. and Torén, K. (2009) 'Fish intake of Swedish male adolescents is a predictor of cognitive performance.' *Acta Paediatrica: Nurturing the Child 98*, 3, 555–560.

Addis, S. and Murphy, S. (2019) '"There is such a thing as too healthy!" The impact of minimum nutritional guidelines on school food practices in secondary schools.' *Journal of Human Nutrition and Dietics 32*, 1, 31–40.

Adolphus, K., Lawton, C.L., Champ, C.L. and Dye, L. (2016) 'The effects of breakfast and breakfast composition on cognition in children and adolescents: A systematic review.' *Advances in Nutrition 7*, 3, 590S–612S.

Bassett, R., Chapman, G.E. and Beagan, B.L. (2008) 'Autonomy and control: The co-construction of adolescent food choice.' *Appetite 50,* 2–3, 325–332.

Blake, H., Stanulewicz, N. and McGill, F. (2016) 'Predictors of physical activity and barriers to exercise in nursing and medical students.' *Journal of Advanced Nursing 73,* 4, 917–929.

Esteban-Cornejo, I., Gómez-Martínez, S., Tejero-González, C.M., Castillo, R. *et al.* (2015) 'Characteristics of extracurricular physical activity and cognitive performance in adolescents: The AVENA study.' *International Journal of Environmental Research and Public Health 12,* 1, 385–401.

Howse, E., Hankey, C., Allman-Farinelli, M., Bauman, A. and Freeman, B. (2018) '"Buying salad is a lot more expensive than going to Mcdonalds": Young adults' views about what influences their food choices.' *Nutrients 10,* 8, E996.

Jackson, D.B. and Beaver, K. (2015) 'The role of adolescent nutrition and physical activity in the prediction of verbal intelligence during early adulthood: A genetically informed analysis of twin pairs.' *International Journal of Environmental Research and Public Health 12,* 1, 385–401.

López-Castedo, A., Domínguez Alonso, J. and Portela-Pino, I. (2018) 'Predictive variables of motivation and barriers for the practice of physical exercise in adolescence.' *Journal of Human Sport and Exercise 13,* 4, 907–915.

Manduca, A., Bara, A., Larrieu, T., Lassalle, O. *et al.* (2017) 'Amplification of mGlu5-endocannabinoid signaling rescues behavioral and synaptic deficits in a mouse model of adolescent and adult dietary polyunsaturated fatty acid imbalance.' *Journal of Neuroscience 37,* 29, 6851–6868.

Chapter 15: Good Stress, Bad Stress

Coan, J. and Sbarra, D.A. (2015) 'Social Baseline Theory: The social regulation of risk and effort.' *Current Opinions in Psychology 1,* 87–91.

Coan, J.A., Schaefer, H.S. and Davidson, R.J. (2006) 'Lending a hand: Social regulation of the neural response to threat.' *Psychological Science 17,* 12, 1032–1039.

Crum, A.J., Akinola, M., Martin, A. and Fath, S. (2017) 'The role of stress mindset in shaping cognitive, emotional and physiological responses to challenging and threatening stress.' *Anxiety, Stress & Coping 30,* 4, 379–395.

Crum, A.J., Salovey, P. and Achor, S. (2013) 'Rethinking stress: The role of mindsets in determining stress response.' *Journal of Personality and Social Psychology 104,* 4, 716–733.

Gilbert, P., Broomhead, C., Irons, C., McEwan, K. *et al.* (2007) 'Development of a striving to avoid inferiority scale.' *British Journal of Social Psychology 46*, 633–648.

Keller, A., Litzelman, K., Wisk, L.E., Maddox, T. *et al.* (2012) 'Does the perception that stress affects health matter? The association with health and mortality.' *Health Psychology: Official Journal of the Division of Health Psychology, American Psychological Association 31*, 5, 677–684.

Kim, J.J. and Diamond, D.M. (2002) 'The stressed hippocampus, synaptic plasticity and lost memories.' *Nature Reviews Neuroscience 3*, 6, 453.

McGonigal, K. (2015) *The Upside of Stress: Why Stress Is Good for You (and How to Get Good at It).* London: Vermilion.

Romeo, R.D. (2013) 'The teenage brain: The stress response and the adolescent brain.' *Current Directions in Psychological Science 22*, 2, 140–145.

Yeager, D.S., Purdie-Vaughns, V., Garcia, J., Apfel, N. *et al.* (2014) 'Breaking the cycle of mistrust: Wise interventions to provide critical feedback across the racial divide.' *Journal of Experimental Psychology: General 143*, 804–824.

Chapter 16: #Social Media and Technology

Blum-Ross, A. and Livingstone, S. (2016) 'Families and screen time: Current advice and emerging research.' *The London School of Economics and Political Science Department of Media and Communications.*

Chassiakos, Y., Radesky, J., Christakis, D., Moreno, M.A. and Cross, C. (2016) 'Children and adolescents and digital media.' *Pediatrics 138*, 5. DOI:e20162593.

Council on Communication and Media (2016) 'Media use in school-aged children and adolescents.' *Pediatrics 138*, 5, e20162592.

Crone, E.A. and Konijn, E.A. (2018) 'Media use and brain development during adolescence.' *Nature Communications 9*, 1–10.

Licoppe, C. (2004) 'Connected presence: The emergence of a new repertoire for managing social relationship in a changing communication technoscape.' *Environment and Planning D: Society and Space 22*, 1, 135–156.

Livingstone, S. and Haddon, L. (2009) *EU Kids Online: Final Report.* LSE. London: EU Kids Online (www.eukidsonline.net).

Orben, A. and Przbylsk, A.K. (2019) 'The association between adolescent well-being and digital technology use.' *Nature Human Behaviour 3*, 173–182.

Acknowledgements

Bettina

I was a bit lost as a teenager, but in my 20s I found a subject I loved, a person to share my life with and some important friends. I couldn't have written a word without my two trusted, inspiring, considerate and brilliant colleagues Jane and Tara. Even when it seemed like an impossible task, we did it. That is the power of friendship and the social brain. It's an honour to have my name next to both of yours. Douglas, our talented and creative illustrator, thank you for finding a way to represent our ideas so beautifully and clearly. Ma, you have been an inspiration and modelled an incredible work ethic, as well as shared a passion for child psychology and education. My sisters and close friends – you know who you are – thank you for your encouragement and for adding clarity through conversation and deliberation.

Without the three people I live with none of it would have any meaning. Martin, I do it all with you at my side. How can you still have the patience to listen to me talk endlessly about psychology, children and therapy? So often you have given a structure to my muddle of ideas that actually you should probably be a co-author. You have taught me what is important in life and kept me steady when I have wobbled (often), while always making me laugh. Ella and Billy, you are the reason I get up in the morning. I just watch in amazement as you work out how to do life. You are both so insightful, tenacious, capable, kind and loving. I don't think there's a thing your incredible teenage brains can't do.

Jane

A great big thank you to my magnificent co-authors, Bettina and Tara. It is rare to find two experts with such razor-sharp intellect who are so unassuming and easy to be around. Well here's a question for you two clever clogs: Why am I missing those wretched Friday Skype calls so much? While you ponder that, here's to Jaffa Cake fuelled all-nighters. I learnt a lot, I laughed a lot. During the writing of this book, the Gilmour family were, as ever, right behind me; especially cheerleader-in-chief Wendy (*That's* your book deadline? Mop my brow...) and my ever kind, ever patient mum (aka the Queen of Emotional Regulation). I'm so very grateful to my husband – whose drawings illustrate this book – for his unconditional love and support whatever my endeavours. I know exactly where I'd be without you, Douglas. Most particularly, I want to thank my two favourite children: the one with the most glorious of curls and the one with the most luscious of lashes. Always gracious when I detailed another 'fascinating' teenage brain fact, actually *you* have taught me everything worth knowing. You are wise, kind and funny beyond your years. How can two such different approaches to the world both be so utterly perfect? It's a privilege to be your mum, giving you a leg up to your future. Reach for the stars, darlings.

Tara

Thanks to Damon for his enduring love, patience and support for all that matters to me. Also, huge thanks to Sinéad, Bella and Manuela for being alongside and sharing the sisterhood. To Amanda, for always being a source of light and a heartfelt inspiration. Lastly, thanks to Bettina and Jane for sharing this journey with me. I have learnt a great deal.

And finally, we would all like to thank Amy Lankester-Owen for seeing the potential in our original paper and for her wonderful light-touch author management and editorship.

Index